D1075026

Death Of A Business: The Red Wing Potteries

By Richard S. Gillmer, Ph.D.

Ross & Haines, Inc.
Minneapolis - 1968

331.89
548

331.89
G48

113661

Library of Congress Catalog Card Number 68-25961

Copyright 1968
Ross & Haines, Inc.

All rights reserved. This book, or parts thereof, may not be reproduced in any form without permission of the publishers.

First Edition

Dedicated to the real loser—the fifty three year old worker who had been at the Potteries for twenty years and is now unemployed.

TABLE OF CONTENTS

PRELUDE

In the face of other current events in the summer of 1967, the Red Wing Potteries Strike and the eventual demise of the company will not appear to most as a particularly important or momentous occurrence. Certainly the riots and social disturbances in Detroit, Milwaukee, Tampa, Buffalo, Newark, Boston, Cincinnati and Phoenix greatly upstaged Red Wing's problems. In the area of labor disputes the Potteries strike was totally insignificant when compared to the United Auto Workers strike at Ford, the teachers strikes in New York and Detroit, the violent walkout of steel truckers in Pennsylvania and Ohio, and even the strike of the Rockettes at Manhattan's Radio City Music Hall. However, to many of Red Wing's people and certainly to this author, the experiences over the summer of 1967 were tremendously frustrating and not easily forgotten.

In some ways the strike could have been termed "the Gillmer family versus Local 6-430 of the Oil, Chemical and Atomic Workers." That is not to suggest that other company employees were not affected drastically by the events of the summer, or did not play a major role in keeping the company's assets intact. However, the major figure on the company side was President and General Manager, R. A. Gillmer, who had been the chief executive officer of the company since 1958, and also the major stockholder. The author, who joined the firm in June of 1966, was Secretary and Operations Manager. The writer's mother and sister devoted most of their summer to waiting on trade in the company's retail salesroom directly across the street from the factory. In the eyes of the community at large, the press and the radio, the company became personalized as "the Gillmers." The fact that the family owned over fifty per cent of the Red Wing Potteries, and that members of the immediate family were intimately involved in the strike, served to heighten the anxiety and gravity of the experience for the author.

In an effort to put things in their proper perspective, it is important to note that the Red Wing Potteries had for years been a marginal company. Plant and equipment were antiquated, manufacturing costs were correspondingly high and profits small. Company management, in the past, had done very little to improve the physical plant or to enhance efficiency through modern machinery and equipment. Had management possessed more foresight in years past, the disaster of 1967 might well have been avoided. That is to say, management might have been in a better position to approach or meet the Union demands in the 1967 negotiations. However, the business in 1967, although some bright spots existed, was not a picture of health. The union demands and the resulting strike were in some ways the proverbial "straw that broke the camel's back."

Ideally, the job of reporting should not be attempted by one so intimately involved and so obviously identified with one side of the dispute. However, if the record is read keeping in mind the frame of reference and probable lack of objectivity on the part of the writer, it can be of interest and hopefully of some value to students of labor relations. It would be impossible for the writer to approach the subject from the standpoint of a disinterested observer. Nevertheless, there would appear to be value in recording, however personal or subjective, the anxieties, hopes, fears and pressures that were experienced on the management side of the conflict, and, further, management's speculation on the feelings and attitudes of the other side. Speculation as to the Union's motives, in itself, can be significant if only as it provided a basis for management's moves and countermoves. Both sides in the conflict reached a point where methods were used which were designed solely to "hurt" their opponents, rather than consideration of the likely effect of these methods on their primary objective - settlement of the strike. Both sides misinterpreted and distorted the motives of the opposition, and both tended to see only "bad" in their opponents and only "good" on their side. Mutual antagonism grew to a point where it was virtually impossible for those involved to act in a completely rational manner. The reader, then, must take into consideration that the author was a key member of one side of the conflict, and must accept the book for what it is - a management view.

RED WING, A CITY

Red Wing, a serene river town of eleven thousand people, is located in Southeastern Minnesota, approximately an hour's drive from the metropolitan complex of Minneapolis-St. Paul. The city lies in the Hiawatha Valley which is characterized by valleys and bluffs overlooking the Mississippi River. Early explorers equated the natural beauty of the area with that of the Rhine Valley in Germany.

Red Wing was settled around 1850 on the site of an Indian village, and takes its name from an old Sioux Chief. It is the county seat of Goodhue County and serves as the medical, cultural and economic center for the surrounding area. The city is bordered by rich farm lands producing primarily wheat, corn and dairy products.

Red Wing is not a typical Midwestern town in the eyes of her citizens. The people are fiercely proud of the natural beauty of their region. The Chamber of Commerce would point out the progressiveness of the city, evidenced in the new or newly remodeled businesses, schools and hospital. The citizens are proud of their well-kept homes, their mayor's Ph.D. in physics, the alertness and forward thinking of their city fathers, and the capabilities of their business and labor leaders. Business, professional and laboring people see themselves as working together to build the city. Many a citizen has been heard to say, rather smugly and possibly from a somewhat narrow perspective, "Red Wing is the only place to live, and the only place to raise a family."

One of Red Wing's major advantages is its diversity of industry. While many cities of Red Wing's size are dependent upon and dominated by one large corporation, Red Wing is definitely not a one-company town. Its five thousand five hundred workers produce flour, linseed oil, fiberglass boats, rock wool insulation, kitchen cabinets, phonograph cabinets, leather, shoes, steel lighting and power structures, diplomas, remote control handling instruments, and, until recently, pottery.

The State's only training school for delinquent boys is located on the edge of the town. Although boys frequently run away from the unfenced grounds and often steal automobiles in the process, the institution's million dollar payroll tends to offset this nuisance for the townspeople.

With their relatively tranquil life Red Wingites have had little experience with social unrest or disorder. The citizens read of the racial riots in the large urban areas with alarm and exclamations of "What's becoming of this country!", but also with considerable depersonalization. The police and civic leaders have had little need to cope with violence or social strife and, with the exception of an occasional teenage beer party, apprehending a group of runaways from the Training School, or policing the Fourth of July parade, seldom deal in group control.

All of these factors - Red Wing's pride in her way of life, her inexperience in matters of social strife, and her generally uncomplicated existence - combined to make it very difficult for the people of Red Wing to comprehend, to face squarely, and to adequately cope with the subject of this book, the three-month Pottery strike.

THE POTTERY INDUSTRY IN RED WING

The earliest recorded pottery making in the Red Wing area is credited to a German immigrant named J. Pohl who in 1861 began fashioning crude crocks on his farm. He used the clay deposits on his own property, and hand-turned his ware on a treadle wheel.

In 1868 W. M. Philleo began manufacturing flower vases in Red Wing using local clay. He manufactured unglazed terra cotta ware until his pottery works burned in 1870. He rebuilt his small factory but ran into financial difficulty and abandoned his business shortly thereafter. D. Hallem, who had worked with Philleo for a short time, continued the manufacture of pottery in a small way in his home.

The ninety year old Red Wing Potteries, Inc. traces its beginnings to 1877 when a group of Red Wing citizens met to consider the subject of organizing a company for the manufacture of stoneware. Incorporated in 1877, the Red Wing Stoneware Company purchased the meager assets of Hallem, and constructed larger, more efficient kilns. The company was a success from the start, digging their clay locally and producing quality stoneware crocks, jugs, and milk pans of all shapes and sizes.

The Red Wing Stoneware Company prospered over the years and the company's apparent success enticed others to enter the field. In 1883 the Minnesota Stoneware Company was organized and began manufacturing across the street from the Red Wing Stoneware plant. Minnesota Stoneware employed over one hundred people and had sales of $125,000 in 1890.

Nine years later, in 1892, another company, the North Star Stoneware Company, was formed. The founders of this business apparently had grandiose plans because they built a three-story plant which was bigger and better than the two older companies. To further complicate matters, North Star's owners chose to build in the immediate vicinity of their two existing rivals. One can imagine the tremendous infighting that must have occurred over sales and manpower among these three firms located literally next door to one another in a small town where labor and management talent was undoubtedly in short supply. Red Wing had a population of only seven thousand six hundred and seventy five in 1895.

To meet the competition of the newer and larger North Star plant, a partial merger was effected between the Red Wing and Minnesota Stoneware Companies in 1894, a joint selling agency entitled "Red Wing Union Stoneware Company." The joining of forces turned out to be a profitable move for the two older companies because the new rival, the North Star plant, ceased operation in 1897.

The year 1900 was a difficult one for Red Wing potters. In February of that year the Minnesota Stoneware plant burned to the ground, and nine months later, in November, the Red Wing Stoneware Company met a similar fate. The fact that both companies burned to the ground the same year challenges coincidence; one might surmise that an embittered former North Star employee was careless with his matches in the year 1900, but this is only speculation.

Red Wing's potters were persistent, however, and both plants were immediately rebuilt. Both companies continued to prosper and, pleased by the success of their partial merger in 1894, chose to merge completely in 1906. They continued the name Red Wing Union Stoneware Company, and the City of Red Wing was left with only one pottery.

In the following two decades the Red Wing Union Stoneware Company enjoyed continued prosperity. Using local clay and shipping primarily by rail, they developed a national market for their jars, crocks, jugs, bean pots, spittoons, milk pans, flower pots, churns, hanging baskets, water coolers, mixing bowls, chamber pots, and bed warmers. Their catalogs boasted "a keen desire and demonstrated ability to look after (the merchant's) requirements in exactly the way (he) expects, a high grade product and a distinctive service." Practically every farm in the Midwest boasted a variety of stoneware items made in Red Wing. Housewives bought their molasses and vinegar in pottery jugs, made their butter in stoneware churns, cooled their milk in heavy crocks, and stored their winter supply of dill pickles, salt pork and sauerkraut in Red Wing jars.

Unfortunately, in the 1920's the market for stoneware began to dwindle. The farm market began to decline with more and more rural people moving to the large urban areas. Fewer and fewer people were churning their own butter, rendering out their own lard, and making their own sauerkraut. The decline of the agrarian economy left fewer individuals in a position to use these "do it yourself" methods, in addition to the fact that these products were available in a prepacked, convenient form on every store shelf in the country.

Thus, the Red Wing Union Stoneware Company was forced to diversify and open up new markets if it were to enjoy continued prosperity. In the late 1920's the company added a line of artware or finer vases. By the 1930's, hurt by the Depression but having experienced some success with artware, company officials chose to diversify further and entered the dinnerware field.

It was soon recognized that the local clay was unsuitable in the manufacture of fine dinnerware. The natural impurities and the unsuitable color of the fired clay did not lend themselves to a quality finished product. From that time on raw materials were imported from Tennessee, Kentucky, North Carolina and Georgia.

Red Wing dinnerware caught on and began accounting for an increasing proportion of sales, with the stoneware products experiencing a proportionate decline. The officers felt that the name of the corporation, Red Wing Union Stoneware Company, did not logically reflect this changing product mix. The company was rapidly leaving the stoneware "jug and crock" field and entering the dinnerware or tableware field. Therefore, in January of 1936, the shareholders voted to change the name from the "Red Wing Union Stoneware Company" to the "Red Wing Potteries, Inc."

While there are no financial records available prior to 1952, the 1930's and 1940's reportedly were prosperous years for Red Wing Potteries. Stockholders received large dividends and very little was put back into the business in the form of capital improvements. By 1947 the company had discontinued all stoneware production and had assumed a leadership role in the dinnerware field.

Around 1950 a trend began that eventually was to be a factor in the demise of Red Wing Potteries. The nation's department stores, which were the backbone of Red Wing's market, began showing increasing quantities of imported dinnerware. However, in 1950 this was not a major source of concern; perhaps only ten percent of the dinnerware patterns in a given department store were imports. This began to change drastically, however, and by 1967 the percentages nearly reversed. While in 1950 only ten percent of all dinnerware patterns displayed were of foreign origin, in 1967 nearly ninety percent were foreign imports.

The available records show that Red Wing's annual sales were historically between one and two million. In 1955 the company experienced its first year of loss. On sales of $1,577,000 the annual statements showed a net loss of $27,000. Company Directors, feeling the need for a change in management, brought in Forest Richardson, an accountant, as President and General Manager to replace Harry Barghusen, also an accountant by background, who was appointed President in 1949 after the death of H. H. Varney.

The situation worsened under Richardson. While sales reached a record level of $1,748,000 in 1956, the company showed a net loss of $49,000. In 1957 sales were $1,674,000, but the net loss for the year increased to $91,000. As President, Richardson had fortified himself with such quantities of management and office personnel that administrative costs made profits an impossibility even with years of record sales volume.

The Directors realized something must be done if the Red Wing Potteries were to continue to operate. In 1958, they brought in R. A. Gillmer to replace Richardson as President and General Manager. Gillmer had been a Red Wing Sales Representative in the Chicago area for fifteen years and was a Vice-President of the company. Gillmer took the job at a $12,000 salary, which amounted to a substantial cut in his annual income.

R. A. Gillmer's first act of office was to eliminate a total of twenty seven office and management employees, and began strictly screening company expenditures. Also, under Richardson in 1956 and 1957 the company had around two hundred and twenty production employees. The new regime began combining jobs and looking for more production in order to reduce the working force.

On the basis of figures, this cost-cutting approach was effective and gave the Red Wing Potteries a new life, at least temporarily. In 1958, the company made a net profit of $63,000 on sales of $1,545,000 and was back in the black ink again. From 1958 through 1966 the company never had a loss year. On the other hand, profits were marginal; they ranged from a low of $7,000 in 1961 to a high of $70,000 in 1959. The average net profit for the nine year period was $36,000. Net sales for the nine year period gradually declined with the exception of 1966 when sales were $1,653,000.

While total sales remained relatively constant, or declined gradually, competition from foreign imports cut deeply into sales to department stores, the backbone of Red Wing's market. In order to keep the total sales volume at a constant level, the Potteries sought out other markets. Red Wing went into the specialty field and began making products specifically for stamp companies and other customers with large potential volume. Diversification was necessary if the Red Wing Potteries was to have any future. Spurred by the need for diversification, a new china body was developed in 1959, and the company began producing a line of casual china dinnerware.

In January of 1961, R. A. Gillmer sent the following letter to shareholders discussing the year 1960 and the company's future plans:

"This has been a disappointing year to some extent to those of us in the dinnerware and pottery industry. Foreign imports continue to grow which has the natural tendency to increase competition and narrow the margin of profit. Because of this situation some diversification is necessary. We manufacture a large variety of dinnerware and pottery pieces. We make both earthenware and china, a complete line of artware which consists of vases, planters, figurines, etc.; also, serviceable things too numerous to mention. In addition to this we are experimenting with the production of ceramic tile, this tile to be applied to concrete blocks serving the building industry as both a utility and decorative wall structure. Considerable progress has been made on this.

"With the help of Minnesota Mining and Manufacturing Company a ceramic abrasive product has been developed. New machinery and equipment has been installed and a contract has been entered into with the 3M Company to manufacture this product for them.

"A new retail store was built in Rapid City, South Dakota, last year. Because of some unforeseen delays in construction, this store did not open for business until the middle of August. We are well pleased with its progress thus far."

The Minnesota Mining ceramic abrasive product proved to be a worthwhile endeavor and a small source of sales. The ceramic tile venture never left the ground and was abandoned shortly thereafter. The Rapid City, South Dakota retail store proved to be a break-even operation, but of undetermined value as a method of disposing of second quality merchandise.

Red Wing was not the only United States pottery seeking diversification and finding it more and more difficult to compete with foreign imports. A 1966 issue of The Reporter, a trade publication stated that "Due to the vast increase of imports from low wage foreign manufacturers, the American earthenware producer is no longer competitive. Cheap imports first grabbed the department store trade and are now making headway with the supermarket and premium business to which the domestic producers have been obliged to turn. . . . Foreign potteries (are) as modern and efficient as those in the U. S., but pay wages only a fraction of the American scale." Gloomy conditions of the American pottery industry in the past score of years were cited: "Employment has dropped from 12,000 in 1948 to 4,152 at present; production is down from 27.5 million dozens to 11.1 million dozens. Of 24 earthenware plants doing business in 1954, . . . seven (are) now functioning. Those remaining . . . have not taken over the business done by defunct firms but have also declined drastically."

Because of the declining department store market Red Wing Potteries went the route of all struggling potteries and turned to the supermarket field as a source of sales. This was a difficult decision for management because supermarkets, while potentially large volume customers, were not a consistent source of sales; dinnerware could be a major premium item in supermarkets one year and completely out the next. Also, making merchandise available to supermarkets or discount houses tarnished a company's good name as far as department stores were concerned. Recognizing the risks and disadvantages, management offered two of their "tried and true" patterns, Pepe and Bob White, to the supermarket field in 1966 and experienced a degree of success. Net sales of $1,653,000 were the highest they had been since 1957. Net profits of $45,000 were better than average.

In a further attempt at diversification, Red Wing began manufacturing a line of restaurant and hotel china in the Fall of 1964. With initial technical and development problems, the company experienced only modest success and was frequently on the verge of abandoning this venture. However, hotel china sales began to increase in 1967 and the long-term potential of the project began to show more promise.

In addition to the marketing problems facing the company, Red Wing Potteries had another very real problem — their physical plant. Built in the nineteenth century, the plant was an industrial engineer's nightmare. Comprising four floors, this manufacturing facility was a maze of narrow isles, posts, ramps and walls. As the need arose for more space over years, an additional section would be "tacked on" to the existing facility, leaving the problem of a ramp to a new level, narrow doorways and obstructing walls. A smooth flow of production was wishful thinking in the Red Wing plant; excessive handling and trucking of in-process ware sent costs rocketing. Storage facilities were inadequate, and in-process ware and finished goods were stored where space could be found — along isles, in niches and crannies along the kilns, on the fourth floor, and in quonset huts outside the plant. Without any system or space for storage, time-consuming long-distance trucking was necessary and quantities of ware were "lost" indefinitely in the little-traveled corners of the plant.

There were a few bright spots in the business, however. The retail store across the street from the factory had become a nationally recognized tourist attraction. Thousands of tourists from all parts of the United States toured the plant and shopped for bargains in second-quality merchandise during a typical summer week. The addition of a new gift shop and a country candy store in the Spring of 1966 brought record sales of $386,000 for the retail store that year, nearly one-quarter of the total company sales.

Despite the many adversities facing the Red Wing Potteries, and the industry in general, R. A. Gillmer felt the business had a future. By 1967, he had accumulated over fifty percent of the stock and had a vested interest in seeing the business progress. Toward this end, he was developing a young management team. Gerry Mewhorter, thirty-three years of age, a man "up from the ranks" was the Production Superintendent. Irving Vick, only forty-three, but with fourteen years' experience in the company, was the Treasurer-Controller. In June of 1966, R. A. Gillmer brought in his son, R. S. Gilmer (author of this book) as Operations Manager. He was twenty-eight at the time, a Ph.D. Industrial Psychologist, with three years of management consulting to his credit. After an extensive year's search a thirty year old, highly qualified Ceramic Engineer, Gerald Ross, was brought into the organization to assist and eventually replace Tom Arnold, sixty-six year old Ceramic Engineer. Ross joined the company on May 15, 1967, just sixteen days before the strike began.

R. A. Gillmer felt he had a nucleus of manpower to make the company advance. There was further talk in 1966 and 1967 of diversification and expansion. The possibility of manufacturing ceramic insulators was being studied. Acquisitions were being considered. Investigations were being made into an additional factory outlet store in the Twin Cities (Minneapolis and St. Paul) area. Plant expansion and the possibility of a pilot plant in Red Wing's Industrial Park were frequent topics of conversation. Red Wing had begun manufacturing two dinnerware patterns for Sears Roebuck and Company which looked promising, and there was talk of several high-volume supermarket deals about to break. There was more than just a "spark of life" in the old company.

UNIONISM AT THE POTTERIES

"The ground-work principle of America's labor
movement has been to recognize that first things
come first. The primary essential in our mission
has been the protection of the wage-worker, now;
to increase his wages; to cut hours of the long
workday, which was killing him; to improve the
safety and the sanitary conditions of the work-
shop; to free him from the tyrannies, petty or
otherwise, which served to make his existence a
slavery."

SAMUEL GOMPERS

Red Wing Potteries had a long history of dealing with organized labor. In 1895, the Stoneware Potters Union Local 8302 was organized to include only the Potteries' skilled tradesmen. This Union was comprised of glaze-dippers and hand-jiggermen or jollymen, the "cocks of the roost" in the early years of pottery manufacture when nearly all products were hand-turned on potter's wheels or jigger wheels. The Stoneware Potters Union persisted for three decades at the Potteries with no record of conflict or disharmony.

According to the old-time potters, however, the employees began to grumble in the late 1920's about the exclusiveness of the Stoneware Potters Union. Why couldn't the Union accept anyone who wished to join, rather than just the jiggermen and glaze-dippers? These feelings grew stronger until 1930, when the employees threw out the old Stoneware Potters Union and brought in the National Brotherhood of Potters Local 150, an AFL Union. While not a Union shop, the NBOP encouraged membership of all employees and Union membership grew to approximately eighty percent of the work force. In fact, over the years Union affiliation became almost a necessity if an employee were to advance to the more profitable skilled jobs. A 1946 contract read:

"Members in good standing in Local Union No. 150 of the NBOP shall be given preference when a vacancy occurs in the trades. Vacancies to be posted on the bulletin board by the Superintendent. By 'trades' is meant any job that requires a preliminary apprenticeship training. Fitness for the job of course is understood, and this fitness is a matter for decision by the company management. Any employee joining the Union with the idea of securing a job more beneficial must retain his membership in good standing or forfeit the job."

By 1948, the Potteries became a Union Shop and a clause in the 1948 contract read:

"The Company agrees to employ only members of the National Brotherhood of Operative Potters except in the case of a new employee, such employee is given sixty (60) days within which to join the Union."

The National Brotherhood of Potters was headquartered logically in the East, for the great preponderance of United States pottery was manufactured in and around the eastern Ohio area. Because Red Wing, Minnesota was isolated from the mainstream of pottery manufacture, Local 150 received infrequent attention from NBOP representatives. Their pleas for advice and procedural guidelines went unheeded or, at best, were attended to through the mails. According to one old-timer "the only time we would see the National representative was at contract time."

This inattention was bound to cause bad feelings, and in 1949 the infighting started among the employees to change Union affiliation. The dissident employees contacted a CIO Union, the United Gas, Coke, and Chemical Workers of America, as a potential replacement for the faltering NBOP. The shop was split down the middle and a terrible squabble ensued. The old-timers on the forming side of the shop - the mold makers, clay preparation, and jiggermen - were loyal to the AFL, NBOP and did not feel a change was needed. However, the glost side of the shop - the decorators, glazers, and finishers - were rabid in their desire to throw out the NBOP and bring in the CIO. These people claimed "the NBOP never did a thing for us; we need a Union that will stand up and fight."

In December of 1949, the company received notification from the National Labor Relations Board that a vote would be held in January in order to determine which Union the majority of employees wanted. In January of 1950, in an election supervised by the NLRB and attended by both AFL and CIO officials, the 426 employees voted by a narrow margin to change their affiliation to the CIO, United Gas, Coke, and Chemical Workers of America. The margin of victory was so small, in fact, that the issue was carried on the basis of an NLRB ruling on a few challenged votes.

The wounds of battle were not easily healed and many of the loyal AFL employees refused to recognize or pay dues to the new Union. A smaller number of workers, while they paid their dues to the CIO, remained loyal to the AFL and continued their dues and memberships. Local Union 436, United Gas, Coke, and Chemical Workers of America, CIO, had their work cut out for them. They had to salve the wounds engendered by the election, overcome the "show me" attitude of the AFL-loyal people, and unite the employees once again under the new CIO banner. The Union was in a tight position; they had to get big things for the people to prove the change was a good one and that they would "fight for the employees." The time was ripe for a strike.

It was under this forbidding aura of circumstances that management began bargaining in March with the Union for a new contract. Bargaining was deadlocked and the Union filed their strike notice with the State Labor Office on April 21. This set a deadline of May 2 before which an agreement had to be reached or the Union could legally strike. The Union was asking 25 cents an hour across the board increase with the increase retroactive to March 1. The company offered increases of 3 cents with no retroactivity. The Union insisted on a Union shop; the company refused to give in on this issue. From the Union's standpoint, it was only logical that they had to hold out for a Union shop; the old AFL had gained Union shop status by 1948, and with employee attitudes what they were the CIO could not expect to gain any measure of unity or strong percentages of membership without winning this Union shop issue. On the management side, President Harry Barghusen had a very practical reason for not granting the CIO a Union shop. The forming side of the shop, nearly fifty percent of the workers, had refused generally to join the CIO and Barghusen had reason to believe that these people would sooner quit their jobs than be forced to join the new Union. The threat of losing almost one-half of his work force made Barghusen determined in his denial of a Union shop.

By the strike deadline, Union and Management were in close agreement on the fringe issues, such as holidays and vacations. The company had come up from 3 cents to 5 cents in their across-the-board wage offer, the Union had come down from their original 25 cent demand to 12 cents, but company and Union were still hopelessly deadlocked on the Union shop issue.

In a desperation move, four days before the strike deadline, the company published their proposal in a paid advertisement in the local newspaper, the Daily Republican Eagle (DRE). The advertisement set forth the Union demands and the company proposals, and pointed out that the company's offer would entail an additional outlay of $57,000, while the Union's package would come to $465,300. In an effort to gain public sympathy, the ad pointed out the fact that the Potteries provided employment for 426 people and had a factory wage of $950,000 in 1949. President Barghusen was quoted: "Our earnest desire to come to a satisfactory conclusion prompted us to make the offers stated. The pottery industry is highly competitive and the market will not permit price advances to overcome the increased cost. In fact, the trend in prices is downward rather than upward."

All to no avail. On Wednesday, May 3, 1950, the DRE headlines screamed:

"STRIKING POTTERY WORKERS REPORT AT PLANT, BUT NOT FOR WORK" The article went on to state:

"Employees of the Red Wing Potteries went on strike this morning and wheels at the plant were idle. The CIO, recently designed as the bargaining agent by the NLRB for the 426 workers at the factory, threw up a picket line. There were no disorders. Picketing started at 5:00 A.M. Negotiations

for a settlement, it is understood, are still in progress . . .
The strike was called by the CIO. Representatives of the
AFL Union, still functioning among pottery workers, said
their members were not on strike but would not cross the
picket lines. AFL spokesman claim a membership of 236
pot shop workers in their Union but admit some of these also
belong to the CIO . . ."

The continued hostility between the AFL and the CIO people
was apparent. It can be imagined that management considered
this hostility their "ace in the hole" and a probable means of
breaking the strike, and it must have come as a disappointment
to find that the AFL employees, while not actively participating,
were honoring the CIO picket lines.

On May 5 the Union countered Barghusen's public statements
with one of their own. In a public letter, signed by Union President Harley Stettingsgard, distributed on downtown streets and
given to the DRE the Union listed "unfair discrimination against
Local 430, CIO, unfair promotional policies, inadequate seniority
and grievance procedures, time study and incentives, shift differentials, premium pay for Saturday, Sunday and holidays, vacations, and negotiating committee pay as major points of dispute." The Union charged the company with various untruths,
and went on to complain about wages: "Wages paid at the Potteries are 29 cents below the average in CIO organized industry
in Red Wing." The letter listed twenty-eight male jobs with a
top rate of 96 cents an hour. The Union declared that "68 men
get less than $1.00 an hour; 184 less than $1.05 an hour; and
counting women, 335 people are paid at rates less than $1.05
an hour." In its charge of discrimination against CIO Local 430,
the Union pointed out that the Pottery management had granted
a Union shop to AFL Local 150 when that Union represented
the company's employees, but was unwilling to give the same
treatment to the CIO organization.

The infighting continued and on May 9 President Barghusen
sent a letter to all employees in which he reviewed the company's
proposal "so there shall be no confusion in anyone's mind about
the offer the company made during the negotiations." Stated in

the proposal was the company's answer to the Union shop issue:
". . . during the life of the agreement (a) all present members
of the Union remain members of the Union, (b) all present
employees who join the Union must remain members of the
Union, (c) all new employees must become members of the
Union after thirty days of employment, (d) dues and initiation
fees will be checked off, for Union members who authorize such
payroll deductions. Those provisions give the Union 'security'.
Present members cannot resign, new employees must join, and
dues are collected for the Union by the company." Barghusen
was holding out on the Union shop by omission of a statement
to the effect that all employees would be required to join the
Union. Under the conditions as stated in his letter, a present
employee who had not yet joined Local 430 of the CIO would
not be required to do so. Barghusen then went on to make the
inevitable, but universally unheeded, plea of company hardship:
"These changes in wage rates and the other employee benefits
in the company proposal would add more than $73,000 to
the operating costs of the company during the next year. This
amount is greater than the average annual operating earnings of
the company for the past three years. The Stockholders should
be able to expect reasonable earnings on their investment. During
the past six months, for the first time in the current history of
the company, it has been necessary to borrow money to carry
on the business. The increased costs cannot be passed on to the
customer by raising prices. Competition in the pottery business
today is too stiff. Higher prices for our products mean fewer
customers — less business — less employment — fewer jobs.
We want this industry to stay in Red Wing. Its annual payroll
of over $950,000 with employment of over four hundred
people means a great deal to the community. The management
is doing all it can to keep it here. We earnestly ask that you
give this matter your very serious thought. Read the company's
proposal carefully, study it, and we are sure you will agree it
is a fair, just and honorable agreement that has been offered
to the Union and the Shop Committee. . . .The offer was made
in good faith even though the company believed the costs of this

program were heavier than could be absorbed under present
business conditions."

Barghusen pushed for immediate acceptance by further adding:
". . . We cannot assure you that this offer, as it now stands, will
be open for acceptance by the Union, your collective bargaining
agent, after May 12, 1950, ... 5 P.M.."

As might be expected, Barghusen's "fair, just and honorable
agreement" was not fair, just and honorable enough and his
plea fell on deaf ears. On May 12, Barghusen's deadline for
acceptance, the DRE stated:

"STRIKE AT POTTERY ENTERS 10th DAY"

"Striking employees of the Red Wing Potteries gave no
indication this afternoon that they were ready to accept
company proposals for a settlement before the 5 o'clock
deadline set by the Management in letters circulated among
workers earlier in the week.

"The company offered employees a five-cent hourly wage
increase, but the letter stated the Management would not
guarantee to adhere to the proposals after 5 o'clock this
afternoon.

"The strike entered its tenth day today. Picketing has been
orderly. This afternoon there were a larger number than usual
gathered around the plant, but the workers had made no
effort to contact the Management for reopening negotiations."

The refusal on the part of the Union to come to terms and
the workers' inability to see the "justness" of the company's proposal must have greatly frustrated President Barghusen. Barghusen, himself, was under the gun, taking on the Presidency, following the death of long-term Pottery President H. H. Varney,
only four short months before the strike began. He was a man
of violent temper, and his executive skills were being given the
utmost test.

Fortunately for Barghusen and all concerned there was no
violence, and picketing continued to be orderly throughout the
strike. The company's retail store, not having reached the magnitude of importance as a source of income that it had in 1967,

was closed when the strike began. In addition, the company had chosen to cease all manufacturing and shipping with the advent of the work stoppage. Thus, with the exception of some rather nasty picket signs alluding to Barghusen's ample waistline, "Management gets fat while workers starve," the strike remained mannerly.

Management and Union remained deadlocked until June 27 when the Union agreed to accept the 5 cent wage package retroactive to February 1, and Management agreed to abide by an NLRB supervised employee vote on the question of a Union shop. The package was submitted to the membership the following night and overwhelmingly approved.

Thus the first strike in the Potteries' long history was officially settled on June 28, 1950, eight weeks after it began, and employees began returning to their jobs on July 5. All things considered, the strike was a victory for the CIO. A subsequent vote by the employees gave them their Union shop by a narrow margin. They had proved to the workers that the CIO was willing to fight for them. While the 5 cent wage increase was not excessive, the retroactive feature was well received by the membership, and approximately 25 workers received inequity adjustments of more than 5 cents an hour. The Union gained six paid holidays where in the past there had been no pay for holidays, an additional paid week of vacation, time and one-half for Saturday work, greater pay differentials for night shift work, and concessions in the area of seniority.

Only one incident occurred to mar the sweetness of their victory. Upon settlement of the strike, the AFL National Brotherhood of Potters announced that a strike benefit of $17,439 was to be divided among 166 pottery workers still affiliated with the AFL. One can only speculate as to whether this was a move on the part of the AFL to assure the continued loyalty of their 166 backers with the hope of eventually regaining control of the pottery workers. While the Red Wing Potteries became a Union shop shortly thereafter, and all employees were required to join the CIO United Gas, Coke, and Chemical Workers of America as a condition of employment, the continuing loyalty of many workers to the AFL National Brotherhood of Potters was a thorn in the Union's side for many years to come.

The relationship between Union and Management was without major conflict for the next few years. In the contract of 1952 the employees were given a 13 cent an hour across-the-board increase. The following contract negotiations in 1954 were settled with an 8 cent across-the-board increase.

The second major conflict between Union and Management was in the year 1956. The preceeding year the company recorded its first net loss, a net loss of $27,000. Early in 1956 Barghusen was replaced by F. D. Richardson as President and General Manager of the Corporation. Richardson began making a concerted effort to eliminate what he perceived as gross inefficiencies in factory manpower utilization.

On January 16 Richardson announced that he was setting up a new kiln firing schedule, and that the around-the-clock kiln firing that had been performed traditionally by thirteen men was now to be performed by only eight men. Seven of the kiln firemen refused to work under the new kiln schedule and were promptly fired by Richardson. This act touched off a series of slowdowns and walkouts that was to cripple pottery manufacturing for a period of six weeks.

The following day, January 17, according to plan, an employee blew the factory whistle at 11 A.M. and 120 workers walked off the job in sympathy. The local newspaper published a Union statement:

> "In our opinion, this (new kiln firing schedule) would be beyond human endurance . . . The Management refused at that time to negotiate this problem with the Union Committee . . . We believe that the employees were discharged unjustly when they stated they were unable to perform their said duties assigned . . . The Union will be willing to meet with the Management at any time to settle this problem."

By Thursday, January 19, only about sixty workers were on the job. Friday more than sixty reported for work, but many in the glazing and spraying departments were sent home for deliberate slowdowns. A week later eleven female decorators were fired for a slowdown, an action which resulted in the entire decorating department staying home in protest the following Monday. And so it went - slowdowns, disciplinary layoffs, and walkouts to protest Management's injustice.

On February 3 the DRE reported:

"Forest D. Richardson, President of the Company, said today that he had been informed by Union officials that neither the walkout nor the slowdowns had been authorized, sanctioned or financed by the Union."

The strike was, then, an unauthorized, wildcat strike.

Both parties agreed to call in Federal Labor Conciliator, Charles Lavalley, and spent all day, February 10, trying to agree on some solution. The original problem - the seven kiln firemen who had been fired - was all but lost in the complicated chain of events which followed.

As evidenced by the number of employees reporting to work the following week the company was losing ground. Only a handful of people showed up for work on Monday, February 15. On Wednesday of that week the first picketing began; sixty employees, mostly women, showed up for picket duty that morning. The company quickly countered this with a restraining order. On Friday, February 17, in Dakota County District Court in Hastings, Minnesota, Judge W. A. Schultz issued a restraining order forbidding Union members from "committing acts of violence, obstructing highways, interfering with vehicles, mass picketing, assaults, threats of violence, coercion, intimidation, and other interference with the company's personnel." The hearing for the temporary injunction was scheduled for the following Friday, February 24, at which time witnesses were to be called from both Union and Management. There was no evidence to suggest that the picketers were performing any of the activities enumerated in the restraining order, and Management's move to obtain this order was either an effort to prevent potential violence or an attempt to intimidate striking employees by means of a court order.

On Saturday, February 18, the first official public concern was seen in the form of a DRE editorial. The editorial entitled

"SIGNS OF DANGER AHEAD," must have pleased Management because it was, for all intents and purposes, a thinly veiled
threat to workers to get back to work or they might not have
jobs to return to.

"Some Red Wing people are beginning to get a little worried
over the continuing stalemate in negotiations between Management of the Red Wing Potteries and the Union representing the plant employees. Outsiders do not pretend to evaluate the merit of the positions taken by the disputants, but
they are becoming aware of the danger to all concerned if
there is a long delay in settling the current issues.

"The danger arises from the fact that the pottery business
is an extremely competitive one with the Japanese out to
capture a larger share of the market. The Japs have mastered
the art of making good pottery and they are able to produce
ware at low prices. As a consequence many American potteries have decided to call it quits.

"Red Wing's pottery has been fortunate in securing a good
market for its wares in the quality field - largely because it
has been a leader in luncheonware design. The company secured a lot of orders at a recent industry show held in Pittsburgh, but, of course, it cannot turn out the orders until the
present troubled waters are calmed.

"What's going to happen? Customers of the pottery can
hardly be expected to sit by and wait until the pottery resumes
operation. The stores who have orders with the pottery
will have to get goods to sell from somebody else. The longer
the stalemate continues the larger the loss of business. That
is serious for the Company. But employees find themselves
in the same boat with company stockholders and officials,
for if the business fades away, job opportunities wither away
too. Both are leaves on the same vine."

The following Thursday at 2 P.M. the conciliator met with
Management and Union. The gruelling session continued until
4 A.M. the next morning with no settlement reached. At the
hearing for the temporary injunction Friday afternoon Sheriff
Lenus Olson testified that no violence had taken place at the

plant and he saw no need for police patrol at the picket lines. Judge Schultz delayed ruling until the following Monday.

On Monday Deputy Sheriff Paul Zillgitt testified that no violence had been encountered by the Sheriff's Department. Judge Schultz, apparently seeing a settlement in sight, further delayed ruling until Wednesday.

As it turned out, the Judge's hesitancy paid off and he never was forced to set forth a ruling. The company agreed to give the kiln firemen an increase of 40 cents an hour to atone for the added work load, and the additional money convinced the Union that the new firing schedule would not be "beyond human endurance." On Tuesday, February 28, the Union members voted to accept the settlement and return to work on Wednesday. The front page of the DRE proclaimed:

"POTTERY IS BACK IN FULL OPERATION TODAY
"The Red Wing Potteries was back in full operation today following settlement Tuesday afternoon of a labor dispute between the Management and Potters Union, which had been under way for a period of 6 weeks."

Thus, the Potteries' second major labor-management dispute came to a conclusion, and the firm turned its energies toward the problems of recovering from the costly setback. But the economic wounds were severe, and the company reported losses of $85,000 in its 1956 annual report. In a letter to stockholders Richardson stated:

". . . The principal cause of the current year's loss was the strike. Our initial efforts in 1956 to eliminate gross inefficiencies in factory manpower utilization were met with misunderstanding and unwarranted suspicion by certain employees. An unauthorized work stoppage of approximately six weeks duration resulted. As reported by a special letter from the Directors on May 23, 1956, our operating loss for the first four months of 1956 amounted to $101,794 only a part of which was recovered in the balance of the year. Everyone loses in a strike but a company's losses continue after the strike is settled."

Prior to the June 1, 1956 contract the AFL and CIO had

merged and the Red Wing Potteries' Union received a new title. They became Local Union No. 6-430, Oil, Chemical and Atomic Workers International Union, AFL-CIO. The fact that they were once more members of the AFL must have given the NBOP holdouts in the 1950 dispute a small measure of satisfaction. The negotiations of 1956 brought the employees a 7 cent wage hike on a two-year contract.

These were shaky years for the Potteries and in 1958 OCAW Local 6-430 signed a one-year agreement with the company for an across-the-board increase of 5 cents. The 1959 contract was for two years and stipulated 7 cent across-the-board increases in 1959, and the same in 1960. Negotiation sessions in 1961 resulted in no increases in that year, and 5 cents in 1962. In the negotiations of 1963, it was agreed to freeze the incentive rates and grant increases of 2 cents in 1963 and 4 cents in 1964. The 1965 contract once again kept incentive rates frozen, and first-year increases of 3 cents were given to non-incentive workers only. Incentive workers received no increases. An increase of 3 cents was granted to all employees in 1966.

These increases were somewhat misleading in that they did not completely represent the wage improvements experienced by the employees over the years. The wage increase of 40 cents over the ten-year period from 1956 to 1966 did not include the gains resulting from the adoption of an incentive program. The company began putting jobs on an incentive basis in the early 1950's, and by 1966 eighty percent of all factory personnel were on incentive. This system guaranteed a man his straight base rate and granted him a bonus if he were able to produce above standard on an operation. Most Red Wing Potteries' employees were able to earn an additional one-fourth to one-third of their straight base rates on the incentive system.

Red Wing's Management and labor had now had two major conflicts since the company originated in 1877, an eight-week strike in 1950 and a six-week wildcat strike in 1956. Despite the inclusion of an incentive program, the base wage increases had been small in the last decade. Sales and profits had been above average in 1966, and the Union was tired of hearing the company's cries of dwindling markets and Japanese competition. The stage was set. Management was expecting problems in their 1967 contract negotiations; they were not to be disappointed.

SETTING THE STAGE

"What are the common wages of labour depends everywhere upon the contract usually made between those two parties, whose interests are no means the same. The workmen desire to get as much, the masters to give as little, as possible."

ADAM SMITH

Management's fears regarding the 1967 negotiations were confirmed when, during a Union-Management meeting in November of 1966, Russell Trout, OCAW International Representative, announced that the Union was through accepting pennies and nickles from the company and that we could expect a real hassle in 1967. He further suggested that, due to the magnitude of problems we were likely to encounter, we begin contract negotiations the first of the year for the May 31 contract expiration date instead of limiting ourselves to the usual two-month negotiating period. Management informed Trout and the Union Committee that if both sides were intent on working toward a settlement the two-month period was sufficient, and to begin negotiations any earlier would only serve to drag things out. Since we had bargained up to the deadline in every OCAW contract previously, there was every reason to believe that 1967 negotiations also would run to the deadline, regardless of when we started.

While the company entered 1967 with trepidation about the coming labor negotiations, they also had some reasons to be optimistic about business conditions. They had brought out four new dinnerware patterns at the Atlantic City Trade Show in January, and Red Wing's new look was well received by department store buyers. There was talk of reviving the dwindling department store business. A contract had been entered into with Sears, Roebuck and Company to manufacture two new patterns exclusively for them. Now that Red Wing Potteries had entered the supermarket field, there was optimism that 1967 would bring additional volume business from this source.

Much to the consternation of Management, 1967 did not progress as well as had been anticipated. Bringing out six new patterns, four for the trade and two for Sears, Roebuck and Company was a monumental task for a manufacturer of Red Wing's size, particularly considering the fact that these patterns called for highly complex treatments, unique in the company's experience. While the orders were in the house, technical problems delayed shipment and it looked as through Red Wing Potteries was going to miss a good portion of the Spring business. With the complexities and red tape involved in dealing with a giant like Sears, this market, while viewed as a strong potential source of sales, had not yet had a chance to take off in the first quarter. The supermarket field proved to be one of the year's biggest disappointments. Cautioned by the housewife boycotts over "unfair prices" in late 1966 and early 1967, supermarket chains were hesitant to take on any new premiums or sales promotion schemes. While there were rumors of interest on the part of this chain or that chain in starting a Red Wing promotion, the company had yet to see its first supermarket business in 1967. To make matters worse, the company had been manufacturing large volumes of the Pepe and Bob White patterns in anticipation of supermarket business. The ware was piling up.

By the end of March these factors had combined to give the company an operating loss of $74,000 for the first quarter. Due to the nature of the business some loss was to be expected in the first three months of any year, but $74,000 was substantially higher than it should have been for a healthy prognosis. The comparative loss in the previous year had been only $28,000. It began to look as though the Potteries needed some dramatic breaks - a big supermarket deal, unparalleled department store sales, or high volume business with Sears, Roebuck and Company - to show a profit in 1967. These circumstances of business and a sense of foreboding about the upcoming Union negotiations gave Management a feeling of anxiety unusual even for the pottery industry.

The company's bargaining team consisted of myself, a novice to anything other than the theory of collective bargaining, and

Gerry Mewhorter, Production Superintendent. Mewhorter, thirty-three, had experience on both sides of the table. Coming to the Potteries in 1956, he worked as a kiln setter and later as a kiln car repairman. He was a member of the Union Shop Committee in 1959 and was President of OCAW Local 6-430 in 1960. He changed allegiance in November of that year, resigning his Union presidency to become Time Study Engineer and a "company man." Recognizing his leadership skills, R. A. Gillmer made him Production Superintendent in 1965. As part of his new assignment, Mewhorter represented the company at monthly Union-Management meetings, handled grievances, and played a major role in negotiating the 1965 Union contract.

On the Union side of the table was Tilfer Chastain, President; Mike Kerg, Vice-President; Vernon Peterson, Chief Steward; Barbara Hove, and Don Hophan. Chastain, forty-four, was a hand jiggerman who had worked at the Potteries for ten years. He had been the Union President in 1965 and, at various times over the years, had been a member of the Shop Committee. Chastain was a transplanted Hoosier, with a record of warning notices over excessive absenteeism and tardiness. He seemed to miss a number of Mondays due to "car trouble, oversleeping and undefined illness." In recent years he had tried his hand at song writing and country and western recording, but apparently had never achieved much success in these avocations because for most of his tenure the company had been sending portions of his paycheck to a variety of loan companies. Chastain had never been able to produce at one hundred percent of standard in his jiggerman's job and, therefore, did not qualify for extra incentive pay. According to the Union contract an employee not producing at one hundred percent of standard could have been transferred to another job, and we were about to do just that with Chastain but thought better of it with negotiations coming up shortly. In Management's opinion, Mr. Chastain was a weak leader. On August 23, 1965, he had turned in his resignation effective September 10 "to look for another job." A few days after signing his resignation slip Chastain had second thoughts and asked Mewhorter to tear it up. With commendable foresight

Mewhorter refused. The Union's International Representative, Russell Trout, called President R. A. Gillmer shortly and asked him, as a personal favor, to reinstate Chastain as he was unable to find him another job. R. A. Gillmer balked at the thought of taking Chastain back, but the possibility of putting the International Rep in his debt was a tempting one. He agreed to present it to his foremen and Production Superintendent for a decision. Feeling he would have no problem in guiding the group to a positive decision, he asked each foreman in turn and none would agree to have Chastain in his department. Further, the Production Superintendent, Gerry Mewhorter, felt it was unwise to reinstate Chastain. Gillmer, at that point, made a decision that was to return to haunt him many times in the summer of 1967; he asserted the power of his office, overruled all present, and proclaimed that the company would, in fact, take Chaistain back.

Mike Kerg, sixty-one years of age, was another member of the Union's Shop Committee in 1967. Kerg, a grandfatherly gentleman, had been with the company thirty-nine years. He was a greenware kilnsetter and was regarded by most as an easy going individual and a conscientious worker.

Vernon Peterson, either sixty-seven or seventy-seven, depending upon which records you chose to believe, was the third member of the Shop Committee. Peterson, with the company thirty years, had been a member of the Shop Committee many times over the years, and had served as Union President in 1966 before turning the gavel over to Chastain. Age was beginning to tell on "Pete"; he wasn't as quick in 1967 as he once was. As for work assignment, Peterson was a power transporter and was responsible for moving finished ware to appropriate storage areas. He had fitted his power fork lift with a foam rubber cushion which enabled him to ride from place to place in the performance of his job.

Don Hophan, forty-four, the fourth member of the Union team, had been with the company only four years. He was a kiln car repairman and a steady and conscientious worker, if not a man endowed with blazing speed. Hophan was a man of few words. In fact, he said little if anything during the negotiating sessions which followed, and his true sentiments remained a mystery.

Barbara Hove, thirty-two, was the only female member of the Shop Committee. She was a hand sprayer with ten years of service with the Potteries. She was an efficient, fast worker, and earned good incentive. Since her husband's back injury in 1965 she had been the sole provider for her family of five children. Despite her assets as a sprayer, she was a person with a low boiling point and one who tended to view things in an emotional, subjective way.

Russell Trout had been the OCAW's International Representative to the Red Wing Potteries since 1958, stepping in for Joseph Karth who left the Union to become the Fourth District Congressman. If it is possible for Management to feel positively toward a Union Rep, Red Wing's Management held positive feelings toward Russell Trout. He seemed to have insight into the problems of the pottery industry, and we had had no major Labor-Management disputes since he had arrived on the scene. Unfortunately, it is next to impossible for an International Rep to be in the good graces of both Labor and Management for any continued length of time. There were rumblings from time to time among the membership that Trout was a "company man" and one who was more interested in keeping the peace than in "grabbing a bundle" for the workers.

In March Chastain dropped a bombshell. Trout was being replaced as our International Rep - by whom he wasn't sure - but thought it might be a man by the name of Joe Hammerschmidt. This announcement came as a real blow to Potteries' Management. We had learned to live with Trout, and now they were bringing in a new man who would be unfamiliar with the industry and with our unique problems, just two short months before the expiration of the contract. Mewhorter added to our concern by stating that he thought Hammerschmidt had a reputation of being militant, short-tempered and stubborn.

Mewhorter and I began careful preparations for negotiations. Working Saturdays in March, we attempted to compile a complete list of company proposals including a number of points that we could easily give up or trade in the heat of bargaining.

One thing we were determined to accomplish was to realign some of the wage rates. Over the years, the across-the-board increases to both base and incentive rates had resulted generally in the incentive workers being paid too much in relation to the non-incentive workers. For example, we had unskilled women making in the neighborhood of $2.50 an hour with incentive, while, at the same time, skilled men on non-incentive jobs such as mold making and glaze making were earning about $2.10. The incumbents in these jobs were getting up in years and we realized it would be very difficult finding replacements for these skills at the wages we were paying. Some method had to be worked out to give most of the increases to the non-incentive jobs, particularly those requiring high-level skills. In meetings with company Directors it was decided to go up to $27,000 in total package cost. Further, it was determined not to present our proposals until we had received the Union proposals and had had a chance to study them.

Our first bargaining session was an all-day meeting on Tuesday, April 18. Expecting the worst, our first impression of Joe Hammerschmidt was not at all negative. A youngish man with an open, deceptively friendly face, he arrived promptly at 9 A.M. and distributed smiles and handshakes around the table. If anything, he carried an air of deference, rather than the open hostility we had been led to expect.

Chastain opened the meeting with a brief statement on the hardships of the working man, the rising cost of living, and the stinginess of the company over the years. Then, without further ado, handed out the Union's proposals:

1967 CONTRACT PROPOSALS

"The following comprises in part those proposals that the Union would make for the current Contract Bargaining Session.

"The Union specifically reserves the right to add to, delete from, or respond with new proposals depending upon the attitude of the company towards the proposals herein spelled out:

"ARTICLE V:

Section 6. Average incentive shall be applied to holiday pay.

Section 7. Amend to provide for the employees working in the kiln operation and the power plant time and one half (1½) for all hours worked on Saturday, and double time for all hours worked on Sunday. (previously read: The kiln operation and the power plant being normally and required continuous operations on all days of the calendar week, there shall be no overtime penalty for work on Saturday or Sunday, if the employee involved works forty hours or less and is given other regular days of rest in lieu of Saturday or Sunday.)

Section 8. Delete language shown and amend to read: The Company shall offer all overtime to the most senior employee. Failure on the part of the Company to comply will result in the employee being compensated for the hours he should have worked.

"ARTICLE VII:

NEW: In the event a job is abolished, the employee so displaced will return to the same relative position of his former classification.

"ARTICLE XI:

Section 2. Increased vacation pay.

1 year - one week - 3% W2 Form
3 years - two weeks - 5%
10 years - three weeks - 7%
15 years - four weeks - 9%

(Previously read:

1 year - one week - 2% W2 Form
3 years - two weeks - 4%
15 years - three weeks - 6%)

Section 5. Add: Every employee shall be entitled to take his full vacation time he has earned.

Section 6. Delete: Two week notice.

(Previously read: An employee whose employment with the employer is terminated for other than just

cause or who terminates his employment for any reason after January 1st and who advises the employer
two weeks in advance of his intention to leave shall
receive and be paid for his full vacation.)

"ARTICLE XII:

Holidays. Add one additional day (Good Friday).
One-half day before New Year's Day.

"ARTICLE XIII:

Section 1. Base rate adjustments.

Adjust: Machine Spray Loader to starting rate three
cents per hour.

Adjust: Ware Handler-female-two cents per hour.

Adjust: Pug Mill Operator ten cents per hour.

Revaluate and provide adjustments for Power Transporter, Engineer 1st class and Watchman-fireman-tool-
maker.

Substantial wage increase.

NEW: Employees required to wear respirators shall be
paid ten cents per hour above their standard rate of pay.

NEW: No loss of incentive pay during a time study.

Section 7. Delete words 'up to' and correct previous
printing error-include mother and father.

(Previously read: Up to three days with pay will be
granted, for the purpose of attending the funeral, in case
of death in the immediate family - wife, husband, children, brother, sister, mother-in-law, father-in-law.)

Section 8. Amend. All inventory work shall be paid at
the employee's standard rate plus average incentive.

(Previously read: all inventory work will be paid at
the rate of $1.68 per hour.)

"ARTICLE XVI:

Section 4. Increase surgical schedule to $300 (from
$200).

Daily hospital benefits shall provide up to semi-private
room rate (from $14).

Company will pay any additional increases in insurance
premiums.

NEW: Sick and accident insurance to provide ⅔ of an employee's base rate commencing on the first day of an accident or upon being hospitalized, on the fourth day of sickness for a period of twenty-six weeks.

NEW: Establish a pension plan.

"ARTICLE XXI:

Amend to provide thirty days retention of seniority. (Previously read: Any employee promoted from an hourly to a supervisory job shall be offered a withdrawal card by the Union. However, the employee shall continue to accumulate seniority and if at a later date is reduced to an hourly job due to a reduction in supervisory staff or reason of ill health, the employee shall be assigned to the job his accumulated seniority entitles him to in the division which he left to become a supervisor, provided he is qualified to perform the job.)

"ARTICLE XXII:

Two year agreement with a wage reopener effective May 31, 1968."

We expressed the appropriate shock and amazement at the Union package, and spent the rest of the day allowing Chastain to clarify and explain the need for each of their proposals in turn. As a matter of courtesy, we kept our evaluations as to the merit of their proposals to a minimum this first day. The Union proposals of greatest economic impact were slipped in almost unobtrusively among the more verbose, but less devastating demands. "Establish a pension plan" and "substantial wage increase" accounted for only seven words in their four pages of proposals. As for the former, we had an average age among our employees of fifty-three. This made the costs involved in establishing any kind of a pension plan prohibitive. As for the latter, "substantial wage increase," we were unable to obtain any specific figure from the Committee. After considerable probing, Hammerschmidt indicated only that "the Union was not talking about nickles or dimes."

Throughout the meeting Hammerschmidt said very little, letting Chastain carry the ball. Chastain seemed to be enjoying his role, and achieved a level of philosophic eloquence heretofore absent in our dealings with him, marred only slightly by his Southern Indiana inflection. It had been our experience up until this point that the International Rep did the talking, particularly in critical discussions of this type, and seeing the Union President as main spokesman was a new twist for Potteries' Management.

Before the meeting was over Chastain put us on the edge of our chairs by announcing that the membership had given the Committee full authority this year for the first time. In other words, the Committee had complete authority to accept or reject any offers we might make or to call a strike without going back to the membership for a vote.

The next meeting was called for the coming Friday at 9 A.M. At this meeting the company was to present their proposals and respond to the Union proposals. A good deal of time was spent the next day in speculating as to what the Union was really after and what kind of a fellow Hammerschmidt really was. While there was no concensus on the former, we agreed that Hammerschmidt seemed to be a pretty reasonable sort with at least not an "uncontrollable propensity toward losing his temper."

On Friday, April 21, I opened the meeting with a brief statement of faith. I said in effect that we had enjoyed good Labor-Management relations in the last decade, that we had always tried to be fair with our employees, and that we, too, agreed the people deserved a raise this year with the rising cost of living, etc. At the risk of oversimplification, I added that the only problem the Union and Management were facing was to reach some agreement as to how much the raise should be. I was to learn that we had vastly differing opinions on that particular point. We then distributed our proposals to the Union Committee.

'RED WING POTTERIES, INC.
CONTRACT PROPOSALS

1. Article 2, Section 3: Delete 'and/or renewals or amendments to this Agreement.' (This was an effort to remove all Union activity from working hours or company time.)

2. Article 2, Section 3: Change 5 members to 3. (An attempt to reduce the shop committee from 5 members to 3.)

3. Article 4, Section 4:

Step 1: Delete 'or within 30 days after it is discovered to have occured.' (To limit the submitting of grievances to within 30 days after it actually occurred.)

Step 2: Change 'If the employees so desire they may be accompanied at such conferences by their Union department steward' to 'Upon the request of the employee, he may be accompanied at such conference by his Union department steward.' (Regarding grievance conferences.)

Step 3: Change 'Within 5 work days thereafter' to read 'At the next regular Union-Management meeting.' (Regarding the third step in the grievance procedure.)

Step 4: Delete 'within the 5 day period' specified in Step 3 above, and 'within 5 work days thereafter.'

4. Article 4, Section 11: To read 'grievances, negotiation of this Agreement or renewal or amendments hereof shall be handled after working hours.'

5. Article 5, Section 4: Delete. (An effort to eliminate paying time and one-half for Saturday work if it was part of the employee's 40 hour week).

6. Article 5, Section 10d: 'A department *or individual* will be required,' etc. (rather than: A department will be required to work on Saturday when a 72 hour notice is given.)

7. Article 5, Section 11: Delete first paragraph. Last paragraph to read 'Kiln Setters and Kiln Drawers shall be subject to the provisions of Section 7 of Article 5 of the Agreement.' (An effort to eliminate the stipulation that when Kiln Setters and Kiln Drawers are employed on a two-shift per day basis or less they receive double time for Sunday work even if part of their 40 hour week.)

8. Article 6, Section 1: Warning notices shall be cancelled after one year. (Instead of 6 months.)

9. Article 7, Section 1: Change 30 to 60. (An attempt to increase the probation period for new employees from 30 to 60 days.)

10. Article 7, Section 6: The company reserves the right to deny voluntary layoffs. (To prohibit a more-senior employee from voluntarily taking the layoff of a less-senior employee if the more-senior employee possesses critical skills.)

11. Article 7, Section 7: Add 'Kiln Fireman Glost Setter Drawer.' (To add this new job classification to the list of skilled 'non-bump' jobs.)

12. Article 7, Section 11: After 'business day' - 'Employees will notify their foreman of reason for absence within 24 hours.'

13. Article 8, Section 1: Change to 4 employees. (This was an effort to reduce the potential number of delegates to a Union convention from 8 to 4.)

14. Article 11, Section 6: Vacations are earned from June 1 to June 1.

15. Article 13, Section 1: Incentive hours will be based on a 2 for 1. (In the past, one hour of incentive was paid at the rate of one hour. We propose that incentive pay be cut in half, two hours of earned incentive be paid at the rate of one hour.)

16. Article 13, Section 3c (New): The new standards will be subject to a 60 day trial period. If a dispute exists at the end of the period they will be submitted to the joint union time study committee for further study. (An effort to lengthen trial period from 30 to 60 days, and make use of Union time study committee rather than immediately negotiating contested standards.)

17. Article 13, Section 3d (New): If a disagreement still exists after Section 3c above, the standard shall be subject to the grievance procedure commencing at Step 5 thereof. (Rather than negotiating standards.)

18. Article 13, Section 3f: Delete. (To eliminate 'All time worked and incentive earned on discontinued patterns will be computed separately and will not be averaged with or charged against time worked and incentive earned on regular pattern.')

19. Article 13, New Section 3f: Quality work is expected of all employees. Incentive workers are allowed to exceed their usual production provided that the quality of their work is satisfactory to Management. The employee will not be penalized where work is rejected through no fault of his own. Work of sub-standard quality will be deducted from the count reported at the end of a job. At no time shall any employee receive less than his base rate.

20. Article 16, Section 1: Add 'as long as employed by employer.' (Previously read 'The employer agrees to continue and keep in full force and effect a one thousand dollar life insurance policy with no change in the present provisions, the life insurance program now in effect at no cost to the employee.')

21. Article 16, Section 2: Delete. (To eliminate one thousand dollar term life insurance on retired employees.)

22. Article 18: Delete last sentence. (Eliminate sex discrimination by deleting: However, work performed exclusively by men in the past shall not be subject to bumping by women, and vice-versa.)

As we reviewed our proposals, the Union Committee blustered and fumed that all the company was doing was "taking away" from the people. Hammerschmidt stated that in all his experience he had never before seen such a list of proposals, that we couldn't possibly be serious, and that if this was our attitude we were not going to get anywhere in negotiations. Chastain added that what we were doing was trying to give them "two sawhorses for a mare."

In responding to the Union proposals we conceded on a few minor items - to offer all overtime to the most-senior employee and that failure to comply would result in the employee being compensated anyway; to allow every employee to take his full vacation time (a practice we felt we had been following); to grant an increase of two cents to the ware handler; that employees would experience no loss of incentive pay the day a time study was taken; and that any supervisor newly promoted out of the bargaining unit could retain his Union seniority for a maximum of only six months.

In the past, employee and company had split the cost of insuring dependents. We agreed to talk about substantial insurance increases if employees would pay all dependent costs. This was our first tactical bungle for, although we retreated from this position at a later date, the Committee clung persistently and noisily to the fact that we had tried to take away the employees' dependent insurance coverage. Our second tactical bungle was proposing the elimination of the one-thousand dollar life insurance coverage on retired employees. We had twenty-four retired employees, three of them over eighty, on whom we were keeping up this term policy. These older employees were raising our overall insurance costs tremendously; in fact, we were paying what was, in effect, a rate of $26.00 per month to keep up the one-thousand dollar life insurance policy on a man over eighty years of age. In proposing that we eliminate retired people from this policy, we had hoped to open the door to the possibility of offering the retired group the alternative of either the insurance or a cash settlement paid by the company. Unfortunately, due to the nature of bargaining, or lack of bargaining, that transpired, we were never able to discuss this point thoroughly. Thus, the company was cast in the dastardly role of trying to "take away" the life insurance of their "old, loyal employees."

Friday's meeting broke up late in the afternoon with very little having been accomplished. The next meeting was scheduled for 9 A.M. Wednesday, April 26, at which time the Union was to respond officially to our individual proposals.

The following Wednesday the two sides assembled in the company's conference room, and Chastain opened the meeting with a statement to the effect that the Union could not go along with any of our proposals, "now or any time in the future."

Despite this rather negative beginning, we requested that we discuss each of the company proposals individually to see if, with discussion and clarification, some headway could be made. At this point I alluded to the fact that Mr. Chastain appeared somewhat "crabby" that day, and he replied with one of his noteworthy analogies, "I'll never be a crab because crabs swim backwards, and that we'll never do." On this note we proceeded to discuss the company proposals. The Union did concede a few minor points: That Step 3 of the grievance procedure be changed to specify consideration of grievances at the "next regular Union-Management meeting" rather than "within five work days"; that the new job classification "kiln fireman glost setter" be added to the list of skilled jobs; and that we comply with Federal legislation and no longer prohibit women from bumping men on what were traditionally men's jobs. Beyond this we were totally and emotionally deadlocked. The Committee's reaction to our proposal that we base incentive pay on a 2 for 1 ratio was one of near-hysterical rejection. We attempted to explain our logic in this suggestion - that this would be a step toward eliminating the inequities that had developed over the years, and would give the non-incentive workers greater gains in any across-the-board wage increase - but the Union's cry that the company was "taking away" or "taking out of one pocket and putting in another" was part of an impervious emotional shield they were building around this topic.

Regarding hospitalization insurance, we brought up the possibility of going from $14.00 to $20.00 a day on room rate, increasing the surgical schedule from $200.00 to $300.00, and adding major medical coverage, but the Committee would make no commitment.

Despite the fact that we had ranked ten of our proposals low priority and were willing to trade or eliminate these in the give-and-take of bargaining, the session remained on an emotional plane, and the opportunity to give-and-take had not presented itself. By noon Mewhorter and I were completely frustrated, and saw no possibility of making any constructive headway. The Union still refused to put a dollar-and-cents figure on the "substantial wage increase" they desired. After the noon break, the afternoon session began in much the same tone as we had left off - bickering, laying blame, and evidencing mistrust of the other side's motives. We felt the Union was being completely unreasonable and had no desire to bargain in the true sense of the word. If questioned they undoubtedly would have expressed the same sentiments toward our position. In any event, we called a short recess, and I expressed my feelings to Mewhorter that the Union was being altogether unreasonable and we were getting nowhere. He agreed, and we decided to call a temporary halt to the whole fiasco. We returned to the conference room and told the Committee that we could see no reason for continuing the meeting with the attitude they had assumed, and if and when they were ready to bargain they knew where to contact us. The meeting broke up on April 26 with no future meetings scheduled, just five weeks before the contract expiration date.

This strategy may or may not have been a mistake. One might speculate that had we continued meeting at that point and persisted in an effort to bring reason to the fore, an agreement would have been reached and the difficult events of the Summer could have been avoided. On the other hand, the tenor of things at the time suggested small likelihood of progress until, we felt, the May 31 contract expiration date was more imminent and the accompanying pressures greater. With the knowledge of what actually transpired and with the benefit of hindsight, it must be concluded that calling a temporary halt to negotiations on April 26 served no worthwhile purpose.

The first week of May passed with neither side approaching the other for a meeting. As time went on, Management came to view a strike as more and more of a distinct possibility. Mewhorter felt that there was no question that the Union would settle happily for across-the-board increases of 10 cents this year and 10 cents next, but we were determined to hold out for a settlement that would at least partially correct the wage inequities existing in the plant.

We scheduled a meeting on May 11 with Mr. Richard Felhaber, St. Paul Labor Attorney, to answer some of the questions that had arisen regarding negotiations and the now-very-real threat of a strike. Felhaber clarified the legalities involved in what constitutes refusal to bargain; the repercussions of the company pleading poverty; supervisors working during a strike; bargaining unit employees working during a strike; shipping merchandise; and the possibility of breaking a strike. I was particularly interested in this latter question. In my contact with the people I was convinced that the majority did not want a strike and, if forced upon them by their fully empowered Committee, some would desire to continue working - strike or no strike. With this in mind, I asked Felhaber just what we could say to employees prior to the strike deadline to indicate we might continue working in the event of a strike. Felhaber indicated that it was safe to say, "If enough people want to work, we intend to keep this plant open." I was also of the opinion that we could hire enough students home for the Summer to keep the plant running.

Felhaber also held the opinion, as we did, that the continued absence of meetings with the Union was unhealthy. Our pride and our last position with the Union would not allow us to contact them personally for a meeting. Therefore, we agreed that Felhaber would contact the Federal Mediation and Conciliation Service, and empower them to contact both sides for a meeting.

Shortly thereafter Mr. Edward Larson, Federal Conciliator, notified us that a joint Union-Management meeting would be held on May 24 at the company offices, one week before the strike deadline. In the meantime, work continued as usual. There were no slowdowns, sabotage, or threats of any kind from the employees. On the contrary, the employees seldom spoke of the current negotiations or of the possible strike. According to Mewhorter, in his eleven years at the Potteries, and R. A. Gillmer, in his nine year tenure, plant morale had never been better. The calm before the storm?

Prior to the meeting to be held on May 24, Management had decided to move off their 2 for 1 cut in incentive stand, and approach the problem in a different way. Since incentive rates ranged from $1.39 to $1.98 with the majority toward the lower figure, the company decided to moderate their position and, instead of 2 for 1, propose that all incentive rates be $1.00 and then concede to move to $1.25. With all incentive rates at $1.25 we would then offer 10 cents per hour across-the-board base rate increases, plus equity raises of from 6 to 20 cents per hour for a total of twenty-four people. On the basis of 1966 hours, this would cost the company in the neighborhood of $17,000, and be a step in the direction of correcting the inequitable wage relationship between incentive and skilled non-incentive workers. This was to be the crux of the first-year package, with another 5 cent across-the-board increase for the second year - but held in abeyance until we had observed the Union reaction to the first-year proposal. The total two-year package would cost approximately $27,000. We reasoned that we could save enough - if we won our point on moving all Union business out of company time - to grant approximately $4,000 in increased hospitalization benefits. The whole thing was settled in our minds. Certainly the Union would yield to the justness and reason of our proposition.

The day of May 24 dawned with a degree of restrained optimism on the part of Management. The leveling and logical influence of the Conciliator was being brought into the picture, and the company had moderated their position to one more likely to be acceptable to the Union. The optimism lasted until we met with the Union in the conference room. Due to the severity of the situation, President R. A. Gillmer was to be present from this point on in negotiating sessions. Both sides briefly reviewed their April 26 positions for the benefit of Conciliator Larson. Larson was quick to still hysterical outbreaks from either side. Having struggled through the preliminaries, R. A. Gillmer took the floor and set forth the company's modified proposal. He opened with the list of equity raises in the hope of putting the Union in a receptive mood. He followed with the proposed $1.00 incentive rate and the 10 cent per hour across-the-board base rate increase. This was met with the now-familiar cries of "taking away" and "taking out of one pocket and putting in another." As far as the Union committee was concerned we had not changed our position significantly - we were still "robbing Peter to pay Paul." We tried to explain to the Committee the reason for our proposal and that it would, in fact, add additional labor costs, but they were not willing to seriously evaluate our proposal. In fact, Chastain indicated that until the company was ready to start giving instead of taking there was no sense in wasting the Committee's time. Larson, feeling that nothing was being accomplished in the face-to-face meeting, decided to separate the two groups and talk with each individually.

We spent the remainder of the day sitting in the President's office while the Union remained in the conference room, alternately discussing our position with the Conciliator, and discussing strategy among ourselves for long periods when the Conciliator left to spend time with the Union. Management was dejected at what we perceived as the Union's lack of reason and unwillingness to talk. The meeting broke up that day with no sign of progress. Federal Conciliator Larson seemed at a loss as to logical avenues of settlement. What he talked to the Union about we had no way of knowing, but he exerted no pressure on us to change our direction. Larson scheduled the next meeting for Monday, just two days prior to the Wednesday midnight strike deadline.

Despite the Union opposition, we continued with our plan. We had not yet conceded to move to $1.25 on the incentive rate, or offered the 5 cents for the second year. We were committed to take a strike over two issues - (1) the realigning of wage rates to improve the relative position of non-incentive workers, and (2) that Union matters be conducted off of company time. Our resolve was never tested on the second issue because it never came up for discussion.

Prior to Monday's meeting the company's Treasurer-Controller, Irving Vick, prepared a record of all employees who worked during 1966; their actual earnings during the year, and what their earnings would have been under the proposed $1.25 incentive rate, 10 cent base rate increase, and equity increases for twenty-four people. We felt that this detailed comparison would demonstrate to the Union that we were not trying to take away anything, but rather were granting increases to all but three people, for whom something could be worked out. The increases ranged from very small for certain high-incentive people to very large, up to $600.00, for non-incentive workers.

On Monday, in the presence of Conciliator Larson, we presented our "revised" proposal to the Union with a statement to the effect that, due to their violent reaction to our last proposal, we had decided to moderate our position from the $1.00 incentive rate to $1.25. The suggestion fell on deaf ears. Barbara Hove indicated that the Union would rather see the company eliminate incentive altogether than cut the rates. In exploring this idea of eliminating incentive altogether it was discovered that the Union would expect the $47,000 the company paid in incentive in 1966 to be distributed in total as part of the general wage increase.

In defense of our revised proposal we gave each member of the Union Committee a copy of the record Vick had prepared showing the effect in dollars and cents of the proposal on each employee. The record was met with mistrust, given a cursory look, and cast aside as supporting information for something that had no merit in the first place.

Chastain was still doing most of the talking for the Union, a situation we began to see as unhealthy. Hammerschmidt seemed to be feeling his way, unfamiliar with the company's history and unique problems. He was giving full authority to the Committee, mainly Chastain, and since we had a low regard for Chastain's leadership ability and judgment, we did not like the way things were shaping up.

Larson chose to split the groups again in mid-morning when it was clear that we had reached a stalemate. The Management team retired to R. A. Gillmer's office and began the nerve-racking ordeal of waiting, speculating, and reviewing. In our opinion the Union was not bargaining. They had adopted a completely defensive posture and, while we had modified our position substantially over the last six weeks, they had totally rejected all of our efforts and, worse still, had offered no constructive solutions of their own. We still did not know what they were after - the actual amount of money they desired, or how serious they were about the various fringe issues.

We learned later that day from Larson that the Committee's thinking was in the neighborhood of 60 cents - 30 cents the first year and 30 cents the second. As far as we were concerned this was preposterous! They were talking about $120,-000 in increased costs in wages alone, when our average net profit in the last nine years had been $36,000. Further, this figure of $120,000 did not include any fringe costs. The 5 cents we were still holding in abeyance for the second year was insignificant if they were truly serious about 60 cents.

While we were hesitant to plead poverty and go through a forced disclosure of our books to the Union, we felt it was necessary to somehow get the point across to them that what they were asking just was not there. Thus, before Monday's meeting was over we disclosed our current financial picture to Ed Larson "in confidence," but with the hope that he would use the information discreetly to bring the Union to reason. He was aware that the Red Wing Potteries, Inc., had losses totalling $90,776 through April of 1967, and that our average net profits had been only $36,000 in the last nine years. The meeting broke up on Monday with a final meeting scheduled for Wednesday, May 31, the deadline date. The meeting was to be held on "neutral ground," at the St. James Hotel in Red Wing.

While Management was totally frustrated by negotiations to date and recognized the high likelihood of a strike, there was still hope. The OCAW had set a pattern in the past of going right to the deadline before arriving at a settlement. In addition, word was out that our financial picture was not a bright one - and we still had another 5 cents we could give to clinch things if a settlement were near. We honestly felt that our last offer was an equitable one, and if the membership had an opportunity to study it they would put pressure on the Shop Committee to accept it rather than take a strike. To this end, we "lost" a copy of the proposal showing the effect it would have on every employee in the plant Monday evening, hoping it would be quickly located and circulated.

We congregated Wednesday morning in a private dining room at the St. James Hotel. Hammerschmidt gave a short speech to start things off, suggesting that Potteries' Management should be ashamed of their miserly ways in the past and, further, that he was actually ashamed of his Union for not doing more for the Potteries' employees over the years. He also accused us of attempting to bypass the Union Committee by deliberately leaving our last proposal in the plant, and warned that the Committee was given full bargaining authority by the membership, and they were considering filing a complaint with the NLRB for our action. When Hammerschmidt had finished, Chastain added that he personally had been threatened by a member of Management and, further, that we had called his Union undemocratic. We remained silent during these accusations, and when the Union had finished Conciliator Larson asked each side in turn if their position had changed. Ours had not; neither had the Union's. At this point, President Gillmer suggested that a strike seemed unavoidable and asked that it be kept orderly, and that statements to the press be avoided if possible. Chastain assured us that that was the Union's intention. Larson split the two groups, and Management retired to the hotel lobby; fatigued, tense, and without much hope. Here it was, the last day before the strike deadline and we had not begun to bargain.

Larson spent most of his time with the Union, and shortly after the noon break suggested that Management return to the office, saying he would spend some more time with the Union, but "there did not seem to be much common ground for agreement." We were to remain on call in case Larson saw some daylight and wanted to get the two groups back together again.

We returned to the company offices, congregating in the President's office to worry and speculate. We agreed that we were not ready to change our approach to the incentive cut, because we firmly believed this wage realignment was necessary for the perpetuation of the business. Even if we were willing to leave incentive rates untouched and give a straight across-the-board increase, we agreed that there was no assurance, because of the Union's hazy position, that an agreement could be reached.

President Gillmer felt certain we would meet again with the
Union before the day was over. He was also willing to bet we
would not see a strike. I felt a strike was inevitable, and a one-
dollar wager was established. Afternoon passed into evening,
and midnight came with no further word from Larson or the
Union. The one-dollar wager was small compensation for the
months to follow.

THE MONTH OF JUNE — THE BUILDUP

"We don't arbitrate grievances, we strike the bastards instead. First, we close down this guy's outfit where the trouble is. Then, if he won't settle, we close him down in the surrounding states. Then, if he still won't settle, we close him down across the whole country . . ."

JAMES R. HOFFA

Arriving at the company offices Thursday morning, June 1, we were not surprised to find pickets at the entrances to the factory and salesroom. While the salesroom clerks were members of the Union and went out on strike with the factory employees, there was never a question that the company would keep the store open. The peak summer season was just beginning for the salesroom, and it would be kept open and staffed by Management, their wives, and office girls. It was to remain open the usual hours, 8 A.M. until 9 P.M., seven days a week.

The salesroom was directly across the street from the factory and had seven driveway entrances along a frontage of approximately two city blocks. The income generated by the salesroom was considered vital to our survival.

We learned that the Union was to have a membership meeting that morning. We hoped that the membership would arise and voice disapproval of the strike. However, this hope soon faded when the picketing resumed after the meeting with no effort to contact Management. Our pre-strike speculation that a certain number of employees would want to continue working, regardless of the strike, was proven false. Only one man contacted Mewhorter and expressed a desire to work. After discussion, we decided that the effect of one man working would be negligible and told him to hold off until we could determine if a back-to-work movement could be started.

While there was an ample supply of pickets, perhaps fifteen or twenty, they were orderly, and made no vocal threats or efforts to prohibit Management and office staff from entering the premises. Nevertheless, it was a source of wonder to see these employees, many of whom I had chatted with as recently as the previous day, engaged in a form of rebellion, however passive at this point. Although others in Management expressed feelings that the picketing could become nasty, I scoffed at the idea of any of our people engaging in violence of any kind. I even found it inconceivable that any of these people would harass me verbally. In the year I had been at the Potteries I had come to regard many of these people as personal friends, and their shouting at me would be an unimaginable violation of this relationship. Unfortunately, I was totally mistaken on this point.

In the course of business, we found it necessary to walk from office to salesroom many times a day. In making this trek it was necessary to pass through the picket line, allowing daily face-to-face contact with the strikers. Initially, and throughout the month of June, I greeted the pickets cordially, conversed on the weather, and agreed that strikes were undesirable. To begin with, this cordiality was natural because we held no animosity toward most employees, but it was also a calculated approach to show employees our good faith and reasonableness. We were to hear shortly that the pickets were surprised to see that we would talk to them in a casual and amicable fashion under the circumstances.

The citizens of the community were alerted to the strike by Red Wing's newspaper, the Daily Republican Eagle (DRE), and the local radio station, KCUE. Representatives of these two media began calling the first day of the strike, and we made an effort to be sufficiently vague and uncritical so as not to arouse the Union's hostility.

KCUE announced the strike:
"Pickets are walking in front of Red Wing Potteries today as the promised strike has begun. Workers did not appear for shifts which started at midnight. The last negotiating session took place Wednesday. A general meeting of the Union membership of the Potteries took place this morning. Ninety-six workers are involved. 'Economic issues' is the stated reason for the walk-out. A Potteries official, R. S.

Gillmer, says the company feels it has been 'fair' in its wage offer but the Union has been unwilling to accept it. No one on either side will venture a guess as to how long the strike will continue. Gillmer said late this morning he wasn't sure of the outcome of the Union meeting. He said there had been no incidents, and picketing had been orderly. Gillmer said he wasn't sure when Federal Mediator, Ed Larson, would set up another meeting between Union and Management."

The DRE carried a picture of two pickets and the following front-page article:

"100 STRIKE R. W. POTTERY; WORK STOPS.

"About 100 workers at Red Wing Potteries were off their jobs today as a strike idled the city's fourth largest industry.

"Members of Oil, Chemical and Atomic Workers Local 6-430 began picketing the plant at midnight as the Union contract with the firm expired at that time.

"The dispute involves economic issues of a new contract. The company contends the union demands are unreasonable and the Union says the company proposals are too low.

"Union representatives said six negotiation meetings have been held and a Federal Mediator was on hand at the last three talks.

"No further talks are scheduled although both sides expect the Labor Conciliator will call another meeting sometime next week.

"R. S. Gillmer, company operations manager, said he did not want to reveal details of the dispute because it might hamper future negotiations. 'We made an offer we feel is fair,' Gillmer said. 'The issue is economic.'

"He commended the workers for their orderly picket line. While the plant is not operating, Gillmer said the salesroom will remain open.

"Joe Hammerschmidt of Hampton, International Representative for the Union, said the company hasn't offered a sound proposal on any fringe benefits.

"The company offered a 10 cent across-the-board pay raise

spread over two years, Hammerschmidt said, but they proposed cutting the incentive pay for workers on piece work. 'Their total offer is less than $17,000 spread over two years for 100 people,' Hammerschmidt said. 'This amounts to four cents per hour per year.'

"Union officials also said they want a pension plan for workers and an increase in hospitalization benefits.

"The company, they said, seeks to remove retired or retiring workers from the life insurance plan and eliminate dependents from medical insurance coverage."

In an effort to keep the situation on an orderly level and to say something of a positive nature, I publicly commended the workers for their "orderly picket line." My motive in this statement was to instill some pride within the people that their picketing was, in fact, orderly; they were not ruffians but reputable citizens who could fight this economic battle in a logical, above-board manner.

Hammerschmidt, as evidenced in the DRE article, revealed more details to the press and went to a greater effort to put the company in a bad light. Our degree of error in the negotiating points of removing retired people's life insurance and not paying dependent medical insurance became clear to us for the first time when Hammerschmidt made these public issues by giving them to the newspaper. This gave the strikers something very concrete at which to point, to make us out as heartless villains, and to justify their strike. For us to claim that these were just starting points in the game of bargaining - issues that we would withdraw, amend, or barter - was useless. For many Unionists this provided the justification for the strike.

The evening of June 1, the first day of the strike, Joe Hammerschmidt arrived to take his turn on the picket line. In crossing from the office to the salesroom, I passed Hammerschmidt and we struck up a conversation. He suggested that we had something up our sleeve and actually wanted this strike. I told him I did not know what he was talking about, and the last thing we wanted was a strike. He added that I personally was doing well financially with an income he knew to be at least

$20,000. I denied this, and added that I had left a job in Minneapolis to come to Red Wing at the same salary and had not received a raise since. He expressed doubt, and said he had friends in Washington who could look up my W-2 tax form and find out exactly how much money I did make. My salary was to be a subject of rumor from this point on. My rumored pay grew in direct proportion to the hostilities of the strike. By August it was rumored that I was being paid $42,000 a year. I could only wish this rumor had some basis in fact.

Our first involvement with Red Wing's police department also occurred on the first day of the strike. It was our understanding that pickets were not allowed to block our driveways in any manner or means. We were feeling our way at this point, and when I noticed one picket who seemed to be standing for brief periods of time in one of the salesroom driveways, I called the police department to report the incident and request that they take corrective action. We wished to see what position the police would take on strike matters, and also desired to stop any border-line illegalities before they got started. A patrol car arrived shortly, officers talked briefly to the pickets, and left. The police complaint report read: "Officers checked with pickets in area. Lady stated that they hadn't been blocking any drives. However, she stated that Mr. Gillmer had almost struck her and another picket as they were crossing the driveway. They were walking on the sidewalk. She said he started to drive in, then speeded up, and they had to jump out of the way."

The lady referred to in the police report was Barbara Hove, Shop Committee member, whom I had driven by earlier in the day. The "speeding up" and "jumping out of the way" were exaggerations, but, as I was to learn, we were involved in a game in which exaggeration was a critical tool. The following week it was rumored that I had run over a picket. Whether I stopped to check the victim's condition or heartlessly drove on, I never learned.

In any event, the prompt arrival of the police, the fact that they talked with the pickets, and the trivial driveway problem had improved, was somewhat heartening to Management. It looked as though we could depend on the police if things should get out of hand.

The following day KCUE reported "nothing new on the strike," quoted me as saying, "Everything is running smoothly, and no bitterness has developed," and quoted Hammerschmidt as saying, "The company has not offered any sound proposal on fringe benefits." My statement that everything was running smoothly was a slight exaggeration in that we were facing the problem of training our wives and the office employees to wait on trade in the salesroom. Further, someone had to become familiar with the lack of organization in the seconds warehouse to enable our locating specific items and filling requisitions for the salesroom. One comforting factor was the vast stockpile of merchandise we had in the seconds warehouse. We estimated the salesroom could operate the entire summer without serious shortages of merchandise.

Friday evening Chastain was on the picket line, and I struck up a conversation with him. We agreed on one point - probably the first since negotiations began back in April - that "nobody wins" in a strike. I commented on the fact that Hammerschmidt had not yet taken his turn on the picket line that day, and asked Chastain where he was. He became quite animated - apparently interpreting my query as an indication Management wanted a meeting - and informed me that Hammerschmidt could be reached at once if needed. Receiving no response, he asked outright if we wanted a meeting. I told him we did not, and that we were trusting Conciliator Larson to call the next meeting when he felt the time was right. I also indicated to Chastain that if the Union, on the other hand, requested that we meet, we would be more than happy to comply. Despite his obvious interest in meeting, Chastain was not disposed to take it upon his own shoulders to call the two groups together. Thus my brief encounter with Chastain ended in a statemate, neither one of us willing to swallow his pride and take the initiative in calling a meeting. Nevertheless, Management wanted the strike to end as soon as possible, and realized that this would not be accomplished in the absence of negotiating meetings. We were

Red Wing Potteries Salesroom

Revoir

View from Salesroom Lot to Factory

Severson

Boat Trailer Hooks Hammerschmidt's Car (Hammerschmidt in Hat)

Taylor

OCAW International Representative Hammerschmidt (Far Right) One Block East of Salesroom Holding Loudspeaker

Company Photo

Pickets Parade in Front of Salesroom after Court Order (Hammerschmidt Center with Tie)

Alpers

Chief Lenway (Plain Clothes in Center Group of Officers) and Police
Observe Parade After Court Order

Alpers

Chief Lenway (Second from left) Attempts to Serve Court Order
on Pickets

Alpers

Two Employees Picketing Factory on First Day of Strike

DRE Staff

Picketing Finley's
Coast-to-Coast Store

DRE Staff

Lone Picket Walks in Front of
Daily Republican Eagle Building

DRE Staff

Two Pickets After News of Liquidation Vote

DRE Staff

President R. A. Gillmer Announcing Stockholders' Decision to
Liquidate

DRE Staff

certain that Larson would call us together the following week.

Entering the first weekend of the strike, Management was faced with the realization that they could no longer be afforded the luxury of a weekend off. Their presence was necessary both Saturday and Sunday to oversee picket activities, and to wait on trade in the salesroom. The weekends, particularly during the summer, were far and away our busiest days, with literally hundreds of cars lining the salesroom parking lot. Management was anxious to see the effect of the picket line on the weekend business.

We were greeted Saturday morning by a substantial increase in the number of pickets. Perhaps forty or fifty patrolled the sidewalk in front of the salesroom. The Union apparently had recognized the fact that Saturday and Sunday were our big days and were generating their major efforts in that direction. While heavy rain off and on both Saturday and Sunday gave Management a degree of satisfaction, it did not discourage the pickets. Those who had the foresight to bring rain-gear remained relatively dry; others were soaked to the skin, but continued to walk the picket line. These people were persistent, unwilling to allow a downpour to diminish their efforts.

Despite the increase in numbers, the pickets remained orderly. Other than calling customers "scabs" and standing briefly on occasion in front of entering cars, the situation remained calm. The police were summoned only once over the two-day weekend. On Sunday at 7:40 P.M. I called to complain that Hammerschmidt was blocking a driveway. The police talked to pickets, and the "Findings and Dispositions" in the police report stated: "Pickets claim they were not blocking drive."

Weekend business had been good, as good as we would have expected had there been no pickets. We felt we had won a major victory. We were surprised to find that very few customers were being turned away by the picket lines.

At this point, it was apparent that there was a vast difference in the picketing techniques of Joe Hammerschmidt and the majority of our employees. He was far more menacing and aggressive in his approach. He would actively wave cars on as they approached his driveway; if they persisted in turning into the drive he would manage to place himself squarely in the middle of the road, forcing them to stop; he would then use various arguments in order to persuade the customer not to patronize the store. Our employees, on the other hand, lacked this boldness of technique and would stand unobtrusively at the sides of the driveway displaying their picket signs, but offering little resistance to the determined motorist. This passivity pleased us, and all things considered, we felt the events of the first weekend gave us an advantage.

The following week George Brooks, owner-manager of station KCUE and president of the Red Wing Industrial Development Corporation, approached us to discuss the advisability of the RWIDC entering the situation as a conciliator in hopes of settling the dispute. Management was reluctant to accept his offer because, (1) we personally were in the best position to know the limits the company could go to settle the strike, and (2) we already had the services of a professional conciliator, Ed Larson. In short, we felt that this approach would not be fruitful at that point. Thus the matter ended.

On Monday, June 5, the DRE and KCUE reported no progress in the strike, no meetings scheduled although Larson was expected to call one later in the week, and noted that the Union had set up headquarters in the house next to the Potteries salesroom at 1844 Main Street. This house belonged to a striking employee who had donated it for Union purposes for the duration of the strike.

On Monday morning a college student entered the company office and announced that he wanted to go to work. After making certain the young man was aware of the potential hazards involved in breaking the picket line, we decided to hire him as a test case. When he left work that afternoon Chastain and ten of the pickets surrounded him. I approached the scene to observe and hopefully prevent threats and violence. The group broke up as I arrived, and I asked the young man to drive over to the salesroom so we could talk in private. I asked him if he was still determined to work. He said that he was and would be at work in the morning. I arrived at the office the next morning in time to see a large group of pickets dispersing and the young man driving away from the plant. By some manner or means the strikers had weakened his resolve and we never heard from him again. This occurrence was a blow to any thoughts we might have had of breaking the strike.

On Wednesday we suffered our first experience of outright defiance on the part of the strikers. We had planned a shipment and had a hauler scheduled to bring in a truck that morning. A supervisor from the trucking company was scheduled to meet the driver in Red Wing in order to drive the truck through the picket line. The Teamster Union drivers had to honor the picket lines or potentially suffer a fine. The truck and driver arrived early and, finding no supervisor on the scene, returned to the local terminal. Before leaving, however, the driver talked to a group of pickets and alerted them to the intended shipment. By the time the truck returned with the supervisor about an hour later, there was a crowd of twenty or twenty-five irate pickets around the back gate. Arvid Johnson, a picket line spokesman, had parked his car across the driveway making it impossible for the truck to gain entry, and other pickets were harassing the supervisor who was to take the truck through. We phoned the police at 8:39 and I went out to the gate to persuade Johnson to move his car. I shouted at him to "get his damn car out of the drive." He refused, and I continued shouting. R. A. Gillmer soon approached the area and added his voice to the din. By 8:45 the police hadn't arrived so we phoned them again. At 9:01, a long twenty-two minutes after our initial call, a squad car arrived containing two officers. We pointed out the automobile, and the fact that it was blocking the driveway. The police seemed unsure of themselves and began an unauthoritarian discussion with Johnson. We were very short-tempered by this time and could not see why any delay was necessary in correcting what was an obvious infraction of the law. President Gillmer asked the officers if Johnson was breaking the law. They answered that he was, and Gillmer told them to have Johnson move his car immediately. They then ordered the car moved and

Johnson complied. The truck proceeded through the gate, and Management was warmed with a sense of victory. The truck then was loaded with about $8,000 worth of our merchandise, while a crowd of angry and frustrated pickets looked on from the back gate. In late morning the truck passed out through the picket line with protests no more serious than verbal abuse. We noted, however, that a car containing two pickets departed with the truck. We were to learn later that the striker's automobile slowed down in front of the truck on the highway in an effort at harassment, and the driver was forced to stop and notify the highway patrol to assure safe escort. Nonetheless, the company had succeeded in making a shipment and we were pleased at the achievement. We were to make six or seven additional shipments during the course of the strike, and met very little resistance after this first confrontation.

Due to our increasingly frequent contact with the police department we thought it best, at this point, to clarify our position and expectations in terms of law enforcement. R. A. Gillmer called Red Wing Police Chief Warren Lenway and informed him that we were sorry to put the police to this inconvenience, that we would try to refrain from calling if possible, and that we did not expect them to take sides, but only to enforce law and order. We felt we could expect this much as taxpayers and citizens. Lenway agreed, and shortly thereafter forwarded the company a copy of his "POLICE DEPARTMENT LABOR DISPUTE POLICY:"

"1. Prevent interference with the free and uninterrupted use of public roads, streets, highways or methods of transportation or convenience, and to use such force as may be reasonably necessary for that purpose.

"2. Prevent disorderly conduct, assault and battery, malicious destruction of property, riot, or other similar crimes and misdemeanors defined by statute or ordinance and to *make arrests for such violations when committed in their presence.*

"3. Have the right and are under duty to use such force as may be necessary to prevent injuries to persons or destruction of property in violation of the general laws of the State codes of Minnesota as distinguished from acts which are merely defined as unfair labor practices and therefore declared to be unlawful.

"4. Have the right and are under duty to make arrests without Warrants for acts of violence committed in their presence and resulting in such injury to persons or destruction of property.

"5. Have the right and are under the duty to make arrests pursuant to Warrants issued by Courts of competent jurisdiction.

"The above items are duties which MUST be performed by Officers when any such occasions arise. The following general policy will be followed when assigned to labor disputes: OFFICERS WILL NOT ASSUME THE RISKS OF MAKING ARRESTS FOR THE PERFORMANCE OF ACTS DECLARED TO BE UNLAWFUL AS UN-FAIR LABOR PRACTICES UNDER THE MINNESOTA LABOR RELATIONS ACT UNLESS SUCH ACTS ALSO CONSTITUTE A VIOLATION OF SOME OTHER STATE LAW OR CITY ORD. FOR EXAMPLE, THE MINNESOTA LABOR RELATIONS ACT FOR FREE *'INGRESS AND EGRESS FROM ANY BUILDING.'* WHEN CASES WHERE THERE IS NOT SUCH FREE *'INGRESS AND EGRESS'* IT WILL NOT BE THE DUTY OF THE POLICE OFFICERS TO ENFORCE SUCH PROVISIONS *BUT IT SHALL BE THE DUTY OF THE INJURED PARTY OR PARTIES TO MAKE A COMPLAINT OF SUCH VIOLATION TO A COM-PETENT COURT* FOR THE PURPOSE OF RECEIV-ING RELIEF FROM SUCH VIOLATION. OFFICERS SHOULD INFORM ANY PERSON MAKING COM-PLAINT OF VIOLATIONS OF THE MINNESOTA LABOR RELATIONS ACT AS THIS THAT HIS RELIEF IS BY COURT ACTION. *OFFICERS SHOULD ALSO FAMILIARIZE THEMSELVES WITH THE LABOR RE-LATIONS ACT AND INFORM PERSONS WHO ARE*

IN VIOLATION OF IT OF SUCH VIOLATION.
"When a Court Order such as a restraining order or an
injunction has been issued by a competent court it is not
the duty of a police officer to see that the provisions of such
order are complied with unless the order specifically pro-
vides that the police department enforce such provisions.
When such order of the Court is violated and it is brought
to the attention of a police officer he will inform the complaining party to apply to the Court which issued the order
for the purpose of 'Contempt' proceedings. In short, the
main duty of a Police Officer assigned to duty at a labor
dispute is to maintain law and order and to enforce all
general state laws and city ordinances. In *no manner of
word or action will he display any partiality toward either
of the parties involved,* but will maintain a courteous but
firm attitude in the performance of his duties."

12/12/66

W. O. Lenway, Chief of Police,
Red Wing, Minnesota

Management was becoming anxious about another meeting,
having expected Larson to call one for the current week. On
Wednesday the DRE reported:

"NO MEETINGS SET IN POTTERY STRIKE

"No meetings are yet scheduled in the seven-day old strike
by Oil, Chemical and Atomic Workers Local 6-430 against
Red Wing Potteries, Inc.
"Tilfer Chastain, president of the local, said that reports a
meeting has been set by the federal mediator for Friday are
'completely false.' 'There are no meetings scheduled and
we have no idea when there will be one,' Chastain said.
"Meanwhile, picketing will continue and the strike headquarters near the pottery salesroom remains in operation.
The telephone number is 388-2669.
"The Red Wing AFL-CIO council Tuesday night voted to
donate $500 to the strikers and pledged their 'moral and
physical support.' They will help with the picketing and
take collections.

"Chastain thanked those who already donated their time for picket line work and said the strike will remain orderly."

In addition to the $500 donated by the AFL-CIO council, KCUE reported a $500 donation from a Pine Bend, Minnesota OCAW local. We had heard that the people were getting only $10.00 a week for picketing and felt at that rate they would quickly feel the economic pressures to return to work. Even the two $500 donations did not worry us because spread over one hundred people this figure amounted to only $10.00 per person.

Thursday, June 8, and still no word from Larson on a meeting. It began to look as though, at best, we could meet the following week.

KCUE carried a story on the dying Red Wing Bus Line and noted concern on the part of Chastain.

"Red Wing Bus Line owner, Robert Vasil, at the end of his financial rope, will get some help from members of the Red Wing Pottery Worker's Union.

"Members of the Retail Division of the Red Wing Chamber of Commerce Wednesday learned that he would be unable to continue his bus line after this week because of lack of patronage.

"He said he is losing from eight to twelve dollars a day and said that part of the current loss of revenue is traceable to the Red Wing Potteries strike. Vasil said the shift of the downtown bus loading point from its former location near 3rd and Bush to in front of the Auditorium Theatre is also to blame for loss of business.

"The president of the Red Wing Pottery Worker's Union, Tilfer Chastain, said, 'It is not the intention of the local or any of its people to be even partially the cause of a discontinuance of service to the Community.' He said, "Therefore as the president of the local I will request permission to take up a collection to help this service to continue and I request that the rest of the community do likewise'."

The idea of Tilfer Chastain expressing civic interest was a source of considerable hilarity for Management, and served as the main topic of conversation at coffee that day. This type of humor was not unusual within the company offices. It provided an opportunity to relieve some of the building tension, as well as a method of expressing hostility toward the other side. In fact, the following day one of the employees located an old Tilfer Chastain recording, "Shoes of a Beggar," and Chastain's melodious voice could be heard most of that day emanating from the salesroom phonograph.

Management was apprehensive about the coming weekend. We had heard there were to be a great many outside agitators brought in by the Union. Saturday dawned overcast and threatening. There were pickets present at 8:00 A.M. when we drove to work. Despite the rain, their numbers began to swell and by noon they were close to one-hundred strong. Our employees were in the minority. There were many faces we could not identify, and assumed they were agitators brought in from Minneapolis and St. Paul. As their numbers grew, they gained courage and became more unruly. Their pauses in the driveways became longer, and their shouting gained volume and became more offensive. Our people, under the tutelage of Joe Hammerschmidt, were learning the art of picketing.

At 1:20 Saturday afternoon President Gillmer called for police assistance. The complaint report read: "Gillmer reports the pickets at the Potteries are stopping cars as they come into the salesroom lot and making insulting remarks to the occupants. Customers have reported this when they come into the store. Gillmer wanted to know if it was possible to have an officer there on duty. Told him we were working short-handed and that it would be difficult to station anyone out there. He said there is talk of going on about a full-scale picket for Sunday." The "Findings and Dispositions" read, "C. Johnson talked to the man in charge of the pickets and also Gillmer."

The police were "too busy" to stay long on Saturday. They stopped briefly in the parking lot and talked to Hammerschmidt. We had no way of knowing what they talked about, but the general disorder on the picket line continued for the rest of the afternoon. At 7:55 that evening we called the police to report a car full of Union sympathizers parked on our parking lot, causing a general disturbance by shouting at customers.

That night, Saturday, I was to experience the first gnawing fear of weekend picketing. Saturday had been relatively bad in comparison with previous picketing activity, and we had every reason to believe that Sunday would be worse. Could we count on the police? We were beginning to doubt it. It was difficult to work up much of an appetite Saturday evening, and harder still to digest the meager portions with the anxieties working on my stomach. The general anxiety I had experienced up to this point was beginning to make itself felt physiologically.

The rain was not to be our ally. The rains came Sunday morning but the weather did not dissuade the pickets. It became clear from the early morning buildup that Sunday would exceed Saturday in sheer numbers of pickets. Some of yesterday's unfamiliar faces reappeared and were joined by growing numbers of new faces. Many of the customers entering the store were visably shaken and related tales of vile language and threats from the pickets—pushing the car over the edge of the bank behind the salesroom and "getting them" on their way out were common threats. A few pickets were painstakingly jotting down license numbers as a means of intimidation. They were becoming more bold in their efforts to stop cars. At 11:20 A.M. I sought the aid of the police. The police report read: "Gillmer reports the pickets stopping cars again and calling the people names." Findings and Dispositions: "Sent car 201 to see if anything could be done. Paulson reports pickets just parading back and forth across the driveways, no one being stopped that he could see."

Rather than cast disparagement at Officer Paulson's report, I would sooner give him the benefit of the doubt and agree that he probably did not see any cars being stopped for any length of time during his brief check. The pickets at this point still had some fear of police action and tended to moderate their behavior in their presence.

After the departure of the police, however, the picketing returned to its earlier level. According to police records, R. A. Gillmer called again at 12:02 P.M. and stated that the "situation is getting more out of hand. The pickets are throwing names at the people when they drive in, and Gillmer is afraid some customer is going to get out of his car and start throwing fists." The "Findings and Dispositions" read: "Send 201 out to hang around there for awhile, and to let me know if more of our men should be called out. Lenway called and advised we keep one of the cars out there after the 1:00 P.M. man comes on duty." Thus, we had a policeman on hand for the rest of the afternoon and, as a result, the pickets were somewhat subdued. We noted with some alarm that the police were visiting in an apparently amiable fashion with the pickets, and at one point accepted an offer of donuts from the strikers. Things were too friendly for our peace of mind.

Observing the pickets throughout the day, it was becoming clear that women, for the most part, were the loudest and most foul-mouthed of the pickets, a somewhat surprising phenomenon. Another factor that never ceased to amaze us was that women would bring their children to the picket line with them. Whether this was for the purpose of gaining customer-sympathy or simply because they did not have baby-sitters, we never determined. Whatever the reason, exposing children (some of whom must have been under the age of five) to the traffic dangers, the language, and the general defiance of authority, seemed a very unhealthy situation.

In spite of the heightened picket activity we were having a good weekend from a sales standpoint. We were amazed, as certainly the Union must have been, at the number of people who ignored the protests of the pickets and entered the store. Some people, I am convinced, became more determined than ever in the face of this harassment, to show these people they could not limit their right of free access. Others had traveled long distances, had been stopping at the Potteries for years, and would let nothing stop their annual quest for bargains in pottery seconds. I told R. A. Gillmer that afternoon that the Union could weather one more weekend with the customers pouring through their picket lines and then "we would have them licked."

This statement turned out to be a gross underestimation of our "foe."

That evening the Union entered our salesroom for the first time. We had been fearing a move of this kind, and when I saw Dale Eggerts, OCAW District 6 President, lay down his picket sign and walk unhesitantly across the parking lot toward the salesroom, a feeling of panic converged on me. I was the only Management person on the premises at the time and was faced with the decision of what action to pursue. Eggerts was alone, and there were very few customers in the store at the time; nevertheless, this was an unprecedented move on the part of the Union and had to be nipped in the bud if possible. Eggerts and I exchanged a few strained words. I asked him what he thought he was doing in the salesroom, and he replied that it was open to the public, and began strolling around examining merchandise. I left the store to talk to the police officer on duty at the time. I told the policeman that I did not want Eggerts on our property and asked him what my alternatives were. The officer replied that he was not sure and would check with the desk sergeant. While he was checking, I returned to the store to find Eggerts tracking a group of customers. The officer came in shortly to inform me that the police department could not advise me of my legal alternatives. A complete novice in the legalities of private property and trespass, I felt I must have a legal opinion before making a move. With Eggerts still in the store I frantically began calling lawyers. Our company attorney was unavailable; the second number answered, but the lawyer I was seeking was not at home; on the third try I reached City Attorney Charles Richardson. I hurriedly explained the situation to him, but he would venture no opinion because, in his words, he was "not a labor attorney." I failed to see why it was necessary to be a labor attorney to rule on this situation, but, in any event, I had exhausted my sources of legal support and was left in the frustrating circumstance of having no legal opinion, with the Union man still in the store. I approached Eggerts, and the customers, sensing a problem from our brief statements, left the store in short order. As the customers were preparing to leave Eggerts asked them, "How are things over in Ellsworth?" which I interpreted as an effort to let the customers know he knew where they were from—a subtle intimidation since they had crossed the Union picket lines to shop. Eggerts left the store shortly thereafter. While the incident was a minor one and no real harm had been done, the fact that the Union had entered the salesroom and left unmolested cast a foreboding sense of things to come.

On Monday, June 12, the picketing returned to normal—only two or three to a driveway, and all of them our employees. There was a definite pattern being established; calm, orderly picketing from Monday through Friday; a big buildup on Saturday; and a peak effort on Sunday with many outsiders. Working seven days a week and experiencing the tremendous tensions of the weekend, Management was sick of the strike already, after less than two weeks. We began singling out individual strikers, discussing their activities, and venting our wrath on their "ungrateful behavior." R. A. Gillmer was particularly incensed that the young high school and college girls who worked in the salesroom would picket. These girls made $1.37 an hour—far more than most summer work in town. With the income they had received during summers at the Potteries, we had helped and were helping many of these girls through college. Gillmer found it difficult to accept the fact that these girls would be so unappreciative as to picket the salesroom. He vowed to "get rid of these ingrates" by some manner or means when the strike was settled.

A further source of concern to Management were the rumors that many of our key employees were seeking work elsewhere. Realizing that most of the employees were at an age where it would be difficult to find another job, we, nevertheless, checked the picket lines carefully each day to find out who was missing, and therefore likely to have found other work.

Another small but irritating problem was our discovery that many service firms would not cross the picket lines. The soft drink machines and candy machines in the salesroom were empty, and the vendors refused to come in and fill them. We eventually chose to pick up the soft drinks ourselves in order to keep the machines filled. The NSP meter reader would not enter the plant to read the meters, and our exterminating service ceased their monthly visits. These things made very little difference one way or the other, but their abandonment of us seemed a matter of principle and was a source of anger.

We were frustrated and could remain passive no longer. We decided to issue a statement describing the negative conditions in the industry, and hinting at the possibility of our going out of business. This type of statement was intended to alert the townspeople, as well as the Union, to the severity of the situation, and the likelihood of a long strike or unreasonable demands making it impossible for us to continue operations. Also, the Union was having a membership meeting Monday night and the statement would give them something to think about.

PRESS RELEASE

"Most of the community is aware that the Red Wing Potteries is in the throes of a labor strike. Because the Potteries has been an integral part of the City of Red Wing for almost ninety years we feel a responsibility to the citizenry to explain our present circumstances.

"A negative condition has existed in the American pottery industry for the past ten or fifteen years. The primary reason for this condition has been the vast increase of imports from low-wage foreign manufacturers and, as a result, the domestic earthenware producer has found it increasingly difficult to compete. By way of illustration, employment in American potteries has dropped from 12,000 workers in 1948 to 4,000 at present. Of 24 earthenware plants doing business in 1954, only 7 are now functioning, and those 7 have not taken over the business done by the defunct firms, but have also declined drastically. To make matters worse, it was decided at the recent international tariff conference to lower U. S. tariffs 10% per year for the next five years on incoming pottery products.

"When these market factors are coupled with the local situation - a labor strike with a settlement unlikely in the immediate future - it becomes increasingly difficult to justify our existence.

"We take some pride in the part we have played in Red Wing's history and in the lives of many of her people. In addition to the obvious fact of providing jobs for over 150 people, our salesroom has become a nationally recognized tourist attraction. In any given week during the summer months, the salesroom brings literally thousands of people to the city. In addition to visiting the pottery these people patronize other establishments and retail stores in the city. Both from a commercial and an historical standpoint, the Potteries has had a place in Red Wing.

"We wish to make it clear that we hold no animosity toward any of our employees. We have made an offer that is dictated by circumstances and which we consider fair. Refusing to accept that offer is their legal privilege.

"Any business organization has three reasons for being: (1) to provide employment, (2) to make a profit, and (3) to provide a fair return for investors or stockholders. When it fails in any one of these three objectives its functional value is lost and its existence cannot be justified."

R. A. Gillmer

The DRE ran the complete statement in their Monday edition, and KCUE reported the story all day Monday. The statement was far more newsworthy than we had anticipated. The Minneapolis-St. Paul media picked up the story, as well as the AP and UPI news services, and interpreted it to mean that we were definitely going out of business. This unanticipated reaction was potentially damaging because trade customers, hearing we were going out of business, would begin closing out our merchandise. Also, we were afraid that the Twin City population would interpret the reports to mean that our salesroom was closed, and critical business across the street would be lost. The telephone was ringing continually, with newspeople wanting to know first-hand what our plans were. Our stock answer was, "It is a distinct possibility we might close down if the strike cannot be settled equitably; however, we have no definite plans at this time to close." Also, we began emphasizing the fact that our retail store was open for business as usual. On Tuesday, June 13, the DRE carried the following story on their front page:

"POTTERY: NO SHUTDOWN SET

"Red Wing Potteries officials today denied reports by Twin Cities news media that the well-known industry plans to close down.

"R. A. Gillmer, President of the firm, said he has issued no statements to the outside press and their reports must stem from a misinterpretation of a release given the DRE Monday. Gillmer said closing down is a 'distinct possibility' if the current strike isn't settled equitably. 'It's possible we would discontinue factory production,' Gillmer said. 'The store won't close as long as we have anything to sell.'

"The President said he has 'no idea' when a decision to halt factory operation might be made. He insisted that the plant couldn't operate under 'the rigid demands' made by the Union.

"Officials of Oil, Chemical and Atomic Workers Local 6-430 could not be reached this morning for comment. Members of the striking Union met Monday night but one spokesman said nothing new came of the session.

"The Union is apparently sticking to its demands for 30 cents per hour increases over the next two years plus additional fringe benefits.

"No further negotiations are scheduled as yet. The strike began May 31 and has idled some 100 workers."

In addition to the time spent planning company strategy we also were occupied with the unpleasant but necessary job of keeping the salesroom stocked with merchandise. Mewhorter and I were spending a good portion of our week trucking ware from the seconds warehouse to the salesroom. We had heard a rumor to the effect that the pickets were going to attempt to stop us from hauling ware, but we were to continue unmolested.

We called our labor attorney, Richard Felhaber, on Tuesday about the possibility of obtaining a temporary restraining order.

The picketing activity of the previous weekend was still fresh in our minds. We felt there had been laws violated, and that a court order would serve to limit the pickets and keep things on a respectable level. Felhaber advised us not to go after a court order at the present time because he felt such action would only serve to antagonize the Union. Also, we wanted a meeting with the Union and asked Felhaber to contact Larson.

We were notified by Larson late Tuesday that there was to be a Union-Management meeting Thursday, June 15, at 2:30 P.M. at the St. James Hotel. Our strategy for the meeting was to listen; our position had not changed, and because the Union had never moderated their position we felt it was their move.

On Wednesday KCUE reported the scheduled meeting, quoted R. A. Gillmer as having "no comment" when asked if the company was prepared to make any new offers, and quoted an anonymous Union member as saying, "They've used this trick before" when asked if he was concerned about the possibility of the Potteries closing down. Felhaber was in contact with Larson behind the scenes on Wednesday.

Mewhorter, R. A. Gillmer and I arrived promptly at 2:30 P.M. at the St. James Hotel on Thursday, and were informed by Larson that Hammerschmidt would be delayed about one-half hour. The Union Committee was absent also, apparently awaiting Hammerschmidt. We used the time to review our position with Larson. By 3:00 we had thoroughly reviewed, and began looking for the Union. By 3:30 we were indignant that Hammerschmidt would be "too busy with more important matters to attend to his little problem in Red Wing." R. A. Gillmer suggested that we leave, feeling that this would be a good opportunity to point out the Union's lack of common courtesy and unwillingness to bargain. At 3:35 we secured Larson's permission to return to the company offices. Arriving at the office we immediately notified the press and radio of the "outrage." KCUE began broadcasting the following report:

"Efforts to reach agreement in a labor dispute at Red Wing Potteries took a turn for the worse today when Union representatives failed to show up for a bargaining session set up for this afternoon by Federal Mediator Ed Larson.

"The President of the Red Wing Potteries, R. A. Gillmer, said they waited for over an hour for them to show up and then Mr. Larson said, 'There's no use in waiting any longer,' and called off the meeting.

"Gillmer said, 'We came to the meeting ready to negotiate, but their failure to show up seems to indicate they're not interested in a settlement.' He said, 'The next move will have to be up to them. Apparently they're not interested in working at the Potteries any longer.'

"The Red Wing Pottery President had 'no comment' when asked about a statement he'd made that the plant would shut down in two or three weeks if there were no settlement.

"Union members are seeking a 30-cent-an-hour increase while the company is offering an 8-and-a-half-cent-an-hour increase.

"Company officials have said increasing low-wage foreign imports, coupled with a labor dispute, with no settlement in sight, makes it difficult to justify their existence.

"There was no immediate comment from Union officials, but it is believed that the International Representative might have been detained in arriving at the bargaining session on time, 2:30 P.M."

Larson called the company shortly after 4:00 P.M. We considered having the girl at the switchboard tell him we had left for the day, but thought better of it and decided to talk with him. Larson informed us that the Union team had arrived, and he requested that we come down to the hotel for the meeting. We explained that Mewhorter had left for the day and, under the circumstances, we were not anxious to meet with the Union. Larson asked that we come "as a favor to him," and we agreed. The meeting commenced shortly after 5:00 with little if any hope for progress considering the strained circumstances.

It was clear from the start that neither side had anything new to offer. The Union looked briefly at our most recent proposal, and the effect it would have on individual employees, but suggested that some of the figures were incorrect and repeated their

contention that it was an effort to "take away." I asked the
Union their feeling on the company stopping the hospitalization
coverage on striking employees. Hammerschmidt replied that
that decision was up to us but that the Union wanted prior notification before we stopped payments. I indicated we would postpone our decision until the end of the meeting. Chastain announced that "due to the company's attitude" the Union's proposals were "no longer proposals, but demands!" Larson split
the groups, sending Management to the hotel lobby. When
Larson came into the lobby I asked him his opinion on stopping
the hospitalization coverage. He said he would not advocate
it because this would serve only to unite the strikers against the
"villainy" of Management. We decided to further postpone the
decision on hospitalization coverage, and the meeting broke up
at approximately 6:00 with no progress; no moderation on either
side; and none of the give-and-take of bargaining.

We heard that Chastain was telling people that the Union was
only "about a half-hour late" for the meeting, and we were
pleased to see the DRE's account of the delayed meeting on
Friday. The newspaper account supported our version and made
Chastain's report out as false.

"NO SETTLEMENT DURING TALKS

"Officials of the Potteries and striking Oil, Chemical and
Atomic Workers held a delayed and unproductive negotiation session Thursday afternoon. Broadcast reports were
erroneous in saying a meeting was not held.

"The Union negotiators arrived late for the session. But
conflicting statements are being offered on the length of
the delay and on the apparent willingness to bargain. The
Federal Mediator's recollection of the length of delay jibes
fairly closely with that of Potteries officials. On this much
there's agreement: No progress was made. No further meetings are scheduled, although both sides are ready to meet
at the call of the Mediator.

"Thursday's meeting was scheduled at 2:30 P.M. in the St.
James Hotel. Ed Larson of the Federal Mediation and

Conciliation Service in Minneapolis arrived about 2:15 P.M. Reached by phone at another negotiation session in Austin this morning, Larson reported to the DRE his version of the afternoon's events. He said he was met upon his arrival by Tilfer Chastain, President of Oil, Chemical & Atomic Local 6-430. Larson said Chastain told him that the Union negotiating team would be about a half-hour late. Larson said he decided against notifying the company by phone of the announced delay and decided he would spend the intervening time alone talking to Potteries officials. Upon the arrival of the company officials, Larson said he notified them that the Union had said it would be ready to talk in about half-an-hour. Larson said he talked with the company officials for about 30 or 35 minutes (until 3 P.M. or 3:05), at which point they 'began looking for the Union.'

"Larson said he was out in the hotel lobby 'looking for the Union' about 3:30 P.M. or 3:35 when the company negotiating unit came out of the meeting room and said they were planning to return to their offices. The Mediator said the Union team reached the hotel about 3:45 P.M. (an hour and 15 minutes late). Larson then called the company and asked the negotiating unit to return, 'which they very obligingly did.'

"Larson said, 'In the business of collective bargaining people are often a bit late.'

"He declined comment on prospects for progress in the strike.

"Potteries President R. A. Gillmer said, 'Management was at the meeting room at 2:30 P.M. prepared to bargain and negotiate.' He said the Potteries group waited for the Union until 3:35 P.M. and then 'Mr. Larson dismissed us.' Gillmer said he received a phone call from Larson shortly after 4:00 P.M. reporting that the complete Union group was on hand and ready to meet. Gillmer said a member of his negotiating team already had gone home for the day. But Gillmer and R. S. Gillmer went to the hotel to meet until shortly after 5:00 P.M. 'Nothing was accomplished,' Gillmer said.

"Union President Chastain said in a statement this morning that the Union negotiating team was only about a half-hour late for the meeting. He told the DRE, 'I can't understand why officials of the company would play up such a thing that we were a half-hour late. The Federal Mediator was notified at 1:00 P.M. that we would be a half-hour late for the meeting.' Chastain said the delayed meeting 'shouldn't be interpreted as a sign the Union has no intention of bargaining.' He continued, 'The company was notified that until they decide not to take money away from the incentive people and give something out of their pocket we will remain on strike.' Chastain said the meeting with Potteries officials took place about 3:00 P.M. The delay was caused, he said, by a Union International Representative who was busy in the Twin Cities. The representative is a member of the local bargaining unit. Chastain said he met Larson at the hotel at 1:00 P.M. to inform him of the delay.

"The strike was two weeks old Thursday. About 100 workers are idled but the Potteries retail store continues to be open their usual hours.

"Some reports have indicated the Union has been seeking increases of 30 cents an hour over two years, plus additional fringe benefits."

On Friday KCUE reported, "Hammerschmidt, in a statement this morning, said the meeting was held but he was a half hour late." He was also quoted as saying, "The company showed no interest in negotiations and it was decided by the Union that until the company decided to give something out of their pocket and not take away anything from the incentive workers the strike will remain." Despite this oft repeated objection to the company's stance, all the Union had done to date was react in a bitter and defensive manner to our proposals. They had not made any efforts to change our position by talking out the problems with us or by offering constructive alternatives. They had adopted a position of angrily protesting our suggestions while clinging rigidly to a 60 cent demand over a two year period, an amount we viewed as ridiculous, particularly when their fringe demands were added to it.

R. A. Gillmer called Felhaber on Friday to report the lack of progress in yesterday's meeting, and to ask again about a temporary restraining order. Felhaber contended that "the only time a restraining order is needed is when the police fail to do their job." He agreed to call Police Chief Lenway to discuss the situation.

We had a meeting of the company Board of Directors that morning at 11:00 A.M. to fill them in on negotiations. All five company Directors were present; Sam Sheldon, retired businessman; S. B. Foot, President of Foot Tannery; Milton Holst, local attorney; R. A. Gillmer; and myself. R. A. Gillmer reviewed the strike and the lack of progress in negotiations. The Board officially approved the conduct of Management to date, and stated approval of their bargaining in good faith. It was the Board's opinion that Management should remain in close contact with Labor Attorney Felhaber. Another Official Board Meeting was scheduled for June 29 even though Gillmer was in almost daily contact with his Board.

Management heard that afternoon that some of the strikers had refused further picket duty because they objected to weekend activity on the picket lines. We also believed that many of the Union members were unaware of what the company had offered. R. A. Gillmer and I briefly discussed our proposal with some of the more reasonable pickets as we walked from the office to the salesroom.

We arrived at work Saturday morning to find a large plate-glass window in the front of the salesroom smashed. Station KCUE reported:

"Police say two pickets on duty at the salesroom last night told them they noticed several boys, believed to be in their teens, around the building between 3:00 and 4:00 this morning. Those on picket duty at the Pottery Salesroom are not stationed near the building but are posted at the driveways to the parking lot. Round-the-clock picketing is deemed necessary by the Union to prevent any hiring by the Pottery or hauling in or out. Police say one of the pickets said, 'We had nothing to do with the rock throwing. We feel this is the worst thing that could happen because people will think the Union is to blame'."

The DRE also carried the story:

"WINDOW SMASHED AT POTTERIES SHOWROOM

"A rock was thrown through a plate glass show window at Red Wing Potteries sometime Friday night. The floor-to-ceiling window is in the showroom and faces Main St. One rock was found inside the showroom and three or four others were found outside by Potteries workers who arrived at 8 A.M.

"The showroom closed at 9 P.M. Friday.

"A police investigation is continuing today. The police have no additional details to make public.

"The Potteries has been struck by Local 6-430 of the Oil, Chemical and Atomic Workers since June 1. Neither police nor Potteries officials have made any public statements connecting the rock-throwing incident to the strike.

"The last strike talks were held Thursday with a Federal Mediator present. No progress was reported and no further meetings have been scheduled."

We felt that it was fairly obvious how the public would interpret the incident and decided against any public statement implicating the Union. However, we met an unanticipated block when we tried to have the window fixed. We contacted a local glass company and they told us they would have to check with Chastain before they could cross the picket line to repair the window. Chastain did not want to be responsible for the decision and referred the glass company to Hammerschmidt. The glass company reported that Hammerschmidt had refused them permission to cross the picket lines, so we were forced to do the best we could with cardboard and scotch tape. It there had been any doubts in our minds about Joe Hammerschmidt, this incident clarified them. We were developing an active dislike for him.

In addition to finding a smashed window Saturday morning, we were greeted with another surprise: The Union had mimeographed sheets they were passing out to all incoming cars. As I accepted a copy I heard Chastain say that we would be surprised when they passed them out on all the Red Wing streets. The Union propaganda sheet read:

"PLEASE DON'T CROSS OUR PICKET LINES

"On June 1st, 1967, the Workers at the Red Wing Pottery Plant and this Company Store went on Strike.

"The Sales Girls are also on Strike. *SCABS* have taken their Jobs, and are running the Company Store. If you make a purchase, you will be waited on by these *SCABS*.

"Our Sales Girls were only receiving $1.40 per hour, which is required under the Minimum Wage Law. The Average Base Wage for the Plant Employees is only $1.70 per hour.

"The Company has proposed *eliminating* Dependents from the Hospitalization Plan, and *eliminating* the $1,000 Life Insurance from Retiring Employees. Their Offer averages *less* than *$.04 per hour* each year of a two year Agreement, and does not include the Sales Girls.

"We cannot live on these Wages!

"PLEASE HELP US in our efforts to get a decent Contract to Support our Families.

"THIS IS A LEGAL STRIKE.

"PLEASE do not Cross our Picket Lines!!!"

We read the Union handout with mixed emotion; partly amused and partly angered. We felt their tactics would do nothing toward keeping customers out of the salesroom. The sheet branded itself as emotional propaganda by starting as it did in referring to us as "SCABS." The average motorist would not have time to read the sheet while attempting to manipulate his vehicle through the masses of pickets. And by the time he managed this, he would have been sufficiently insulted by the hooting and name-calling that it would be impossible for him to raise any sympathy for the strikers anyway. Further, the average customer did not care if he was waited on by "scabs" or not as long as there were bargains to be had. The sheet angered us by the twisting and one-sideness of the facts it presented. Regular salesgirls received $1.49 per hour rather than $1.40 as claimed by the Union. Part-time or summer girls received $1.40. Their claim that the company offer did not include the salesgirls was true as far it it went. We had at no time denied raises for the salesgirls - only requested that we consider this group separately from the factory employees. To that date we had not even discussed raises for the salesgirls during negotiations. While the average base wage was $1.70 for plant employees, they overlooked the fact that with incentive the average wage was around $2.00. We deserved to be criticized for proposing to eliminate dependents from the hospitalization plan and eliminate the $1,000 life insurance from retired employees. Although these were always considered bargaining points, we had made a tactical error in including them and were suffering for it. The Union's statement that our offer averaged less than 4 cents per hour each year was false; it averaged slightly over 4 cents per hour, a small discrepancy.

On Saturday, whenever R. A. Gillmer or I appeared outside the salesroom the picketers shrieked "liar" at us. We assumed that they had reference to last Thursday's meeting and the time discrepancies reported in the newspaper. How anyone could interpret the facts as presented as "lying" on our part was beyond us. This was an example of the irrationality engendered by the conflict - a condition that was to increase with the antagonism and duration of the strike.

Saturday we must have have hosted close to a hundred pickets in the peak-afternoon period. Working at the front counter wrapping customer purchases, gave us an excellent view of the driveways and picket activity. Every car attempting to enter the parking lot was a new emotional experience for us. We tended to identify with every driver as though we were in the car with him. We tensed as the driveway was momentarily blocked, encouraged the driver mentally as he edged his way in, and felt our anger and frustration rising as we saw the pickets shout and threaten.

Sunday was approaching - the day we were coming to dread. By late morning on Sunday it was clear that the picket line was going to reach new peaks in both hysteria and numbers. At 11:50 R. A. Gillmer called and pleaded for police presence because the pickets were becoming very abusive. The police report "Findings and Dispositions" read: "Advised Gillmer that intentions were to have officer there this afternoon if it did not conflict with regular duties." Apparently it did not conflict with regular duties because one policeman was present most of the afternoon.

As I returned from lunch that afternoon and was walking from my car into the salesroom I could hear Chastain shrieking at me. "Junior - Sonny Boy," he shouted at the top of his lungs. While it was no more than I expected from Chastain, I was mad enough to stop short and head out to the picket line. I walked up very close to Chastain and told him if he had something to say to me I didn't want him to have to shout all the way across the parking lot. "Get back in your scab hole," he screamed, and Hammerschmidt pulled him away from me. I turned and walked back into the store. In retrospect, going out on the picket line - which I was to do many times in the course of the strike - was a mistake and never accomplished anything other than to allow me to release some of my building hostility. It put me on the picket's "level" and let him know he was "getting to me." I was to learn later that the pickets reported to company Director Sam Sheldon that I had tried to start a fight with Chastain.

The number of picketers reached one hundred fifty by the middle of the afternoon. The detainment of cars gradually became longer, the shouting increased in volume, but the lone policeman did very little. When it became clear that a mob was refusing to let a car enter, the policeman would saunter slowly in that direction. This action, at that point, was enough to make the pickets grudgingly move aside. Customers would enter the store shaking with anger, and relate tales of threats and harassment. Many would ask why we stood by and let this sort of thing go on, a remark which we regarded as indicating a marked lack of intelligence, but which we tried to answer patiently. We explained that we certainly did not want this activity to go on and were doing everything within our power to stop it. We pointed out the presence of the policeman and suggested they take it up with him.

In the middle of the afternoon Red Wing Mayor Demetrius Jelatis arrived to observe the activity. In Red Wing's form of city government the Police Chief takes his orders from the Mayor, and Jelatis apparently felt a responsibility to find out first-hand what was going on. He was standing in the parking lot talking with Director Sheldon when R. A. Gillmer and I decided to walk out to them in order to demonstrate the mob's unrestrained hostility toward us. As we left the salesroom and began walking toward Jelatis and Sheldon the crowd rose to the occasion and began jeering and cat-calling. By the time we had reached them the din had grown to such a point that the few abortive efforts we made at conversation were completely drowned out. Feeling our point had been amply made, we returned to the salesroom.

Despite the efforts of the pickets a great many customers had braved the picket lines, and our weekend business had not been hurt to any great extent. Neither had the rumor that we were closing hurt our business as we had feared. In fact, there was some likelihood that the rumor may have helped business. It seemed that many Twin Cities customers had driven down to fill in their dinnerware sets with the fear that we would be closing and they might be unable to fill in at a later date. We were very surprised at this continued business under the circumstances, as well the Union must have been.

Between 5:00 and 6:00 Sunday afternoon Lorraine Taylor, Salesroom Supervisor, called her daughter (who was working at the salesroom at that time) to report that someone had ransacked their trailer home. Mrs. Taylor had worked until 5:00 that afternoon, and found her home ripped apart upon returning from the store. I offered to drive her daughter home, and upon arrival there found Mrs. Taylor distraught and her home in terrible disarray. Clothing, bedding, suitcases, and other personal property were thrown about, and human feces were liberally distributed on curtains and bedding. Other than a plate of fried chicken, nothing appeared to be stolen. Under the current circumstances, our suspicions could not help but be drawn to the Union. Mrs. Taylor calmed down somewhat, called the Sheriff, and I returned to the store. Upon my arrival there, I asked Hammerschmidt to come over to my car as "I had something to tell him." I related the story and he seemed surprised; said the Union had nothing to do with it, and thanked me for telling him. I made no accusations, feeling the incident was enough in itself.

The arrival of Monday and the return of "normal" picketing was, as always, a relief. KCUE reported:

"The pickets are reduced in number, when compared with the large crowd of union workers who converged on the Potteries last Sunday. Not only did more than 150 men and women picket at various times around the Potteries salesroom and plant, but the full executive board of the Oil, Chemical and Atomic Workers Union showed up at Red Wing to meet with officers of the Potteries local, and take their turns in the picket line."

KCUE went on to report more contributions to the Union cause:

"The president of the Potteries local, Tilfer Chastain, reports more than $1,350 has been banked from contributions made by other unionists around the area. Chastain says a half-dozen checks come in every day to help the Potteries local handle what is termed 'hardship cases.' The Potteries Union has a three man committee on welfare matters. While those who are on strike do get benefits from a fund, the strike, to use Chastain's words, is 'rough' for some people. Those who have large families to support and substantial power and phone bills to pay can deal with the Union's Welfare Committee to get additional payments."

It is likely that Chastain's public statements regarding contributions were intended to serve a dual purpose: (1) to let the company know the membership was not starving and had financial support, and (2) to further encourage donations from the local community. We had heard the $10.00 strike benefit checks were not being distributed promptly, and began subtly needling pickets. On our walk from the office to the salesroom we would inquire if an individual was being paid for his efforts by the Union.

We called Felhaber on Monday to report the events of the weekend. Still no move to obtain a temporary restraining order. No Union-Management meetings were scheduled.

On Tuesday our St. Paul Branch truck was to come down to deliver a load of garden merchandise for the salesroom. The teamster driver was to stop outside of town, call us, and Mewhorter and I were to bring in the truck. The transfer was handled smoothly, but our arrival at the salesroom sent a number of pickets scurrying off to their strike headquarters. In the process of unloading the truck the police arrived to report that they had received a complaint that we were driving the truck without a chauffeur's license. True, we did not have a chauffeur's license but did we need one? The officer was not sure but would find out. He returned shortly to inform us that we did need a chauffeur's license for the large truck in question but not for the pick-up truck we used for hauling seconds to the salesroom. We assured him we would either obtain a proper license or refrain from driving the truck. He seemed satisfied and left. The fact that we were not placed under arrest came as a disappointment, no doubt, to the pickets. The next time a load of garden merchandise was needed, we had the St. Paul Branch Manager, complete with chauffeur's license, bring it down. The pickets apparently alerted the police, because a patrol car was lying in wait for him as he left town.

On Tuesday, June 20, Chastain again made the newspaper. His strong sense of civic responsibility had motivated him to bring a convention to town.

"RED WING UNION TO HOST CONVENTION
"A six-state district convention of the Oil, Chemical and Atomic Workers is scheduled in Red Wing in early August.

"Tilfer Chastain, president of Local 6-430 said dates for the two or three-day convention will be announced in about a week. He said past district conventions have drawn any-where from 50 to 500 delegates, depending upon the action of locals throughout district 6. Each local is eligible to send up to five delegates.

"Local 6-430 is now on strike against Red Wing Potteries. Chastain said the decision to hold the district convention in Red Wing was in no way influenced by the existence of the strike. 'I've been working two years to get this convention here,' he said. 'It has nothing to do with the strike. I'd like to settle the strike tomorrow.'

"(No new strike negotiations have been scheduled. The last session was held Thursday. It was unproductive.)

"Chastain said district President Dale Eggers of River Falls, Wis., has been visiting Red Wing at intervals over the last two weeks. Members of the district executive board also have made visits.

"Chastain said the board voted unanimously to hold the convention in Red Wing, 'even though Red Wing is one of the smallest locals in the district.'

"Arrangements for rooms, meals and meeting places are being investigated by a committee of local 6-430 headed by Chastain.

"Chastain said he will seek the assistance of city and com-merce officials in arranging the convention. Sessions will be held in the Trade Council auditorium or in the VFW hall, depending upon the number of delegates.

"District conventions are held twice a year. The last session was at Cumberland, Wis."

The thought of an OCAW convention in town in early August, with the possibility of the strike still unsettled, did not please us.

On Wednesday, June 21, R. A. Gillmer left for a Canadian fishing trip. He was to return the following Sunday. He had been debating the advisability of going for the preceding ten days, and was finally persuaded to go. It was agreed that he would take this trip and I would leave on a previously planned vaca-

tion the first week in July. With the increasing tensions of the
strike the break would be a welcome and necessary relief for
both of us.

That afternoon Mrs. Taylor informed me that the current
rumor on the picket line was that her home had never been
ransacked because if it actually had been, there would have been
something in the newspaper about it. It was all a plot on the
part of the Gillmers to intimidate the Union. Mrs. Taylor initially had requested that no publicity be connected with the
incident, but agreed that the press be notified in light of the
current rumor. After some thought I phoned the newspaper to
report the incident, and said they could quote me as saying,
"I cannot believe any of our people would do anything so malicious." The statement was made with "tongue in cheek," and
I knew that anyone reading the account would assume Union
involvement. The DRE carried the story that evening on page
one.

"LORRAINE TAYLOR TRAILER HOME
IS RANSACKED

"Investigation is continuing in the ransacking of the trailer
home of Mrs. Lorraine Taylor, Rte. 3, Red Wing.

"She reported the vandalism to Goodhue County Sheriff's
officers at 3:30 P.M. Sunday. Preliminary investigation by
Deputy Clifford Witt has revealed only damage to property.
Apparently nothing of value was taken.

"Mrs. Taylor is salesroom supervisor of the struck Red
Wing Potteries. The strike of Oil, Chemical and Atomic
Workers Local 6-430 has idled about 100 production work-
ers. But the salesrooms have remained open regular hours.

"No public statements have been made linking the trailer
vandalism in any way with the strike. R. S. Gillmer, Potteries Operations Manager, said, 'I can't believe any of our
people would do anything so malicious.'

"Preliminary investigation has revealed no forceable entry
to the trailer. Inside, all clothes, bedding, suitcases and other
personal property was strewn about. Human waste also

was found. A plate of cooked chicken had been left atop the refrigerator. It was all gone except for one piece.

"Sheriff's officers have made no monetary estimate of damage."

The newspaper article accomplished something in that it stopped the rumor that "it never happened" but a new rumor was to take its place - "the Gillmers hired the job done to make the Union look bad." It was beginning to look as though it was better to shrug off the rumors, rather than to try and counter them with fact.

On Thursday we ran into trouble on our candy delivery. We required a weekly delivery of candy to keep our Country Store stocked. The driver had experienced substantial harassment on his previous week's delivery, and had even been followed out of town by some of the strikers and warned that it was not in his best interests to make the deliveries. Thus, he called on Thursday to inform us that he no longer desired to deliver directly to the store but would agree to meet us out-of-town. We agreed to meet at a truck stop on the edge of town to make the transfer. This meeting place served its purpose for the next few weeks, but eventually was discovered by the strikers. Our remaining rendezvous with the fearful candy man were to be held at an obscure bar about seven miles north of town; an inconvenience, but the candy store remained stocked.

We were somewhat taken by our own cleverness and tenacity. We had succeeded in making factory shipments; we were keeping the salesroom well-stocked with candy, garden merchandise and our own wares; and were operating our retail business successfully. It was heard said within the confines of the company office that Hammerschmidt was getting more than he bargained for; that he had "a tiger by the tail;" and that he had expected us small-town boys to fold up as soon as he hit us with a strike. Our confidence was shaken only by the anticipation of the approaching weekend.

On Friday the DRE carried Chastain's story on the contributions the Union was receiving. We were beginning to see less and less of Chastain on the picket line during the week.

We took the opportunity to needle the pickets about his absence, asked them where Chastain was keeping himself, and implying that he was not carrying his fair share. One of the pickets told us that Chastain had to take care of the paper work and stay close to the telephone. From this point on, Chastain's "importance" and "executive stature" provided a source of humor and an outlet for our mounting hostility at the office coffee breaks and Management meetings.

Friday evening Hammerschmidt and I had our first overt conflict. I received a call at home that evening informing me that Hammerschmidt had been in touch with our salesroom custodian and had attempted to dissuade him from continuing his service to us. This man and his three or four teenage children performed a very critical service for us. Arriving at closing time, 9:00 P.M., seven days a week, James Lifto and his family would spend one to two hours thoroughly cleaning the salesroom. Lifto called himself an "independent contractor" and was not a member of any Union. He had agreed to meet Hammerschmidt and Chastain at 9:00 P.M. that night at the salesroom to discuss the matter. Motivated by the principle of the thing, as well as the practical realization that the evening cleaning job could well fall into my lap should Lifto quit, I decided to represent the company at the 9:00 P.M. meeting.

Hammerschmidt and Chastain were on the picket line and I was in the salesroom when Lifto and his family drove into the parking lot promptly at 9:00. The two Union spokesmen reached the car first and were talking to Lifto as I approached. Hammerschmidt told me to "get back in the store where I belonged," and I told him he had no business on the company parking lot. There followed a frenzied series of shouted accusations and finger-waving. When the attention returned to Lifto, Hammerschmidt suggested the Union would make it up to him financially if he stopped cleaning. I added that he had better see the money before he agreed to anything. Lifto said he needed the money the job provided and did not intend to give up the income. There being no Union money forthcoming, he proceeded to enter the salesroom for the nightly cleaning. The incident was closed, at least temporarily, with a company victory, but the bitterness of the encounter added to the mounting antagonism between Union and company. Lifto was to be contacted again from time to time by the Union, but a man of some resolve, he was not to be turned away from his nightly duties.

Rain was predicted again for the weekend, but despite the small measure of pleasure we derived in seeing the pickets drenched, we held no false hopes that the weather would deter the picketing. On Saturday we were confronted with a new technique - Hammerschmidt was carrying a loud-speaker. Throughout the day he and Chastain would trade off carrying the loud-speaker, noisily demanding that approaching automobiles stay out of our parking lot, shouting "scab" and "yellow belly" at customers who had broken their picket lines, and jeering at Management whenever we left the store. Their efforts were supported by about a hundred other pickets. With a few exceptions, the really noisy and offensive pickets were not our employees. Although the police would cruise by occasionally, we had essentially no protection on Saturday. The pickets were becoming bolder, and occasionally a few of the more aggressive would cross the parking lot and walk the sidewalk immediately in front of the store, commenting to customers and gesturing at Management.

It was a hectic day but, as always, we could be certain that Sunday would be worse. Sunday morning the strikers had their cars right up to, and sometimes extending into, the driveway entrances. At 10:45 I reported the situation to the police, explaning that customers had very little room to maneuver their cars and that, in my opinion, this presented a real safety hazard. The police report "Findings and Dispositions" read: "People were informed to move them out of the way." At least the police had managed to move those cars which were extending into the driveways. They accomplished this, then left.

The language of the pickets was becoming more abusive, and, meeting no opposition, they were becoming more aggressive in stopping and detaining entering automobiles. They would stand well into the street, forming a line and waving cars on past the

drive. If a car attempted to enter, they would either stand immobile or move very slowly in front of it yielding only if the
driver persisted in inching forward. In our estimation this behavior constituted blocking a driveway and was clearly illegal.
Also, customers told stories of receiving obscene insults and
vicious threats - a clear violation of the law, although more
difficult to detect and prove. For the most part, customers were
badly shaken and astounded that such behavior was allowed to
continue. "This would never be allowed in my town," and "What
is the matter with your police department?", were frequent comments.

At 11:20 A.M. I again called the police department to complain of "strikers standing in the driveway waving their arms
and not letting cars get in." The "Findings and Dispositions" read:
"Gene (police officer) reports nothing out of ordinary when he
checked." It all depends on what one would consider "ordinary",
but it was becoming clear to Management that we could not
count on the Red Wing Police Department to maintain what we
considered to be law and order, pure and simple.

By 1:00 that afternoon we still had had no police officer
on duty, and I called police headquarters to report a boat trailer
had collided with one of the striker's cars. A customer, flustered
by the angry mob, in turning into the driveway had cut the
corner too sharply, and the corner of his boat trailer had hooked
the fender of a car that proved to be too close to the driveway
for safety. Some degree of satisfaction was derived from the fact
that the damaged car belonged to Joe Hammerschmidt. I had
called the police fearing the incident might lead to physical violence. When the police arrived I walked out, amid the jeers
of the pickets, to the scene of the accident to complain again
about the closeness of the strikers' cars to the driveways. Despite
the concrete evidence of the accident to support my complaint,
the police did nothing. However, one or two policemen remained
on duty at the Potteries for the remainder of the day. They added
nothing other than the effect of their presence.

Later in the afternoon, forty or fifty strikers laid down their
picket signs and entered the salesroom. Although this was to

become a weekend tradition, it never ceased to frighten and anger us tremendously. They would parade through the entire salesroom, making remarks about the prices and "junk" we sold, and making disparaging remarks to customers and those of us working in the store. We initially expected them to damage or steal merchandise but, to the best of my knowledge, they never attempted this. We would follow closely behind them as they toured the store; business stopped as customers stood gawking at the situation. The police, rightly or wrongly, never made a move to stop them or, up to this point, enter the store with them to assure order.

The company added a new twist to the afternoon's activity. Mrs. Taylor's brother, vacationing in the area, offered to spend the afternoon in the parking lot taking pictures of the strikers. We wholly supported the idea, feeling the presence of a photographer would inhibit the pickets and, further, that we might at some time find the photographs useful as evidence of law violations. His presence did not do much to subdue the pickets, but bothered them enough that he was followed upon leaving later in the day. A car full of strikers threatened to "smash his camera," but he succeeded in leaving the area safely.

R. A. Gillmer returned from his Canadian trip that evening, reported immediately to the salesroom, and was pleased to find that the weekend business had, once again, held up despite the picketing. Although his brief absence had renewed his spirits somewhat, the company's precarious situation had nagged at him, made sleep difficult, and precluded a restful, health-restoring vacation.

On Monday, June 26, we again experienced the relief of having the weekend behind us. We had heard nothing from Conciliator Larson about another meeting and, at this point, were not really anxious for one. Our annual vacation was scheduled for the first two weeks in July and, assuming the employees would demand their regular vacations, there was no possibility of starting production before July 17. We had, from the beginning, set the middle of July as the most logical time for settlement, feeling the Union would push hard for an agreement in order to return to work after the regular vacation period. Since we would have shut down the plant for two weeks in July regardless of the strike, this would leave only the month of June lost due to the strike. We made the mistake of counting too heavily on this logic, and were not well-prepared emotionally to watch the strike go beyond this point.

Toward the end of June we reached the stage of talking a great deal about retribution once the strike was over. There were certain employees we were going to "get" one way or another when the strike was settled. We asked ourselves, "Could we work with all these people again after what they have said to us, and the way they have behaved?" We even vowed there would be no company Christmas Party that year. We would recount scenes we had witnessed on the picket lines, and by the third and fourth telling they became very old stories. This retelling of "outrageous incidents" was to become for me one of the most difficult aspects of the strike. R. A. Gillmer would recount an incident in my presence to a listener who was more than likely hearing it for the first time, but I would have heard the story over and over again and reached the point of mental exhaustion with the redundancy. One of the oft repeated true experiences was the one about the female striker whom R. A. Gillmer overheard telling customers she only made $1.40 an hour. Gillmer looked up her hourly rate and found that in 1966 she had averaged $2.65 with incentive. He then approached her with these facts and asked her if her incentive pay was "script or confederate money - something she could not spend." I was to hear this story two-dozen times by conservative estimate in the course of the strike.

One evening during the week of June 26, I received a call from one of the foremen (who were not unionized in our plant), complaining that Chastain had called him and reported that the picnic was over and they were going to get him that night when he arrived at work. He was working the 11:00 P.M. to 7:00 A.M. shift, and, while doubting the likelihood of Chastain following through on the threat, I agreed to follow him to work. I kept about a block behind him and was almost disappointed to find no one waiting for him at the plant.

We called Felhaber on Monday to decry the behavior of the pickets and to broach the subject, once again, of seeking a temporary restraining order. He reiterated his opinion that a court order would increase the antagonism, making a settlement more difficult; and, should we attempt to get a court order and fail, the failure would give the Union license for even greater misconduct.

We felt very much alone in the battle. The public seemed apathetic to the havoc that was occurring at the Potteries on weekends. It seemed the city of Red Wing was ignoring the situation, hoping somehow it would go away. The local newspaper and radio station had almost no coverage of the strike the last week in June.

On Thursday, June 29, a Board of Directors meeting was held with Labor Attorney Felhaber present. The Board was becoming increasingly concerned about the absence of meetings and general lack of progress in the conflict. Felhaber explained to Board members that, in his opinion, the strike was not "ripe" for settlement. Hammerschmidt had worked the people up to a fever pitch, there was tremendous animosity toward the company, and now it was Hammerschmidt's task to let them down slowly until they returned to some level of rationality and were ready to listen to talk of a reasonable settlement. Until Hammerschmidt did this, Felhaber explained, there would be little likelihood of ending the strike unless, of course, we were willing to meet their demands. The Board decided, with the blessings of Felhaber, to send a letter to all employees stating that we were discontinuing their hospitalization coverage, but including their regular vacation checks. On Friday, June 30, the letters went out:

"We are enclosing a check which represents the amount due you for vacation pay. While we do not have a labor contract at present this would ordinarily have been paid to you on July 1 and we desire to make payment without delay.

"We must stop coverage under the life and hospitalization insurance, as of the morning of July 1. Obviously the employee work relationship does not exist at present but we are asking your union whether they wish to pay for such coverage during the strike period."

R. A. Gillmer

We also sent the notice to Hammerschmidt with the following cover letter:

"Enclosed is a letter which went out to all employees on Friday, June 30th. As you will note, we mentioned the possibility that the Union may wish to pay for the insurance coverage. If you desire to do this, please get in touch with us at once."

R. S. Gillmer

The decision to stop the monthly insurance payments of $1,196 was both a method of reducing costs and a reflection of our disappointment in our employees. We reasoned, "why pay insurance coverage for these people when they are no longer working and who are, in fact, doing everything they can to hurt our business?" Since their loyalty was obviously to the Union rather than the company we suggested that their Union pay for the coverage, fully expecting the Union to decline the offer and, as a result, lose some face. Our strategy backfired somewhat when the Union agreed to pick up the insurance payments for June and July.

Regarding the vacation payment, we were obligated for this amount and would be forced to pay it sooner or later. While technically we could have withheld this check until the strike was over, we reasoned that payment at the regular time would show the good faith of the company and, further, if they had it to spend it would be gone by the middle of July, increasing the probability of settlement at that time.

The last day of June the DRE carried a brief statement on page 1 summing up the situation to date and the marked lack of progress.

"NO PROGRESS REPORTED IN POTTERIES STRIKE
"No progress has been made in the strike by the Oil, Chemical and Atomic Workers at Red Wing Potteries.

"The last meeting between the Union and Potteries Management was held June 15 with a federal mediator. No progress was reported at that session.

"Both Management and the Union said today no meetings have been scheduled. Union officials, however, said they will issue a statement within a few days.

"The strike is now a month old. About 100 workers at the Potteries remain idle, but the Potteries retail store continues to be open."

In retrospect June was a month of buildup. The picketing advanced from a lackluster effort to high-pitched chaos by the end of the month. Union-Management feelings, while far from good in the beginning of June, had reached the point of open hostility and antagonism. We had chosen to keep the salesroom open and had done almost $43,000 in sales over the month in comparison to $44,000 in June of 1966. Despite the all-out efforts of the Union to cut off this source of income, we had all but equalled the sales volume of the previous year. This fact, no doubt, was a source of constant irritation to the Union. They were becoming desperate as June passed into July.

THE MONTH OF JULY — OPEN WARFARE

"No single union nor the body of unions federated together in the AFL-CIO can afford to take the attitude that their only responsibility and purpose is to advance the interests and economic well-being of their members alone, regardless of what happens to the rest of society. Not only is this true as a matter of morality and social responsibility; it is a hard, cold economic fact. Labor cannot advance and make progress at the expense of the rest of the community. . . . I share the belief that the position of labor leadership is now and always has been a position of public trust."

WALTER REUTHER

It became important to us to discuss our theoretical acceptance of unionism: "Unions kept communism out of this country," and "Running a plant with a responsible Union, one who works with Management toward common goals, is an asset and even preferable to no Union at all." Statements such as these then allowed us to criticize our Union as an exception, but not as a reflection of our overall antipathy toward unionism. "But our Union and its leadership are unreasonable - just no good," we would add. The Union people, no doubt, were making comparable statements about Management, and the antagonism continued to grow.

The round-the-clock picketing and the picketing of the plant stopped in the first days of July. The Union apparently felt their manpower could be put to better use exclusively at the salesroom during the business hours. They had been unable to stop the four shipments we had made in June, and there was no logical reason for picketing through the night. Also, their numbers were dwindling slightly as a few additional employees had taken other employment and some had stopped picketing because they objected to the Union tactics.

Early in July we began receiving increasing pressure from our trade customers and salesmen for merchandise. While we were able to fill critical orders in June, our supply of first-quality merchandise had become depleted to the point that orders were nearly impossible to fill. Sperry and Hutchinson, as well as other large volume users, began calling almost every other day to inquire about their orders. Our salesmen, operating on straight commission arrangements, were on the phone with increasing frequency, wanting to know when the strike was to be settled. Our standard reply was, "We expect a settlement around the middle of the month." Pressure of this type was to increase with each passing day.

On July 1, I left with my family for a week at a lake cottage. It would be difficult to remember a vacation I had anticipated with more enthusiasm, but actually had a worse time. It was impossible to force the strike out of my thoughts. The temperature reached record lows the first week in July, and the cold forced us to spend most of the week in the confines of the cottage. The lack of activity enabled me to spend nearly all of my time worrying. I could not help wondering what voice the OCAW had in determining weather conditions.

The first weekend in July was on a par with the previous weekend: Hammerschmidt with his loudspeaker leading his troops in tormenting customers; the threats, the shouted obscenities, the blocking drives; and no police present on Saturday. Sunday was the same, but with the added confidence of greater numbers. One and sometimes two policemen were present to witness the havoc on Sunday afternoon. At 6:08 Sunday evening the officer on duty called the desk sergeant to report, "The pickets had dropped their signs and were entering the Potteries salesroom." At 6:09, R. A. Gillmer called headquarters and advised the same and was told, "The police would not get involved unless it was necessary. If pickets caused trouble he should advise and state the complaint."

On Monday, July 3, the newspapers revealed the Union's growing bitterness. The Minneapolis Tribune reported a statement by Hammerschmidt threatening a nationwide boycott:

"RED WING POTTERIES FACE BOYCOTT ACTION
"The following report on the strike by Local 6-430, Oil,
Chemical & Atomic Workers, was submitted this week by
Joseph L. Hammerschmidt, District 6 international repre-
sentative:

" 'The strike is in its sixth week. The plant is still completely shut down - no production. Picketing of the salesroom has been real effective and sales have been cut to a
minimum.'

" 'Our concern, and particularly from the standpoint of the
International Union, is the series of statements being made
by the management to our people: They will starve them out
and there will be no Union when this strike is over. We
wonder if the company realizes the seriousness of these statements.'

" 'This International Union has never run any company out
of business over economic issues. In fact, this same Union
has, in the past, negotiated agreements with the company
with no monetary amounts involved just to allow them to
continue operations.'

" 'However, when a company takes a position this company
is taking, it no longer is a matter of economic issues, and
this International Union will have to take another approach
to the problem.'

" 'Certainly, the Oil, Chemical & Atomic Workers International Union is large enough, with 170,000 members, to
see that a company does not carry out its threats.'

" 'At the present, a nationwide consumer boycott on Red
Wing Potteries, Inc. is being considered. It is probably only
a matter of time. We are generally hesitant in applying a
nation-wide ban on any company because once this is resorted to, it is pretty difficult to stop even after the parties
reach an agreement.'

" 'The morale and the determination of these people on
strike is the strongest ever seen in a situation like this.' "

Both KCUE and the DRE carried essentially the same story,
but quoted President Gillmer as denying any statement on the

part of the company that our intentions were to starve the people and break the Union. While we had never put it in so many words, we had talked repeatedly of our chances of breaking the Union, but had never gone beyond the wishful thinking stages to the actual formulation of a plan. Thus Gillmer's denial was accurate.

As far as the threat of a national boycott was concerned, this possibility did not bother us in the least. Rightly or wrongly, we were relatively certain that a Union boycott would have little if any effect on sales. Hammerschmidt's statement that "picketing of the salesroom has been real effective and sales have been cut to a minimum" was proven false by our records. That he actually believed this is doubtful, but we were not about to refute him and risk the consequences of heightened violence on the picket lines. Neither did we believe his statement that "the morale and the determination of these people on strike is the strongest ever seen in a situation like this." The DRE also quoted him as saying, "They'll (the strikers) come out of it with a better way of life regardless of what happens," and, "If they're (the company) going to break us, they're going to get broke." This was the Union's first all-out public attack on the company, and alerted the community to the fact that there was a war going on.

The Union was pulling all stops, and that same day placed a paid ad in the DRE explaining their position:

"THE FACTS INVOLVED IN THE STRIKE
"Between Local 6-430, Oil, Chemical and Atomic Workers, AFL-CIO, and Red Wing Potteries, Inc.
"The members of Local 6-430 O.C.A.W. went on strike against Red Wing Potteries, Inc., June 1, 1967 and at this time remain on strike.
"During this period of time the company has made numerous statements to the News Mediums and to the general public. Many of these statements have been FALSE and MISLEADING.
"The Union does not believe that this dispute can be re-

solved by the News Mediums or the general public, but
ONLY at the BARGAINING TABLE. However, realizing
that the people in the Community are concerned and could
be affected by the outcome of this dispute, we are going
to make an attempt to tell them about the SHAME and
DISGRACE that exists in the dispute which is reflected on
the whole Community.

"We are convinced that the majority of the people in the
Community are aware of the EXTREMELY LOW WAGES,
INADEQUATE BENEFITS and POOR WORKING CON-
DITIONS that do exist and have existed for many years at
Red Wing Potteries. This company has proposed to DIMIN-
ISH these conditions even further.

"They have proposed eliminating the retiring employees
from an inadequate $1,000 life insurance feature which
was granted to the employees in place of no wage increase
in prior negotiations.

"They have proposed a different Hospitalization plan that
WOULD NOT include the employees dependents, which
are included in the present plan.

"They have proposed cutting the incentive workers' rate
from their present rate down to $1.25 per hour.

"They have also proposed 24 other changes in the contract
language pertaining to time studies, standards, vacations
and many other issues that would take away from the employees.

"In return for all of this take away the Company made an
offer to adjust 18 Classifications and grant an increase in
wages (does not include sales girls). In determining how this
would affect each employee the Company submitted a list
to the Union bargaining Committee, showing what an employee had previously earned and what an employee COULD
EARN with the cut in the incentive rate and then applying
the increases offered. A number of employees would receive
less.

"This list included several deceased employees, retired employees and others who were not employed at the time of

the strike. This list showed 176 employees. THERE ARE
ONLY 100 EMPLOYEES.

"The Union has not been able to determine exactly what
it would cost the Company for the 100 employees. The
Company's own QUOTED FIGURE for the 176 employees
on the list is $16,996 total cost and NO wage INCREASE
the SECOND YEAR of a 2 year agreement. Even if the
amount of $16,996 were to be divided by the existing 100
employees it averages only $.08 per hour average cost to
the Company and NO increase for the second year of the
agreement. If this amount were to be divided by 176 employees it would amount to less than $.05 per hr. In arriving
at these figures the Union has used the Company's OWN
numbers and amounts of monies that were submitted to the
Union.

"The present average BASE rate is $1.70 per hr. The Com-
pany has NOT DENIED this figure. Their claim that the
women average $1.93 per hr. and the men $2.16 per hr.
is completely FALSE. Again using the Company's own
figures and adding the average incentive earned, there is no
way possible to reach these rates unless there was overtime
pay added to them.

"There have been many misleading statements as to what
the Union demands are. In view of the existing conditions
we believe our demands are of the bare necessity to exist.
The Union's basic proposals included increased hospitalization with dependent coverage, increased vacations, the start
of a pension plan, fair standards on incentive work and a
substantial wage increase. There was NO SET figure on
wages due to the Company's position on CUTTING the IN-
CENTIVE worker. However, the Union did indicate to the
Company that we expected wage increases comparable to
the last increases provided for by the Federal Minimum
Wage Law, which were $.20 per hour Feb. 1, 1967 and will
be another $.20 per hour February 1, 1968.

"The Union never had an opportunity to readjust its demands in negotiations. All of our efforts were applied to

fighting to retain what we had.

"There are a number of facts that many people in the Community can probably recall. Nine to 10 years ago there were over 400 employees at Red Wing Potteries. Two years ago there were approximately 120 employees. Today actually 97. The Union has allowed this Company to combine jobs, speed up production, increase the work load to the extent these 97 employees produce approximately the same amount of ware that was produced 9-10 years ago.

"For the past 13 yrs. wage rates have only averaged .026 cents per hr. increase per yr. The past 2 year agreement provided $.03 per hr. for non-incentive workers each year of the agreement and $.03 per hr. for the incentive worker for only one year with a reduction of some 20 employees in the 2 year period.

"Several other interesting facts were printed by this same newspaper in the February 13, 1967 Progress Edition. It stated that Red Wing Potteries enjoyed a good year in sales, with an increase of 24 per cent. It also stated that imported ceramics were a problem. However, many American firms are returning to domestic suppliers.

"We also know that Red Wing Potteries is one of, if not the largest producer of domestic ware.

"Finally the Company has AGAIN indicated they may close down their operations. This has been stated every time the Union has approached the bargaining table. They have NOT said that the Union demands would force them to close. They HAVE SAID before they would meet our demands they MAY close. We are of the opinion the Company is again attempting to blackmail the people in the Community and the employees. We will ASSURE the Company that this method WILL NOT work this time. We are DETERMINED to continue this strike whatever LENGTH OF TIME it takes to gain a just and necessary settlement.

"If the company is serious in closing, we are concerned, but we are NOT AFRAID. 'A quick death is better than the slow death we have been suffering for years.'

"The strike has now drawn nationwide attention from the Oil, Chemical & Atomic Workers International Union and all AFL-CIO Unions. They have pledged their support to us. If the Company is serious in their comments about starving us out and breaking the Union all of this support will be directed against the Company. The O.C.A.W. International Union alone has approximately 170,000 members and they are not about to see 100 of its members beaten down by any Company whether they happen to be in Red Wing, Minn. or not.

"To all of the people in the Community and especially to the various Union Groups who have supported us we extend to you our sincere appreciation. We know you will continue this welcomed support."

MEMBERS OF LOCAL 6-430, OCAW, AFL-CIO

In evaluating the Union's treatise we felt they diminished their impact by a somewhat hysterical tone and the use of emotionally charged words such as "shame" and "disgrace." We felt the community had not reached the level of emotional involvement to comfortably digest and unquestioningly accept such an angered attack. What bothered us most was the distortion of facts and the absence of certain points in order to strengthen their position and weaken ours. Their implication of subterfuge because our list included 176 employees and there were only 100 employees working, was something we had carefully explained to them at previous meetings. The 176 people were all employees of the Red Wing Potteries at one time or another during the year 1966. At any given point in time there would be only 100 employees, but due to retirement, death, and general turnover of personnel there would be many more than 100 over a year's time. Whether this number was 150 or 175 made no difference in total wages paid, as long as there were 100 workers at any point in time. Their claim that some employees would earn less under our proposal was false because we had offered to "red circle" those three individuals guaranteeing them no decrease. We learned in the article that the Union apparently was lowering their demands from 60 cents over two years to 40 cents.

This was the first we had heard of it. Their claim that wage rates had advanced an average of only ".026 cents" an hour per year over the last thirteen years was false. Our records show the average increase to be nearly 4 cents an hour per year, and they failed to mention the vast increases in take-home pay due to the addition of the incentive program. As far as the Company was concerned the majority of their presentation involved gross distortion of the facts, and their statement that "a quick death is better than the slow death we have been suffering for years" failed to call forth the intended feelings of sympathy on our part.

The DRE, in addition to the paid ad and the threatened boycott, carried an article citing further donations to the Union cause:

"POTTERIES STRIKERS RECEIVING HELP
"Various organizations have been contributing to Local 6-430, Oil, Chemical and Atomic Workers Union since their strike at Red Wing Potteries began a month ago.
"Pierce County's NFO has contributed an undisclosed amount of cash. Sunbeam Bakeries has left sweet-rolls and donuts three times a week. Arol's Bar has furnished canned pop and ice weekends for pickets. West Wing Speed Bowl has contributed passes for the pickets.
"Local 31 of United Rubber Workers have given support on the picket line."

If the house next to the salesroom was the "official" Union headquarters, Arol's Bar was certainly the "unofficial" headquarters. Located about two blocks east and on the same street as the salesroom, strikers could be seen entering and leaving Arol's most any hour of the day or night. If we were queried by anyone as to the whereabouts of a striker, we would suggest they try Arol's. Supplying canned pop and ice for pickets was the least Arol's could do, considering the business the strikers were bringing their way.

The Fourth of July was traditionally a good business day for the salesroom and, recognized as such by the Union, pickets turned out en masse. July 4 brought the first evidence of nails in the salesroom driveways. The nails came as a shock to us.

While the Union's methods had been distasteful up to that point,
the nail-strewing was the most blatant and potentially harmful
tactic we had witnessed to date. KCUE reported:

"Tempers are apparently growing short in that strike at
Red Wing Potteries, which is now in its fifth week. Red
Wing Police say they received a report that someone had
strewn nails into the road leading to the Red Wing Pottery
Salesroom. A tourist talked with a KCUE reporter at a
filling station just before noon and told him there were
eight or so nails in his tires. The Red Wing Police Department is investigating the incident."

We were very concerned about the effect of the strike on the
future business of the salesroom. While customers were outraged at the earlier tactics of the pickets and vowed never to
return to the Potteries, we were afraid that the nails in the drives
would be a determining factor in turning regular customers away
for years to come. Therefore, we were pleased when the Mayor
and Chief of Police arrived on the afternoon of July 4 to talk
to the pickets about the nails. The next day KCUE announced:

"The Red Wing Street Department, Mayor, and Chief of
Police spent part of their Fourth of July Holiday clearing
up a nail strewing incident at the Red Wing Pottery Salesroom. Red Wing Police received a call that a large quantity
of nails had been placed in the road leading to the Salesroom, the Potteries' main source of income during a strike
which is now in its 5th week. Company President, R. A.
Gillmer, says he thinks that the lecture given by the Mayor
and Chief of Police to the pickets about the nail strewing
may have done some good. He added, 'I hope there will be
no recurrence of such incidents because this is the sort of
thing that is giving the community a bad reputation.'
"One tourist told KCUE that he counted 16 nails in the
tires of his car and a woman from Rochester reported she
had to stop at a filling station to have five nails removed
from tires on her vehicle. President Gillmer said he is sending a check from the company to the Rochester woman to
pay for the repairs to her car. Red Wing Police believe that

the nail scattering on the road to the Pottery Salesroom was done by an outside strike sympathizer.

"Gillmer said he is expecting a call sometime soon from Federal Mediator, Ed Larson, over the date of another meeting. You may recall that one meeting has been held since the strike began on June 1 but no progress was reported.

"Several other incidents have also been reported earlier in connection with the Pottery worker's strike. A window was broken at the Salesroom, President Gillmer said a few bullet holes have been found in office windows, and the trailer of one of the clerks at the Salesroom was ransacked.

"The strike has also produced an impact on Chamber of Commerce tours of the Potteries, one of the main attractions in Red Wing. Secretary of the Chamber, Mrs. Dorothy Nelson, says she's been running up a large phone bill calling groups planning tours, telling them to cancel-out because of the strike. She said, 'It's a loss of tourists and their dollars in addition to whatever else the pottery strike means to the community.' "

It is unknown how the police concluded that the nail scattering was done by "outside strike sympathizers," rather than the pickets themselves. In any event, the picketing and the potential effects of the strike were beginning to gain the attention of the community. On Wednesday, July 5, Philip S. Duff, Jr., Editor and Publisher of Red Wing's DRE, wrote an editorial on the strike:

"A WORRISOME STRIKE

"It's time, in our opinion, for the Red Wing community to start doing some serious worrying about the long continuing strike at Red Wing Potteries.

"Now nearing the end of its fifth week, the strike gives no evidence of an approaching settlement. Words were still being spoken in anger through the DRE's columns Monday. A good deal of mistrust is apparent between labor and management. So far as one can determine, the two sides have engaged in very little serious, down-to-earth, realistic-type bargaining to date.

"It would serve no purpose here to attempt any judgment of the strike issues or to try to assess 'blame' for the impasse. Really it's the difficult situation of the U. S. earthenware industry that is at fault. Potteries workers are understandably unhappy, especially in these times of inflation and big wage boosts elsewhere, because Potteries wages are not high. At the same time, the company has managed to make only very modest earnings and faces a precarious financial future. In truth, this is a depressed industry.

"Imports have hurt seriously, and from a national standpoint it probably makes little difference if Red Wing Potteries goes out of business like most other pottery manufacturers in the country. But to us in Red Wing it makes a great deal of difference.

"For it's not only 150 jobs that are at stake. That in itself is substantial. But Red Wing Potteries is a major part of our community's public image. The Potteries salesroom is a magnet with power to draw thousands of visitors from near and far at all seasons of the year. It would be a major loss, one that every Red Wingite would feel, should Red Wing Potteries go out of business. And we think that's not impossible as a result of the current strike.

"To say this is unfair to the workers is true, in a sense. They ought to have the right to bargain - and strike if necessary - without facing a constant threat that the company will close. At the same time, there are the financial realities. Like management, the workers bear a responsibility for the company's welfare. They ought to make sure they have a realistic understanding of the company's position, and the company ought to make sure the full facts are available.

"It is not a tenable position, in our view, to argue that, if the Potteries must pay such low wages, it might as well close. The wages aren't really that bad. If an individual wants to leave to improve his earnings elsewhere, he certainly can and should. But he should be careful about pulling down the whole house of cards when others, because of personal circumstances, may very much want these jobs to continue for the rest of their working lives.

"It's time, we think, for a new approach to practical, realistic bargaining from both sides. If this is not forthcoming, if emotions are running too strong, we wonder whether it would be helpful to have an outside group of Red Wingites, composed at least half of people who are active in the labor movement, examine the whole situation and make an independent evaluation of what wage levels the company can afford without imperiling its existence."

Duff was sincerely concerned about the strike and, earlier in the week, had visited with Gillmer about the company's position. Gillmer had shown him the company's profit history and revealed the pessimistic figures on the first quarter of the current year. It became clear to Duff that Management was not bluffing when they claimed a distinct possibility of closing down if the strike could not be settled equitably and within a reasonable time. We could find little fault with Duff's editorial and that fact, in itself, would suggest it was "pro-Management" in its leanings. However, as for his suggestion that an outside group of Red Wingites evaluate the wage levels the company could afford, we were not ready for such a move. This was the role the Federal Conciliator was supposed to be playing and, in addition, we felt that we were logically in the best position to make this determination - not a group of outsiders unfamiliar with our problems.

Conciliator Larson was in Red Wing Wednesday and briefly met with both sides individually. Finding neither side willing to move, he chose not to schedule another joint meeting in the immediate future. Our mid-July settlement date was approaching, and if we were to gain any settlement by that time we would have to begin meeting. Thus, Management was very anxious for a meeting if it would contribute anything toward a settlement.

The picketing Monday through Friday, with the exception of the Fourth of July, was relatively mild as we had come to expect on the weekdays. Most of the pickets were our employees and, with a few exceptions, did very little shouting and harassing. Chastain was rarely present on the picket line anymore and we asked pickets if Chastain was "too busy" to carry a sign. Also, in our brief talks with the pickets we found that most knew very little about the company offer. Those who had been scheduled for raises up to 30 cents an hour with our proposed equity adjustments seemed unaware of these facts in our conversations with them. We were still entertaining the hope that the masses would rise up and overthrow their leadership when told the facts.

Saturday evening my family and I returned from the week at the lake. While the week had been far from restful, I felt somewhat recharged and capable of facing the picket line again. I learned that Saturday had been vicious and, as usual, we were expecting trouble on Sunday. Business had begun to fall off somewhat. The pickets were succeeding in turning away nearly thirty-three percent of the automobiles by our rough estimates.

We were expecting a difficult Sunday, and the Union was not going to disappoint us. Early Sunday morning it became apparent that nail setting was to be standard operating procedure. The pickets would not aimlessly throw nails in the drives, but rather would carefully stand them on their heads to assure their being picked up by entering autos. Roofing nails were standard equipment; with their large, flat heads they suited the purpose beautifully. From time to time we felt compelled to walk out to the picket line to gather up the set nails. The mob would take the opportunity to call us names and accuse us of setting the nails ourselves to make it look like the work of the pickets. No police were present that morning and we were becoming very hesitant to call them. We knew by that point they hated the sound of our voices, and we were getting very little satisfaction from them anyway. Therefore, rather than phone the police ourselves, we did everything we could to persuade outraged customers to call them, and many of them did. However, by late morning I had had all I could take and phoned the police. The police report showed the call at 11:49. I reported that "another customer had picked up several nails in his tires as he drove in." The

"Findings and Dispositions" read: "Keith (officer) reported that he had been out there early this A.M. and that he checked every driveway, and in one there were about a half dozen, the rest of the driveways were all clean."

Rather than leave the confines of the store for lunch, we were finding it less stressful to send just one person out for sandwiches for the group. In that way only one person had to suffer the abuse of driving out and then returning through the picket line. It cannot be denied that a certain element of fear was associated with exposing oneself to the picket line.

At 1:50 that afternoon R. A. Gillmer called the police and reported that "the pickets were throwing nails in the driveways again, and that some of his customers saw the party throw the nails but wouldn't sign a complaint." The "Findings and Dispositions" read: "Galvin (officer) will check when he goes to the pottery for the afternoon." We felt the situation required immediate police attention, and the seemingly casual attitude on the part of the police greatly angered us.

We had one, and at the most two, policemen on duty the remainder of the day. While we would not have thought it possible, the pickets were going to even greater lengths to block the driveways. If a group would successfully wave a car past one driveway, many in the group would run frantically to the next driveway to make certain the car did not gain entrance there. The number of people standing within a driveway had increased, making it more and more difficult for customers to slowly inch their way into the lot. After one particularly obvious blocking incident I left the salesroom to ask the one officer on duty, "How can you stand by and not do anything to stop that?" He replied, "There is only one of me." This seemed a totally inadequate answer.

Later that afternoon I approached one of the two officers on duty at the time to suggest that it would be advisable for a policeman to enter the building with the pickets when they all entered the salesroom. I told him I felt that this would help to insure law and order in a potentially explosive situation. The officer saw it differently, and informed me that "if an officer went inside it might stir the pickets up more, and possibly incite them to do some vandalism more readily." So, later in the day when a large group of pickets entered the store, the police remained outside. Two of the pickets picked up merchandise, and after it had been wrapped exclaimed loudly that they would not give us a nickel for it, and walked out leaving the wrapped merchandise on the counter.

This attitude seemed typical of the police throughout the strike. They would refrain from doing anything in a situation because of their fear of the mob. Whether or not they had received formal orders to remain passive we had no way of knowing. Any speculation as to the sympathies of the police - whether with the Union or with the company - would be purely a matter of opinion.

That afternoon I found one old man on the picket line particularly offensive. This individual spent his entire afternoon trying to catch my eye as I waited on trade at the front counter. When he noticed me looking in his direction he would grin insanely, mouth words, and make obscene gestures. While his persistence was commendable, I found his actions extremely annoying. This, I suppose, was his purpose - to annoy me - and he was very successful in his role.

Customer reaction that afternoon reached new peaks of bewilderment and outrage. Elderly ladies had to sit down once they made it into the store, their dignity and self-composure shattered. People would ask us jokingly, in order to cover their real alarm, "Will they do the things they said when we try to leave?" Many of the customers would approach the policeman on duty and angrily assail their failure to correct the situation. The stock answer of the police was, "Would you care to sign a formal complaint?" None of the customers would involve themselves to the point of filing a complaint. Many times throughout the day the customers would line the front windows, stopping all shopping efforts, to watch the antics of the pickets. Our nerves had been strained to the breaking point by the end of the day.

That evening I received my first strike-inspired phone call.

The phone rang twice before midnight, revealing only heavy breathing on the part of the caller. This was coming too close to my home and family for my comfort and sleep was difficult that night.

On Monday, July 10, the company Directors met at the St. James Hotel. Director Foot was out of town and could not be present. Directors Sheldon and Holst were becoming increasingly anxious for a settlement, and could not understand the lack of meetings. There had been only one Union-Management meeting since the strike began. They objected to our passivity in allowing Conciliator Larson sole determination of if and when a meeting was to be held. Our feeling was that Larson would call a meeting only if he felt some progress could be made, that one side or the other was willing to modify its position. For us to call a meeting would weaken our position, we felt. Holst and Sheldon inquired as to the feasibility of our raising prices in the salesroom to enable us to move closer to the Union demands. President Gillmer replied that a plan of this type was, in his estimation, a gamble at best, and certainly not something upon which to justify greatly increased labor costs. In any event, Directors Holst and Sheldon insisted that we make the necessary contacts to initiate a meeting.

As far as Management was concerned our most immediate fear was the anarchy we were witnessing on the picket line. I had two flat tires that week from nails, and Gillmer had had his tires repaired twice since the first nails were set on July 4. The fact that the Red Wing community was doing nothing to stop the picketing activity bothered us, but, of more concern, was what we perceived as almost complete lack of police support. Also, the relief from harassment we had come to expect during the week days was no longer complete. Angry pickets began arriving in mid-afternoon after the first shifts let out from other plants in town. The nail setting was no longer confined to weekends. The strike was an excellent opportunity for every Red Wingite with an authority problem to unleash his pentup hostility in a semi-legal manner. It is not often that a working man has the chance to cuss out the President of one of Red

Wing's largest industries. The situation to many provided an emotional catharsis.

In light of growing anger of pickets and the lack of police intervention, we called Mayor Jelatis for a meeting. Over lunch at the St. James Hotel, Sheldon, R. A. Gillmer and I reviewed the picketing activity with Jelatis and decried the police department's failure in coping with the situation. Knowing Jelatis' strong DFL involvement and his liberal leanings we did not expect him to adopt an autocratic position with labor. What we did expect, however, was that he would see to it that law and order was maintained in Red Wing. We felt no worthwhile goal would be served by discussing the negotiating positions behind the dispute, so concentrated mainly on what we contended to be the illegalities of the picketing. Jelatis admitted that the blocking of the drives as well as the nail strewing was illegal. If illegal, then, why didn't the police make an effort to stop these activities? We requested that we have more than one and occasionally two policemen on duty on the weekends and that the policemen actively put a stop to the violations and, if unable to do so, begin making arrests. Jelatis refused our request for more than one policeman, using the now well-worn justification that more than one policeman would likely incite the mob to more violence. I told him of the day the officer informed me he could take no action because "there is only one of me." Jelatis' argument did not hold up as far as we were concerned. If there were laws being violated, as he admitted there were, then the responsibility of the police force was to correct the situation, apprehending the law breakers if necessary, regardless of whether it required one man or ten men to do the job. The Mayor would not agree with this point, claiming the main function of the police department was to make certain no one was physically injured. We felt we deserved more protection than this and, in any event, an automobile tire punctured by a nail could cause serious injury if a blowout occurred on the highway. Jelatis could see the merit in our arguments and agreed to discuss the matter further with the Chief of Police and the City Attorney. He said he would get in touch with us later, and we left the meeting feeling we had made some headway. Jelatis called President Gillmer later in the week to inform him that we "would get police protection." We breathed a sigh of relief at his assurance.

In the first weeks of July we received a report that increased our feeling that we were in this conflict alone, and that to expect any active community support was wishful thinking. The story that reached us was that Chastain had entered Nybo's Cafe, Red Wing's major restaurant, and demanded that owner Nybo remove his display of Red Wing Potteries products which lined his restaurant walls. The alternative was that Chastain would see to it that Local 6-430 would throw up a picket line around Nybo's place of business. The display was removed. A healthy portion of Nybo's business was a result of the masses of tourists the Potteries drew to the area, and we felt that removing the display, while unimportant from a practical standpoint, was letting us down on principle. If Red Wing's businessmen would not stand together, there were very few sources upon which we could depend.

In light of the Board of Director's suggestion that we initiate a Union-Management meeting, President Gillmer called Felhaber on Tuesday, July 11. After being informed of the Board's feeling, Felhaber asked if the company was ready to change its bargaining position. Learning that we were not contemplating any change at this time, Felhaber saw no purpose in our initiating a meeting. His opinion was that feelings were still running too high - the people were still too militant to move toward a settlement. In a word, the time was not yet "ripe." We informed the Board members of Felhaber's opinion and they had little choice but to defer to his superior experience in such matters.

On Wednesday my sister had a blowout, caused by nails picked up in salesroom driveways, on her way to summer school classes at River Falls, Wisconsin. She had been dividing her time between working in the Potteries salesroom and taking summer classes at Wisconsin State University, River Falls. This upset her mother greatly and when, on the following day, the tires were going flat on their other automobile she was incensed. She called the police department from the service station and

requested the presence of an officer. Mrs. Gillmer, slow to anger
under most circumstances, told the officer in no uncertain terms
of her displeasure with the police department. The complaint
report read: "Mrs. Gillmer very irately complained about nails
in the tires of her car picked up at the Pottery. Seems to think
it is our fault that nothing is done about it. Says an officer was
shown where nails were placed in the driveway at the Pottery,
and all he did was to look at them and then walk away." The
"Findings and Dispositions" section of the report went on to
say, "Mrs. Gillmer very irate. Reported this is second time she
had to have tires repaired. Reported nine nails in three tires.
Reported daughter had blowout on way to college. Felt it was
disgraceful and that something should be done right away."

The phone calls from trade customers and salesmen regarding
delinquent orders continued with increasing frequency. On Friday, July 14, R. A. Gillmer sent a letter to all salesmen with
a note of optimism he did not feel:

"Would like to bring you up to date with regard to our
labor difficulties. The strike was six weeks old yesterday.
Two of these last weeks we would have been shut down
anyway because of our annual vacation shut-down. There
have been no meetings called up until now, probably for
a couple of reasons: One is the vacation shut-down; the
other being that probably any meetings called prior to this
date would have been unproductive in a case of this kind.
We are told by our labor attorneys that you have to wait
the thing out and wait until the workers have a desire to
come back to work. I think we are approaching that situation. We will be having meetings next week and it is
our hope that we will have it settled after a meeting or two.
"We have been analyzing just what damage the strike has
done, and with the exception of some of the special items
we make for Trader Vic and for the stamp companies, we
feel there has been very little lost, in that we have made
shipments all during the month of June and some shipments
in July. We have a trailer-load leaving our factory today.
Another place that it has probably hurt us is that we did

not get our shipments out on all of our Adobestone, and being shut down we were forced to curtail further development on this pattern.

"As far as future business is concerned, we do have a good stock of jardinieres, artware, and ash trays, also a good stock on all our new patterns plus Bob White, Pepe and Damask. Ray Swanson told me this morning that we are running low on Damask creamers and cereals, but we have these items in bisque and will be able to produce them immediately when the plant resumes operation. Suggest that you take orders just as you have in the past. It might be well to advise customers that we have had a strike so if there should be any delay (and I shouldn't expect the delay to be a week or two more than normal) they will understand why.

"It is my sincere hope that we will have good news, possibly by the end of next week."

R. A. Gillmer

Although nothing specific had been scheduled, we had reason to believe Larson would call a meeting the following week. However, our earlier speculation that the strike would be settled, and the people would be back to work on July 17 after the regular two-week vacation period was not holding true. This was a difficult realization for Management because we unwisely had prepared ourselves for a settlement by July 17. We were forced to readjust our thinking and strengthen our emotional resolve for a longer strike.

The end of that week Chastain released a statement to the local media containing an "ultimatum" to the company. KCUE reported:

"The Red Wing Pottery faces a nation-wide boycott of its products unless company officials move toward the bargaining table in an effort to settle a six-week strike. In the latest development local president, Tilfer Chastain, of the Oil, Chemical and Atomic Workers Union has issued an ultimatum to company officials. Chastain said in the ultimatum, 'Unless company officials set a date for negotiations and fulfill their obligation to the people they employ they will face the full impact of a nation-wide boycott of pottery products.'

"You may recall that July 3rd, International Representative, Joe Hammerschmidt, issued a statement threatening a nation-wide boycott in answer to company statements, according to the Union, that Red Wing Pottery would starve out Union members leaving no Union after the strike is over. The company has denied making any such statement and has had no comment over the threatened boycott.

"Thursday Chastain in another statement called upon all the labor force in Minnesota to support the some 100 pottery workers on strike in their efforts. Chastain said, 'In effect this means that efforts are already underway in Minnesota to boycott Pottery products.'

"Only one meeting has been held among Union and Management in the Red Wing Pottery strike and there were no results from that bargaining session. A company official said Friday they are waiting for Federal Labor Conciliator, Ed Larson, to set the date of the next meeting. Operations Manager, R. S. Gillmer, said, 'It's our understanding that Larson will not call another meeting until it is evident to him that one side or the other has something to offer.'

"Basically Union members are seeking a 30 cent an hour increase, while the company is prepared to offer an 8 cent hourly increase in some cases. The Union has charged that the company offer would take money away from some to give raises to others at the Red Wing Pottery."

The DRE also carried the report, and added:

"Meanwhile, Red Wing police were called to the Potteries again Thursday to remove nails which had been placed in the driveway of the salesroom. Source of the nails was not determined."

We found it rather humorous that Chastain would have the "gall" to issue an ultimatum. We continued to take lightly the Union's threat of a nation-wide boycott - not because we felt they would not attempt it, but because we felt it would have little effect on business.

We were more interested in the position the police would take in the coming weekend. With the Mayor's statement that we "would get police protection," we were anticipating a much easier time.

Early Saturday it became clear that the pickets were becoming increasingly desperate and, therefore, engaging in more brazen harassment. In every likelihood, they had anticipated a settlement, as we did, on or before July 17. It was now clear that there was no settlement in sight and, further, their money undoubtedly was in short supply. Most had seen the last of the vacation checks we had sent out the first of the month. With this realization came greater efforts to stop our salesroom business and make us yield. Pickets were more bold in delaying entering customers, more threatening in their shouts, and more apt to contact cars with their hands or picket signs. Nails were in almost constant evidence in driveways. I had seen the police drive by a time or two that morning, but by noon it was clear they intended no drastic action. Earlier that morning I had collected a handful of roofing nails in the driveways, so on my way home at noon stopped at the police department with the evidence. I stomped into police headquarters, placed the nails noticeably on the counter, and attacked the desk sergeant for allowing this type of activity to continue. I made no effort to hide my anger. My attitude made him angry, and we conversed in loud and accusing tones. After receiving no satisfaction I left, and the desk sergeant proceeded to compose a report on the incident: "Mr. Gillmer brought in roofing nails that he had picked up at the Pottery lot. I advised him there was little that could be done unless this was witnessed. I advised him that I had been to the lot and warned pickets. He stated that all we did was drive by. At 11:00, after receiving a complaint that a motorist was forced to park outside the lot, officers Krause, Edquist and myself went to Pottery lot and spent several minutes there warning pickets. Also advised pickets to have man in charge (Hammerschmidt) contact this department when he returns."

The nail setting continued throughout the remainder of the day; yet the police department did not intervene other than to cruise past a time or two during the afternoon. That evening, upon leaving, R. A. Gillmer and wife noted a conspicuous number of nails in one drive. They called the policeman over. The officer, without saying a word to either Gillmer or the pickets, turned and walked back to his car. As Gillmer gathered up the nails one of the worst pickets told him he "was going to get a nail in the head before this was over."

At 6:43 P.M. Mrs. R. A. Gillmer entered police headquarters and angrily displayed a handful of nails, evidence of the above incident. She also notified the police of the threat to her husband. The resulting police report read: "Mrs. Gillmer came in with some roofing nails she had picked up at the Pottery. Was very upset. Wanted to know why they couldn't have some protection out there. She said no police officer had been at the Pottery most of the day. I advised her that Officer Schmidt had been at the Pottery and had talked to the pickets. I also advised her that we had escorted a party to the Pottery and patrolled the area heavily all day. After talking to her for some length of time she calmed down and said she was sorry she had come in the way she did." (It is interesting to note that no mention was made of the threat in the police report.)

The situation was becoming one of mob rule. The pickets entered the store that evening, parading around making derogatory comments about merchandise, customers, and employees. We felt the police, by looking the other way, were allowing the nail strewing to continue. They apparently felt they were doing what was expected of them by briefly warning pickets once or twice Saturday that they should not set nails. Unfortunately, the warnings did nothing to curtail the enthusiasm of the picketers. We reasoned that, since laws obviously were being violated, the police should do everything within their power to correct the situation even if it meant stationing one policeman at every driveway. We imagined the public outcry and the concerted police action that would take place should someone or some group begin setting nails on the downtown streets. Our only logical conclusion was that the police were taking the side of the strikers.

Saturday nights were unquestioningly the most tense and anxiety-producing evenings in the week. That Saturday night was no exception. At my home the phone rang twice before midnight with only heavy breathing as a response. After the second occurrence, we decided to take the phone off the hook, as we were to do for most of the remainder of the summer.

Sunday's picketing promised to rival all previous experience if Saturday was any indication. We were seething with anger at the police passivity. On Sunday, July 16, the action started early; at 9:43 R. A. Gillmer called the police to report unruly pickets. According to the complaint report: "Pickets at the Pottery lot attempting to tip over camper. Also picketing in the street." The "Findings and Dispositions" read: "Squad went to Pottery lot and warned strikers. Hammerschmidt contacted on this also." The police quickly left again after talking with Hammerschmidt. But a new element had clearly been added to picketing - the pickets were making physical contact with automobiles. They would hit the sides of cars with their fists or signs as they drove past. Occasionally they would let the wooden sticks on their picket signs scrape the length of the car, leaving nicks and scratches in the finish. They were feeling their way, going further and further to see how much they could get away with. On infrequent occasions they would rock cars. Many customers would stand in the lot and shake their fists and return the shouts of the pickets. This never failed to arouse the mob to new heights in insults and obscenities. A well-dressed Negro family from the Twin Cities entered the lot, and a few of the pickets shouted remarks about "serving niggers" and the store "being fit for niggers." The Negro mother, holding one of her children by the hand, turned to the crowd and shouted, "We've driven a long way and we're going in." The husband, embarrassed by his wife's outburst, turned and ordered her on. We would look on from within the store, and suffer with every man, woman and child as they were disgraced by the pickets. Small children could not understand the situation, and many entered the store in tears.

As I returned from lunch that day the mob greeted my arrival with shouts of "son of a bitch," "god damn bastard" and other such subtleties indicating their feelings toward me. Being called a "son of a bitch" by a crowd of over a hundred people is a unique experience. The first and most natural inclination is to run into their midst, arms and fists flailing. If able to conquer this compelling urge, you must walk naturally and at all times unhurriedly to your destination, as though nothing out of the ordinary was occurring. A faster-than-normal pace might reveal the tremendous fear and tension you are experiencing. At times like this I would frequently stop to knock the ashes out of my pipe as proof of my casual disinterest. The experience brings forth a variety of emotions. Underlying the outright fear is a vague feeling of self-importance. Here are over a hundred people who care enough to shout at you and about you at the top of their lungs. Although it would be preferable to have them shouting your praises rather than referring to you as a "son of a bitch," the fact remains that you are important to these people.

I was not alone as the target of the mob's verbal wrath. My sister reported that they had called her a "bitch" that noon, and Mrs. Taylor's daughter had the same experience. This upset Mrs. Taylor immensely and she was able to talk of little else for days. She was finally able to secure a private apology from Tilfer Chastain later in the week.

One and sometimes two policemen remained on duty in the parking lot Sunday afternoon and evening. Their presence calmed the crowd only slightly, although we were grateful for even a slight curtailment. In the presence of the police the driveway blocking continued as did the shouting of "scabs" and "yellow bellies." However, the more obscene phrases and the threats were spoken in lower tones. The nail setting continued, but was reduced somewhat to occasions when the officer's back was turned. On one occasion I observed a picket bending over apparently setting a nail. I hurried out the door and walked directly toward the driveway where I had observed the maneuver, motioning for the policeman to join me. Approaching the drive, I saw the metal spike glinting in the sunlight, and saw the picket attempt to kick it over after witnessing my approach. He failed in his effort to kick the nail on its side, but the feat was accomplished by another picket who observed his plight. I retrieved the nail, showed it to the officer, and pointed out the man I had seen performing the act. I noted with some satisfaction that the picket was quite nervous at the confrontation, and anxiously denied setting the nail, saying he "had only bent over to pick up some papers." The officer, confronted with a witnessed crime and the evidence, was nervous also. A jeering crowd of pickets began to gather so I told the officer I wanted to file a formal complaint, and asked him to return to the salesroom with me. Within the confines of the salesroom the officer informed me that "it would be my word against the picket's" in any court appearance. Seeing no other alternative I dropped the complaint, but hoped that at least the possibility of a complaint would serve to make the pickets uneasy for a few days.

During the peak afternoon activity a female picket was slapped in the face by an irate female customer. The customer claimed the woman had blocked the driveway and called her foul names. This was the first incident of actual physical assault between customers and pickets. We were surprised that more of this had not occurred. Later in the afternoon the pickets laid down their signs and made their traditional parade through the salesroom.

Business was down some for the weekend. We speculated that word had gotten around the State that Red Wing Potteries was a good place to avoid because of the many abuses tourists had received. By Sunday evening it was all too evident that the police had not changed their approach in any way; we had seen no greater number of policemen, nor had those present been more aggressive in stopping violations. Jelatis' statement that we "would get police protection" was a complete farce as far as we were concerned, and we were thoroughly disgusted with the Mayor, as well as the police department.

At home that evening my anger grew and I seriously considered writing Jelatis a letter outlining my lack of confidence in him. Instead, I composed a very hostile press release attacking the Union's propaganda leaflet and their paid advertisement in the DRE. Writing the press release in itself relieved a good deal of the tension I had built up over the weekend. However, the following day, upon less-emotional reflection, I decided not to release it.

"PRESS RELEASE

"We compose this letter with some regret. While any Labor-Management dispute is bound to affect the community to some extent, we had hoped to keep our differences among ourselves as much as possible. However, certain actions on the part of the Union have forced us to make our side of the story public knowledge. The Union has distributed leaflets and released information to the media of a one-sided nature in an apparent effort to gain public sympathy and influence public judgment against Management. If Union spokesmen find it necessary to seek public judgment of our situation, then Management, of necessity, must release certain facts in order that the public may avail themselves of both sides of the story.

"A leaflet recently composed and released by the Union states that the average base rate of our employees is $1.70 per hour. While this is a true statement, it fails to point out that 80% of our employees have the opportunity to earn incentive pay for above average production. Therefore, the average take-home pay of our people is $2.07 for male and $1.93 for female employees. The Union president, Tilfer Chastain, has been vocal in claiming that our people do not have sufficient income for the necessities of life. This may be true in Mr. Chastain's case. The man who held his job previously (before his retirement in July last year) averaged over $3.00 per hour with incentive. Chastain has been unable to achieve the performance level necessary to qualify him for incentive pay and, therefore, has been limited to the base rate for the job.

"We have a number of female employees who earned over $5,000 in 1966. We believe this is higher than Red Wing's nurses and many of the elementary school teachers earn. By the same token, we have a number of employees earning less than this, providing sole support for their families, and carrying as much if not more responsibilities in their jobs. They are not making enough money. Therefore, rather than proposing an across-the-board increase we have offered a plan to correct some of these existing inequities. The plan includes setting a standard incentive rate of $1.25 and increasing base rates from 10¢ to 30¢ an hour. The result of this plan would be to keep the people who appear to be making an adequate wage at approximately the same annual salary level. Others who have not been paid adequately for their skill and responsibility would receive various adjustments up to $600. The average increase would be 8½ cents.

"The Union leaflet accuses Management of offering no fringes and eliminating dependents from hospitalization coverage. We would suggest that the whole story on this matter has not been objectively presented. Our negotiations broke down in the very early stages and, as the Union committee most certainly realizes, most of these matters did not receive adequate discussion. However, we did have the opportunity to bring up a substantially improved medical plan for discussion. Also, only 50% of our employees carry dependent coverage on our present medical insurance. Because of the fact that presently we pay a portion of the dependent insurance, the 50% of our employees without dependent coverage receive less dollar value in fringe benefits than others. This factor has caused complaints from the employees themselves. We attempted to point out these facts to the Union committee and, further, to suggest that (1) the matter would appear to be more equitable for all concerned, and (2) the insurance package could be

that much better for the employees if the 50% with dependents would agree to pay for them themselves.

"Union statements suggest that we desire no raises for our
salesroom employees. This is false. Because of the obvious
differences in responsibility, working conditions, number of
part time employees, etc., we did request that increases for
the factory employees be discussed separately from increases for the salesroom employees. The Union has somehow interpreted this to suggest that we desire no increases
for our salesroom employees.

"As for the claim that we desire to take the life insurance
policies away from our retired employees, this is another
matter that received little if any discussion. Certainly action
on our part of this type would be grossly inhumane and
quite possibly illegal. On the other hand, paying term
insurance rates on people in their 70's and 80's is nearly
prohibitive. If there had been less hostility and more co-
operative problem solving in our few negotiating sessions,
the Union would have learned that we were considering
an optional cash settlement for these people.

"We want to again emphasize that writing this letter is an
unpleasant task; certainly one we would have much preferred to avoid. However, when information containing gross
omissions and obviously representing only one side of the
story is being disseminated to the public for their judgment, we are forced to defend ourselves, present our side,
and plead that the situation be judged objectively.

"We also wish to make it clear that we hold no animosity
toward the vast majority of our employees, and recognize
that they find the present circumstances as distasteful as we."

On Monday the DRE carried a small statement on the Sunday
picketing:

"POLICE CALLED TO POTTERIES SEVERAL TIMES
"Red Wing police were called to the pottery salesroom
several times Sunday by reports of unruly pickets. One
woman picket was reported slapped in the face by an irate

customer who claimed she blocked the driveway entrance to the salesroom lot. Other customers said strikers hit their cars with signs and called them names as they entered and left the salesroom.

"Police talked to Union officials who promised to keep the picketing orderly.

"No new developments were reported today in the strike, now entering its eighth week."

In reading the article it seemed incongruous to us that the holocaust we had experienced would be treated so briefly and nonchalantly by the press. The statement that "Police talked to Union officials who promised to keep the picketing orderly" was a joke as far as we were concerned. We called Felhaber on Monday to inquire about a court order and the possibility of meeting that week. Felhaber was of the opinion that Larson would schedule a meeting for the end of the week, and in light of that possibility advised against pursuing a court order.

The Union revised their propaganda leaflet that week, and changed from white to sunshine-yellow paper. They toned down their statements somewhat and the message appeared less hysterical. While we considered this a better effort and more likely to accomplish its intended purpose, we still felt the leaflet would have very little influence on customers.

"PLEASE DON'T CROSS OUR PICKET LINE

"The Pottery Workers of Red Wing went on Strike on June 1, 1967.

"The Issue mainly is Low Wages! The Company's offer of *less than 4 cents per hour* for each year of a two year Contract caused the Strike.

"The Pottery pays the *Lowest Wages* of any Organized Plant in the Community.

"The Sales Girls, are also on Strike. SCABS have taken their jobs, and are running the Company Store. If you make a purchase, you will be hurting our efforts to win Decent Pay for Ourselves and Our Families.

"Please *don't buy Red Wing Pottery* until the Strike against
Low Wages is ended.
            "THIS IS A LEGAL STRIKE
"PLEASE do not cross our Picket Line."

We took issue with their statement that the company's offer
was less than 4 cents per hour for each year of a two year contract; it was slightly more than 4 cents per hour and, further,
we had offered to allow them to take the entire increase the
first year. We also disagreed with their statement that the
Pottery paid the lowest wages of any organized plant in Red
Wing. We knew for a fact that at least one other major Unionized manufacturer was lower. On the other hand, they had
eliminated certain other items contained in the original leaflet
such as eliminating insurance and the implication the sales girls
were to receive no raises.

By this time we were running low on first quality merchandise, and were finding it exceedingly difficult to ship even the
most critical orders to trade accounts. The phones were ringing almost continually with customers and salesmen inquiring
about critical merchandise. It became more and more difficult
to put them off; our claims of an imminent settlement began
to take on a hollow, unconvincing ring. Reports of major department stores closing out their Red Wing lines began to filter
in. While some of these disgruntled customers undoubtedly would
come back, Red Wing had been losing ground over recent years
in the department store market and could ill afford the loss of
any of these major accounts.

The telling and retelling of picket line incidents continued,
and was beginning to wear on my nerves. Not only did the stories
play a major role in the daily working hours, but also were a
main topic of any after-hours social function. Friends uncon-
nected with the Potteries were interested in getting the "inside
report" and the conversation topic would inevitably turn to the
strike. It would be wrong to suggest that I was never responsible for turning the conversation in this direction. Despite the
fact that I found the topic distasteful and intended to avoid it

if possible, the pressures accompanying the strike were a twenty-four hour a day reality and I found myself with a near-compulsive need to talk about it. No matter how sick I became of the subject, talking about it provided a kind of catharsis and seemed to release some of the building tension. Undoubtedly some of my acquaintances began to regard me as somewhat of a bore. However, I did attempt to avoid the constant retelling of "outrageous" picket line incidents, discussing instead the broader implications and strategies of the situation. I found myself thoroughly fed up with oft-repeated stories of picket "Mary Smith" doing this, or picket "John Jones" telling customers that, and experienced a growing urge to leave the room whenever someone else broached the subject.

Regardless of the emotional wear-and-tear we were all experiencing we had to continue, and when Conciliator Larson called to announce a meeting for Friday, July 21, our hopes were raised at the thought of settlement. Larson, for some reason unknown to us, had scheduled the meeting for the West End Grill. The West End Grill was located next to Arol's Bar, the reputed Union gathering spot, in a low-rent section of town. None of Management had ever set foot inside the establishment, and could only speculate that the reason Larson had called the meeting there was to encourage Union receptivity by putting them on familiar ground. The meeting was to commence at 10:00 A.M. KCUE reported:

> "Federal Mediator, Ed Larson, has set up another meeting between Union and Management for Friday morning in Red Wing, in an effort to settle a strike at the Red Wing Potteries which began June 1st. There has been one meeting since the strike began and that one produced no results. It is not known if either side in the dispute is prepared to make any concessions."

In light of the growing complications and multiplicity of unsettled issues, we requested that Labor Attorney Felhaber be present at the meeting. Also, because of the insurance issues and complicated wage and hour questions, company Treasurer Irving Vick was to be present in negotiations for the first time.

The company was bringing all of its resources to bear when
Felhaber, Vick, Mewhorter, R. A. Gillmer and myself entered
the West End Grill Friday morning. We picked our way past
tables, counter stools, and booths into a small semi-private dining room in the rear. The strong smell of fried foods, the chat-
tering of the waitresses, and the clinking of dishes being washed,
somehow detracted from the solemn, businesslike atmosphere
typical of negotiating sessions. A folding plastic screen placed
in the doorway gave a sense of some privacy but did nothing
to alleviate the noise. It crossed my mind that we had best not
raise our voices or the cafe patrons would become the proud
possessors of choice topics for gossip. Had Larson had a lapse
of sanity in picking this spot for a meeting? On the other hand,
it made no difference at all where we negotiated if some progress
could be realized.

It was decided prior to the meeting that there were to be no
angered references to Union picketing tactics on our part. Such
attacks would contribute nothing toward a settlement, and more
likely than not would turn the meeting into a series of emotion-
ally-laden reproaches. We entered the room with a series of
mumbled "hellos" and sideways glances. Larson began the meeting by asking both sides to review their past positions for the
benefit of Mr. Felhaber. Larson then asked the Union for their
present position, and Hammerschmidt reviewed the Union's original list of proposals. He was interrupted only once when a man
in coveralls entered the room unannounced to search briefly
for some kind of a tool in a side closet. Judging from his emphasis the Union was still serious about a substantial wage
increase, a pension plan, added hospitalization coverage, an
additional day-and-a-half holiday, and added vacation allowance with pay. President Gillmer took the floor for our side
and stated that he wanted to clarify something before we went
any further; that the company was proposing raising regular
sales girls from $1.49 to $1.60, but keeping the part-time summer girls at $1.40. He felt that $1.40 was a good wage for these
students and if pushed to raise them further, the company would
be forced to stop factory tours and thus eliminate the classifi-

cation. Mewhorter then went on to review the company's proposals. He made it clear that the company was still serious about conducting all Union business off of company time, reducing incentive rates to $1.25, but granting the equity and across-the-board increases. Gillmer offered to increase insurance costs by twenty-five percent in any form the Union desired. Since twenty-five percent was only $3,000 the proposal sounded better than it actually was.

At that point any potential progress that might have been realized was put in serious jeopardy by Chastain taking the floor and expounding on "poor company management." He elaborated on past incidents that proved to him the poor quality of Potteries management. The plant was not kept clean enough, the incentive system was no good, and all the foremen were tyrants. The gist of his lengthy discourse was that Management was both unfair and incompetent. I am certain that most of the company team was wondering, as I was, why, if Chastain was so intelligent as to be in a position to judge Management's business competence, he personally had not managed to achieve more of life's rewards. However, we managed to refrain from attacking him personally, and broke in only to dispute some of his allegations, which to us were only figments of his active imagination. We agreed later that Chastain was way out of line, that what he was saying had little bearing on the issues at hand, and wondered why Larson did not stop him.

When Chastain had finished his discourse - a fact for which we were all grateful - the discussion turned to hospitalization insurance. Felhaber, sensing an opportunity for progress, chose to commit the company to what we considered to be a very generous hospitalization package. He offered to pick up all dependent coverage, including that which employees were contributing under the previous plan, and give the Union their choice between a $20 hospital rate with major medical coverage or a $25 daily hospital rate without major medical coverage. Both of the alternatives would increase the surgical schedule from $200 to $300. Considering the fact that the previous plan had a daily hospital rate of only $14 with no major medical

coverage, either of the two alternatives the company was proposing offered vastly improved coverage. The Union's reaction
to the new hospitalization proposal was noncommittal. We broke
for lunch, still smarting from Chastain's accusations and with
little feeling of accomplishment.

The brief afternoon session was no better. Most of the time
was spent with the Union attacking the stinginess of our wage
proposal and our effort to "take away." Larson sent the company back to the Potteries offices in mid-afternoon and remained with the Union at the West End Grill.

We were very discouraged to find nails set in the salesroom
drives on our return to the company offices. We reasoned that
the least Chastain and Hammerschmidt could do would be to
call a halt to this type of activity while we were in the process
of negotiating. Larson returned in late afternoon to inform us
that he had dismissed the Union, that he had found no weak-
ening in their resolve, and that we would likely have another
meeting the following week. He suggested it was time for the
company to put their proposal in writing, and we agreed to do
so the following Monday. Before Larson left for the day he and
Felhaber met alone for a brief time. Falhaber gathered that
Hammerschmidt had given Larson a rough time for not seeing
that things were moving toward a settlement. We interpreted
this as a good sign and speculated that Hammerschmidt might
be feeling some pressure from his superiors to get the strike
settled.

Thus, the second attempt to negotiate a settlement since the
strike began seven weeks earlier ended in another stalemate.
Station KCUE reported the meeting:

"Members of Local 6-430 of Oil, Chemical, and Atomic
Workers Union met all day Friday with officials of Red
Wing Potteries in an effort to hammer out a new contract.
The bargaining session began at ten Friday morning, and
ended at five o'clock with a break for lunch in between.

"After the day-long session Federal Mediator, Ed Larson,
issued a brief statement. Larson said, 'I was satisfied with
the meeting and we'll probably meet again some time next

week.' Larson said that this was not the time to make an evaluation of what progress has been made.

"Some one-hundred members of the OCAW at the Potteries have been on strike since June 1st. The only other meeting held, with Mediator Larson, produced no results."

On Saturday there were fewer pickets than usual - only fifty to seventy-five - but those present were an unruly group. Perhaps angered by the lack of results in Friday's meeting, it soon became clear that we were in for a rough day. With seven weeks of picketing behind them the strikers were becoming adept at harassment. Further, they had received little if any censure from the police, which could be interpreted as license to go to greater lengths of violence. As usual, the police were not present on Saturday, although they would cruise by infrequently in their squad cars. We had all but given up phoning the police for protection.

Nails were present in quantity, driveway blocking lasted for three to five minutes or until the customer backed up to leave, and incidents of scratched cars became more frequent. Also, a few of the men had developed a new technique. They would run menacingly at a car, jabbing the end of their picket signs through the open window, stopping inches short of the driver's face. After watching this type of behavior for any length of time, it was all one could do to refrain from going out and physically attacking the picket. The pickets were highly effective in turning cars away with these tactics, and business was severely off.

The middle of the day a woman from Davenport, Iowa, called from a local gas station to report that her tires were full of nails. Gillmer agreed to pay for the necessary repairs. A few days later we received a letter from her:

"I am writing in regards to an incident that happened to us Saturday July 22. Maybe you remember our conversation when I called you from the gas station about the nails in our tires. Two brand new tires (our car is only a few months old) and 4 new nails which punctured both tires completely through. We appreciate the fact you paid for the repair of the tires but you realize this lessens the wear of our tires now. It also delayed us 1 hr. & 45 minutes. It upset both of us to think what would have happened if we hadn't noticed the one tire going flat before we got on the highway. After that tire was fixed my husband asked the service man to check the other tires for any more, then he found the other nails. We could have had a blow out. Don't those people realize the danger in this sort of thing. Grown men and women doing this is outrageous. It was bad enough they scared the three children telling them things like - they would cut their legs off. We can ignore them, the children don't understand. They were sitting in the car, until they came running in crying, telling us what the men had said. "We did not know your company was on strike or we wouldn't have stopped, but when you go out of your way to come, you're not going to leave.

"We bought $45 worth of dishes. We would not have bought a penny's worth had we known this.

"We drove 50 miles out of our way to stop in Red Wing. We had been in Bemidji for 2 weeks and had a 12 hr. drive. My husband did not want to take the extra 50 miles as it was.

"We have bought dishes in Red Wing before and I always enjoyed going there. I would always mention to anyone going to Minnesota to be sure and make a trip to Red Wing Potteries. A lot of people from Iowa have stopped there and gotten things. After this incident I will never send anyone there again, nor will we come again unless something is done about our new tires, our embarrassment, and inconvenience. Since we arrived, one of the tires we had fixed went flat again."

The molestation of customers became so blatant during the afternoon that we called the police in desperation. The police would then cruise by, stop and converse briefly with pickets, and continue on their way. Our frustration and anger were nearly unbearable. In late afternoon a lady and her two children attempted to enter the parking lot in a small foreign car.

The pickets rocked the car severely, and when she managed to find an opening to pull out of their clutches three or four pickets chased the car the length of the parking lot, shrieking and swinging their picket signs at the car. This was too much and, in desperation, we set off the burglar alarm, knowing full well it would bring the police in a hurry. The police called us and I answered the phone. Completely losing my temper, I told the police in no uncertain terms what I thought of them, and hung up. While I was doing this, a squad car had arrived with lights flashing to investigate the "burglary." R. A. Gillmer was shouting at the two officers that setting off the burglar alarm was the only way we could get any police attention. We angrily told the officers what had happened to the lady in the foreign car. The police approached the distraught woman and her tearful children. They told her that she was on her own when she crossed the picket line. They asked her if she wished to file a formal complaint, but that if she desired to do so she must know the names and addresses of her attackers, and further she could not file the complaint until Monday because the judge would not be available until then. The lady explained that she was from Washington, D. C., and could not possibly wait in Red Wing until Monday to file a complaint. The matter was dropped and the officers left, but we could not help wondering how she could be expected to know the names and addresses of her assailants under the circumstances. We felt the police had handled the matter incompetently and, worse, with a pro labor bias.

A few minutes later when one of the worst offenders on the picket line began jabbing his sign through an automobile window, I lost my head and started for the picket line. R. A. Gillmer was close behind me, not to detain me, but to help out if needed. We reasoned that we had no other alternative but to take the law into our own hands. While this reasoning was grossly unsound, our nerves had reached the breaking point. I noticed with some satisfaction that the picket was obviously apprehensive about our approach. I reached him, drew my face up to within inches of his, and began shouting, "god damn coward - you're tough when it comes to women and children." I was hoping I

could provoke him to take a swing at me, but he muttered something about "picking on me," and "you can't hit me, I'm wear-
ing glasses." Finally, after I had shouted in his face for a few
minutes, he pushed me. I grabbed him by the shirt collar and
drove him back into the street, ripping most of the buttons off
his shirt. He stumbled, nearly fell, and dropped his picket sign.
He made no move to counter-attack so I stifled my rage. He
reached down to retrieve his picket sign and I stood on it. He
mumbled something more about "picking on me." By that
time all the pickets had gathered around the driveway and I told
them what I thought of their methods. They told me "to stay in
the store where you belong," and accused me of attacking the
picket. I told them he shoved me first and they, as expected,
claimed I had made the first physical contact. One woman started
slapping me on the arm. At this point the police arrived. Someone in the salesroom had called them, fearing the situation would
turn into a full-blown riot. The presence of the police cooled
things off and we returned to the salesroom. No one filed a
complaint with the policeman, and he did not question anyone
regarding the incident. The pickets were quite subdued for the
rest of the evening and, while taking the action I did was no
doubt unwise, it gave me a marked sense of relief and satisfaction. Any relief was short-lived, however, when I considered that
Sunday was still to come bringing, as always, new forms of
harassment.

When I drove into the parking lot Sunday morning, July 23,
there were more pickets present than ever before. Chastain was
later to claim the presence of two hundred pickets that day.
Upon leaving the car, the pickets led by Joe Hammerschmidt
unleashed a tremendous verbal attack on me. Referring to the
scuffle I had had the previous day, they shouted that I was a
coward and afraid to come out to the picket line now with all
of them present. I could hear Hammerschmidt's voice rising
above the din. My anger rising, and noting the presence of a
policeman which gave me some assurance I would not be torn
to bits by the mob, I turned and walked toward the picket line
directly at Hammerschmidt. I moved up close to Hammerschmidt

and said to the mob, "You said I was afraid to come out here, and here I am." Hammerschmidt said, "One move from you and you'll be down." The officer moved over and dispersed the crowd and I returned to the salesroom amid the jeers of the pickets, but I had derived satisfaction from calling their bluff.

In addition to Hammerschmidt's loudspeaker, the pickets were armed with a variety of noise makers including whistles and cowbells. The result was pandemonium. The few customers that gained entrance to the salesroom reported vicious verbal attacks; they were referred to in a wide range of obscenities and suffered enumerable threats.

Despite the fact that two or three policemen were present all day, the picketers had their way. Strikers were seen lying across automobile hoods, and falling in the drives in front of oncoming cars. They were well into the street, forming a nearly impervious wall, gesturing wildly as a car approached. If the car passed the drive, many would run frantically to the next to make certain the driver did not find easier going there. Those drivers who courageously inched their way into the lot were likely to pick up nails in their tires, have their cars scratched by picket signs, and find themselves and their families the target of the most vulgar verbal abuse. Early in the afternoon the pickets initiated a new technique; they would fill empty beer cans with water and throw the contents on the cars' windshields and, if the driver did not think to roll up his window, through the open window onto the occupants. Many customers, unable to gain entrance to the salesroom parking lot, would park their cars on the street or across the street in the factory parking lot, and walk through the picket line and into the store. They, of course, were victims of continual verbal abuse during their walk. All of this was occurring with little, if any, censure from the police. When an incident became too bad - such as a striker lying across a car hood - a policeman would usually walk slowly in that direction and the activity would ordinarily cease by the time he reached the drive. We were amazed that such activity could continue in the presence of the police.

Watching the proceedings from within the salesroom was like

going through the turmoils of hell. Our anger and frustration were nearly uncontrollable, but we were helpless to find an outlet or a solution to the dilemma we were facing. A plan began to form in my mind: If the pickets could block our drives, why could we not block the entrance to the salesroom when they attempted to enter, as they most certainly would later in the afternoon. I talked to Gerry Mewhorter, and he agreed to join me in blocking the double doors to the salesroom. I waited expectantly for the pickets to lay down their signs and head for the salesroom. About 5:00 P.M. they made their move, and Mewhorter and I were in front of the entrance before they could reach it. At that particular time there were no police present, and I fully expected and half-hoped for a full-scale battle. The pickets initially were somewhat bewildered by this unexpected move, and there were references to "open to the public," and "they have to let us in." Only three of the thirty or forty people at the entrance were our employees. After the initial uncertainty the pickets made passes at door handles and engaged in some minor shoving, but we were determined not to yield. It soon became obvious that there was one flaw in our scheme - while the pickets were kept from entering the store, the circumstances also made it impossible for the customers to enter. While we were weighing this dilemma, the police arrived and approached the scene. I had decided that I would force the police to arrest me if they ordered me to move. However, the police informed the pickets that they could not move us, and that it was our privilege to block the doors if we so desired. They did not disperse the mob, however, and retreated in order to observe. Another five minutes of impasse and I tired of the game, and re-entered the store followed by the pickets. My anger and tension had not subsided, however, and I decided to harass the pickets individually within the store, reasoning that on our property if something broke out they would receive full blame. I picked out a few of the most offensive strikers whom I had grown to thoroughly dislike over the weeks, and proceeded to harass them one by one. At that point my reactions were strictly emotional and I would have welcomed an incident.

I would meet one of my "targets" in an aisle and block his progress, telling him he was a "worthless, no-good who was tough when it came to scaring hell out of old ladies and children." This bothered them, but they made no efforts to respond physically. After most of the strikers had returned to their posts on the picket line I spotted one particularly offensive young man lingering in the gift section of the store. As I approached he sat down in a nearby chair and lit a cigarette. To me, this man of twenty odd years - not one of our employees - represented all the nastiness and vulgarity of the long summer. He had a police record and held no job, and I tore into him with these facts, referring to him as a "worthless troublemaker, foul mouthed, etc." He apparently thought better of engaging in any kind of a scuffle within the salesroom because all of my tactics failed to arouse him to action. He left shortly, leaving us all drained both physically and emotionally.

The weekend had been a nightmare. Not only had our business been cut severely, but the increasing hostility and aggressiveness of the pickets had taken its toll on our stability and resolve. We could not go through another week-end like this one. We were absolutely determined to seek a court order.

My sister received an obscene phone call that evening. Whether or not it was strike-inspired we will never know. R. A. Gillmer phoned me that evening before I had taken my phone off the hook for the night, and brought up the possibility of liquidation for the first time. He was at the end of his rope with the weekend picketing, the growing loss of trade customers, and the rigidity of the Union demands. We were convinced that to meet the current demands of the Union would assure the death of the company, seriously depleting the assets in the process. If the Union refused to soften their position, liquidation was the only logical alternative. We decided to discuss it with Felhaber and the company Directors at the first opportunity.

Monday morning Mewhorter, Vick, R. A. Gillmer, and I drove to St. Paul to meet with Felhaber. In conjunction with Felhaber we prepared a letter for the Union detailing our proposal at last Friday's meeting:

"This is a proposal by Red Wing Potteries designed to settle the current strike.

"We propose a new agreement for two years effective August 1, 1967, incorporating the following changes from the expired agreement.

"1. All incentive rates would be changed to $1.25 from the rates otherwise listed in the expired agreement.

"2. All factory employees would receive an increase to their base rate in the expired contract of 10¢ per hour.

"3. Certain job classifications would receive further increases based upon equity adjustments. They are as follows:

	EQUITY RAISE	TOTAL RAISE
a. Slip maker	15¢	25¢
b. Filter press opr.	15¢	25¢
c. Car scoop opr.	15¢	25¢
d. Block & caser	20¢	30¢
e. Ram die maker	20¢	30¢
f. Hand spray tr.	7¢	17¢
g. Mold maker	10¢	20¢
h. Machine spray opr.	10¢	20¢
i. Wahl jigger opr.	7¢	17¢
j. Glaze maker	12¢	22¢
k. Asst. glaze maker	10¢	20¢
l. Hd. pick-up man	10¢	20¢
m. Hd. 2nd man	10¢	20¢
n. Maint. group ld.	7¢	17¢
o. Maint. Man sp.	6¢	16¢
p. Hand sprayer	7¢	17¢
q. Watchman	6¢	16¢
r. Caster	7¢	17¢

"4. All regular sales personnel will receive a base rate of $1.60 per hour. Sales personnel hired during the summer season will receive $1.40 per hour.

"5. To the extent the readjustment in incentive rate appli-

cation would result in a loss to an estimated three
or four individuals, said loss to said individuals will
be avoided by 'red circling' their names.

"6. The company will improve medical-hospitalization insurance through offering two alternative choices to
the employees with either one acceptable to the
company.

(a) The first choice would add major medical together with X-ray and lab coverage as explained
at last week's meeting.

(b) Present plan of benefits would be continued plus
an increase on the daily hospital from $14 to
$25 per day.

Both of the above alternatives include an increase
in the surgical schedule to $300 and that the com-
pany would pay all of the cost both for the employees
and their dependents. There would be a clause added
whereby in the event of a spouse also working or
the husband is working in another place covered by
insurance there would be no duplication of benefits.
We also wish to repeat what was stated at last Friday's meeting that none of these alternatives would
affect the $1,000 life insurance benefit for retired
employees. This benefit would be continued the same
as it has in the past.

"7. Section 11 of Article 4 shall be changed to read:
'Meetings with the Shop Committee for the purpose
of considering grievances or negotiations will be held
after the end of work for the first shift without re-
inbursement for time so spent by the company.'

"8. All pay computed in Article 2, Section 2, drop the
last four words 'percentage of W-2 Form' and sub-
stitute 'percentage of pay received in the twelve
months prior to June 1 as follows.' Make the same
change in the last clause of Section 3.

"9. In addition there should be a written commitment exchanged between the parties that neither one will

impose or exact upon any employees any penalties
or discrimination of any kind or nature whatsoever.
It is regrettable that incidents have occurred including the maltreatment of customers, use of threats
and abuses, damage to personal property which cannot be justified by the current bad human relations
otherwise existing in the country. Red Wing has prospered because it has been a small closeknit community with a high degree of civic pride. We trust
this can be restored. Without such restoration, this
company's future cannot be sustained, particularly
when it is coupled with higher wages than the pottery
industries pay throughout the United States, and
differences of opinion on how to handle our problems without resort to the application of basic economic facts. The company cannot quarrel with the employees' desire to be represented by a union outside
of the traditional union which has represented employees in the pottery industry, but it does quarrel
with any belief that this enables a different set of
economic arguments to be given to the content of
negotiated labor agreements."

R. A. Gillmer

We also discussed with Felhaber the possibility of liquidation
if a settlement could not be reached in the near future. After
describing the agonies suffered over the weekend Felhaber agreed
to pursue a court order.

On our return to Red Wing we heard KCUE's description
of Sunday's chaos. This was the first public recognition of the
level the picketing had reached.

"It was again an ugly Sunday at the Red Wing Potteries
salesroom parking lot. Tourists coming into Red Wing to
visit the world-famed Potteries were again subjected to a
variety of name-calling, cuss words, and physical movements
by the Union pickets around the entrance to the parking
lot. A Red Wing police prowl car spent much of the afternoon parked in the area to, as one officer put it, 'baby

sit the pickets.' Most law officers seem to feel the situation
is growing worse every weekend.

"The Potteries Union has been on strike since the fore-
part of June. A negotiating session held last Friday did
not appear to move either the Union or the Pottery's ownership closer to a solution. At one time wages and working
conditions appeared to be the major points of dispute. Now,
after weeks of name-calling, hate words and bitter criticism, no one seems to be able to define what it is that is
keeping the Union and the company apart.

"Cowbells and even loudspeakers were brought into play
Sunday as pickets at the Potteries tried to discourage
people from buying. One man who was there said, 'You
practically had to run over the pickets to get through the
picket lines.' Police officers say most of the trouble is being
created by pickets who come in to Red Wing from other
towns to bolster picket lines on weekends. Law officers say
the Red Wing workers themselves act much better than
some of the out-of-town volunteer pickets. Sunday the Pierce
County NFO sent over some farmers to join in the cat-
calling, and individual Union pickets showed up from points
as far away as Duluth. Some Pierce County highway department maintenance workers also appeared on the picket
lines Sunday. They were recruited through NFO efforts,
one said. A policeman who spent some time at the scene
Sunday said, 'It is getting to be like Plymouth Avenue.' 'They
can't keep on like this,' he said. 'Some day it'll get to be
really unruly.' Today's Minneapolis Tribune says the pickets
are known for shouting things like 'yellow bellies' and 'scab'
to those who drive onto the Potteries parking lot. Many of
the people who have gone through the picket lines to shop
have phoned police afterwards to complain that pickets
rocked their cars, poked picket signs at them, and called
them filthy and unprintable names.

"The president of the Pottery, Richard A. Gillmer, says
he may have to close the plant if he loses accounts because
of the strike. Gillmer claims he has enough backlog to keep

his sales going for a year and a half, and it appears the Union, too, is digging in for a long strike. The president of the Union local, Tilfer Chastain of rural Hager City, feels that the effects of imports on pottery sales is not important. He discounts this. Says Chastain, 'If Gillmer feels he must close the place, we'll pick a committee and help him nail the doors.'

"The 89-year-old Pottery company is the fourth largest industry in Red Wing. Many Red Wing people feel it would be a major loss if Red Wing Potteries should go out of business. Tourist flow has been dwindling because of the strike. Dick Karsten, owner of the Standard service station near the bluffs at the edge of the business district, says he feels business is off about a third. Karsten says he normally gets about 25 requests a day from people who want to know where the Pottery is. The secretary of the Red Wing Chamber of Commerce, Mrs. Dorothy Nelson, says the strike has forced her to cancel Pottery tours. She says, 'Many people have planned the tours as part of their summer vacations.' While the salesroom has remained open during the strike, Mrs. Nelson points out there are a lot of people who will not cross picket lines."

Chastain's statement that he would pick a committee "to help nail the doors" was greeted by Management, as were most of Chastain's statements, with combined humor and hostility. However, in this latest edict we felt he had reached new levels of pomposity.

Returning to the company offices from St. Paul, we distributed our written proposal to a number of the pickets, asking that they see that it reached Chastain or Hammerschmidt. We judged that this tactic would not please the Committee, but wanted to make certain the membership was fully aware of the company proposal. We guessed it would be read and thoroughly discussed before it ever reached Chastain or Hammerschmidt.

Monday morning the Minneapolis Tribune carried a lengthy piece on the strike.

"POTTERY STRIKE SLOWS TOURISM IN RED WING
"Visitors to this town's most famous industry have faced
shouts of 'Yellow-bellies!' and 'Scabs!' for more than seven
weeks.

"Pickets began parading near driveway entrances to the
Red Wing Potteries, Inc., salesroom June 1 after a strike
was authorized by the 120 members of Local 6-430 of the
Oil, Chemical and Atomic Workers International Union.

"Negotiations between Richard A. Gillmer, company president, and Tilfer Chastain, president of the local, resumed
Friday after a break of five weeks.

"Federal Mediator Ed Larson said he was 'satisfied' with
the meeting and plans to schedule another one this week.

'Gillmer said in an interview before Friday's talks that
the Nation's pottery industry is slumping, injured by imports.
If he loses accounts as a result of the strike, Gillmer said,
he may have to close the plant.

"Chastain discounted the effect of imports, adding, 'If he
must close the place, we'll pick a committee and help him
nail the doors.'

"Prime issues in the dispute include wages, insurance, medical benefits and working conditions.

"The 89-year-old pottery company is the town's fourth
largest industry, according to the Red Wing's Daily Republican Eagle, which editorialized: 'The Potteries salesroom
is a magnet with power to draw thousands of visitors . . .
It would be a major loss, one that every Red Wingite would
feel, should Red Wing Potteries go out of business.'

"Already, because of the strike, the tourist flow is dwindling.
'Business is off about a third,' said Dick Karsten, 32, owner
of a Standard service station near the bluffs at the town's
southern edge. 'We're the first station off the highway, and
we normally get about 25 requests a day from people who
want to know where the pottery is.'

"Mrs. Dorothy L. Nelson, executive secretary of the Red
Wing Chamber of Commerce, said the strike has forced
her to cancel pottery tours. 'Many people have planned the

tours as part of their summer vacations,' she said. And although the salesroom has remained open during the strike, 'There are a certain number of people who won't cross picket lines,' she said.

"The pickets themselves - including many women - are vociferous as they try to discourage drivers from entering the salesroom's parking lot. But aside from tacks strewn in the lot on July 4, there has been little physical harassment by the strikers.

"Gerald Niebling, 23, a desk clerk at the St. James Hotel said he believes most Red Wing citizens favor the workers - and not only because he, like many others, had a relative or close friend working at the pottery.

"The wage scale is low here,' he said. 'And if the Pottery raises salaries, other factories will have to go along.'

"One woman on the picket line said she thought the plant's employees were 'worse off than 10 years ago. Compared with other workers around here, our salaries have slipped.'

"Another picket said, 'Man we'd rather the company died a sudden death than drag on like it has been.'

"Ralph Finley, 60, president of the Chamber of Commerce and a stockholder in the pottery, had little sympathy for the strikers. 'They haven't got the best class of people working there,' he said. 'If they're not satisfied, why don't they go somewhere else?'

"Despite cautious optimism after Friday's meeting, both sides seem to be digging in as the strike lengthens.

"Gillmer claimed he has enough backlog to keep his salesroom open for a year and a half. Union leaders have received both financial help and extra pickets from other locals throughout the state.

"City officials, though worried, seem reluctant to interfere in the dispute.

"Jack Adams, 65, president of the City Council, said a group of business leaders who belong to the 11-year-old Red Wing Industrial Development Corp. voted to have no part in the negotiations. That was during the five-week breakdown in talks when Adams said, 'We found very little real desire to bargain.'

"Mayor Demetrius G. Jelatis, 50, expressed special concern for the effect the strike will have on the town's reputation. 'This is one part of the Red Wing image,' he explained. 'People all over the country know about Red Wing pottery.' But Jelatis, too, contends the city government must wait for the disputants to resolve their own difficulties. 'My own feeling is that if this is prolonged, both sides stand to lose a great deal. But I think they're both right; it's their problem, and the only thing the town can do is try to keep order. We can't do anything until they ask us to.' "

The statement that "aside from tacks strewn in the lot on July 4, there has been little physical harassment by the strikers" was something, we felt, the reporter must have learned in his interview with the Union. Finley's alleged statement that "they haven't got the best class of people working there" was to cause him a great deal of trouble in weeks to come, although he vehemently denied having made the statement.

Letters were still pouring in from irate customers. From a Robbinsdale, Minnesota man came the following:

"We were in your fine city today to visit your Pottery to buy some items which the wife uses in the winter for prizes and gifts, etc. We did not know about the strike at the plant and we found it hard to get into the driveway as the crowd of people blocking the driveways to the store. I finally found one driveway with one man standing in the middle waving people on but he had to jump as I drove my car right at him, and did he cuss me out. I let my wife go into the store and I stayed outside hoping he would come after me but he knew better. In leaving we drove out another driveway and the women standing there said 'ain't you ashamed of yourselves for driving through the picket lines' and at the next driveway the man hollered out, 'How does it feel to be a Scab?' I wanted to go back and call for the squad car and have him picked up and charge him with slander. I wrote your Chief of Police at Red Wing

today also. I hope they are giving you some protection.
"The way they are going about this strike I hope they don't get a dime raise. It's not pleasant, I know."

From a Harvard, Illinois woman:

"On July 15th we visited your lovely city and having heard for years of Red Wing pottery stopped for some. (I have owned a set of your dishes for years.) The place was being picketed but we drove in. I don't understand why the police do not protect your salesroom. It is one thing to keep people from going to work but to take their grievances out on the tourists is bad. We didn't see they had thrown nails around the road. The next morning (Sunday) we had two flat tires. One had five nails in it and the other two. We only have three thousand miles on our car and you can imagine the feeling. Luckily our motel was near a gas station so cost us only three dollars for repairs. I had spent twenty dollars for pottery for gifts. Perhaps you can tell your police department the hazard this is. Imagine getting a flat on a busy highway. The best of luck to you. I sympathize with you due to all the cheap imports."

From a Minnetonka, Minnesota woman:

"We are new to Minnesota, from Mass., and took advantage of your TV invitation to visit your salesroom last Sunday. It has taken all of us this long to get over that visit. We were greeted by strikers pushing our car, pounding on the hood to keep it out of the parking lot. After a trip through your beautiful rooms we sent the children to the car so that we could look around alone. While they were alone in the car they were called Scab rats, Scab brats and all but molested orally. When we came out they were in tears.

"Before we could leave the parking lot we had to be subjected to ignorant name calling again. This was all too humiliating and has left a distinct taste as to the type of people you hire. These were women. Our company would no sooner hire stupid uncouth people, although how could you tell.

"I do not need a reply! Actually this letter is merely to blow my stack. We will never come again."

This last letter was such an ideal illustration of the inhumane treatment of customers that I had a copy made and gave it to the pickets in an effort to shame them. The letter reached Chastain in short order, and the next day we received a note from him on official OCAW stationery:

"Reference is made to letter you received from a customer from Mass. We do not feel this is at all true. However you must try to realize that you yourself are to fault if you ask your customers to enter your STRUCK store to line your pockets while we watch on. We did not enter this strike to see how nice we could be to you or the SCABS you call Customers."

Tilfer E. Chastain, President Local 6-430

We felt that Chastain's letter in essence condoned the contemptible behavior described in the letter and put him in a vulnerable position. We could not resist taking the three letters and Chastain's reply to the DRE.

That evening the DRE reported that Finley, Chamber president and owner-manager of the local Coast-to-Coast store, denied making the statements attributed to him in the Minneapolis Tribune:

"FINLEY DENIES TWIN CITIES PAPER STRIKE STATEMENT

"The president of the Red Wing Chamber of Commerce today denied making a pottery strike statement attributed to him in a Twin Cities newspaper this morning.

"I didn't make that statement,' said Ralph Finley of the quote which drew the ire of strikers. Finley said he talked with a man from the Minneapolis paper and told him it would be good to see the strike settled. He denied saying unsatisfied workers should go elsewhere. 'What I did say,' Finley contended, 'was that if some workers didn't want to return to the potteries I hoped they could find other work here.' "

Finley was not to get off the hook that easily.

Monday afternoon at 3 P.M. we had a Board Meeting with all Directors present. President Gillmer discussed the lack of progress in negotiations and brought up the possibility of liquidation. The Directors agreed that liquidation was a very real possibility should the lack of progress continue and the Union refuse to moderate their current position.

That week a number of rumors were circulating: (1) That R. A. Gillmer had been bragging loudly at the country club that he "had the workers under his thumb;" (2) That old man Gillmer was not so bad - it was the son who was the stubborn one; (3) That they were going to "get" my sister and wreck the company car the next time she was seen out anywhere driving it; and (4) That I was a communist.

We were talking very little with pickets anymore on our walks from the factory to the salesroom. For our part, feelings were running too high to muster so much as a greeting to those people. Regardless of whether or not an employee had actually participated in the weekend harassment, we reasoned that he was guilty by association and condoning that type of behavior by continuing to picket.

R. A. Gillmer's doorbell began to ring at all hours of the night. When he would answer the bell there would be no one present. Also, both of us had to take our cars in that week for tire repair. They had taken thirty to forty nails out of R. A. Gillmer's tires by that time and about half that number out of mine.

Conciliator Larson called on Tuesday to schedule a meeting for 9:30 A.M. Thursday at the Court House. We were pleased to discover he had moved the meeting place from the West End Grill.

KCUE reported on Tuesday Finley's alleged statement in the Minneapolis Tribune and the Union's reaction to it:

"Finley said he was as surprised as anyone to see the quote in print. He says, 'It doesn't sound like me. It is not my type of thinking.' Finley went on to say that he 'hopes they settle the strike soon. It is not doing the town any good.'

"The quotation attributed to Finley in the Minneapolis Tribune produced a statement from Tilfer Chastain, president of the Union local at the Potteries. Chastain said, 'I don't think there is any statement necessary on Finley's comments. I think Abraham Lincoln made a perfect answer to this situation more than a hundred years ago when he said, 'Better to keep your mouth shut and be thought a fool than to open it and prove yourself a fool!'

"At least one Union member made the rounds of many Red Wing business places on Monday, carrying a copy of the Tribune article with him, to point out to Chamber members the irritation of Union workers at the Potteries with what was said to be a statement by Finley."

That Tilfer Chastain would be quoting Abraham Lincoln seemed somehow a great paradox to Potteries Management.

Tuesday evening the DRE carried a front page article on the letters we had given them:

"STRIKE TACTICS HIT —
WE WILL NEVER COME AGAIN

"Complaints of alleged unruly tactics by strikers at Red Wing Potteries are being received from as far away as Massachusetts by local officials. Visitors to the pottery salesroom say their cars have been damaged, their children frightened and their integrity slandered by the pickets.

"In answer to the charges, Tilfer Chastain, president of striking Oil, Chemical and Atomic Workers Local 6-430 wrote pottery officials: 'We did not enter this strike to see how nice we could be to you or the scabs you call customers.'

"A woman from Harvard, Ill., wrote that she visited the salesroom on July 15. She claimed her car encountered nails in the driveway and received two flat tires. 'It is one thing to keep people from going to work, but to take their grievances out on the tourists is bad,' she wrote.

"A couple from Minnetonka said their car was rocked and pounded by pickets as they visited the salesroom one Sunday. 'After a trip through your beautiful rooms we sent the

children to the car so that we could look around alone.
While they were alone in the car they were called scab
rats, scab brats and all but molested,' the couple wrote.
'When we came out they were in tears. Before we could
leave the parking lot we had to be subjected to ignorant
name calling again. This was all too humiliating and has left
a distinct taste as to the type of people you hire. These
were women. I do not need a reply. Actually this letter is
merely to blow my stack. We will never come again.'
"A man from Robbinsdale said the way the pickets are
going about the strike, 'I hope they don't get a dime raise.'
He said he had to almost run over a picket to get him out
of the driveway and then was cussed out. 'I let my wife
go into the store and I stayed outside hoping he would come
after me, but he knew better.' On leaving, the man said
there were more insults and he strongly considered filing
slander charges. He complained to the chief of police, he
said.
"In his letter to pottery officials, Chastain said he did not
feel the complaints were true. 'However,' he wrote, 'you
must try to realize that you yourself are to fault if you
ask your customers to enter your struck store to line your
pockets while we watch on.' "

We were thoroughly pleased with the article, feeling it would
alert the Red Wing community to what had been going on at
the Potteries. Also, we felt the article cast Chastain in a "fool's
role," and made him out as condoning the described abuse.

The media were carrying more and more news on the strike,
and that evening the DRE printed a letter to the editor:

"STRIKE HURTS BOTH SIDES

"To the Editor: In your editorial of about a week ago you
were writing about the Pottery situations. You stated that
the main contributing factor was foreign competition. In
this case I think that it might have very little to do with it.
I think that it has been a case of very poor management.
You can't learn how to make pottery by reading it in books

and then try to make it on paper and IBM punch cards. With the quality of the labor turnover in the last year or so, good help has been hard to get.

"Again, I think that the administration payroll has near succeeded the plant payroll.

"As to the Union, they have not got the workers' interest at heart. The most of their local officers have not got any great stakes in the town of Red Wing or they are in a position to retire and forget about the Pottery. And the International organization, they are just using this strike to scare some of the bigger unions into better contracts. The lousy $10 a week strike benefits and maybe a bag of beans thrown in by the various locals, what does that amount to? The union agents would have their jobs and get their big salaries if the Pottery closed.

"You pay $4.50 a month dues and all you get back is $10 a week for a few weeks - isn't much. Figure it out.

"I think the smart thing to do would be to go back to work and see if you couldn't make a go of it.

"A few of the workers could maybe get by but there is some who couldn't find work any place else.

"A strike always hurts everybody. I know I have been through a couple of them."

A Reader

While anonymous, the letter sounded suspiciously like one of our old-time employees. He seemed to know too much about the situation to be an "outsider."

Chastain and Hammerschmidt paid a visit on Mrs. Dorothy Nelson, Chamber Secretary, on Tuesday. They indicated their displeasure with the Chamber's stock answer to tourists that "the Pottery is on strike, but their retail store is open." The Union's hostility was spreading to other points in town, a situation that we felt would do nothing to help their cause. In fact, we were beginning to detect a swell of public sympathy in favor of the company and against the Union.

We had heard that Chastain had been showing his W-2 form around town, protesting the low wages at the Potteries. We also

knew that other employees were misrepresenting their wages
to the public - townspeople and customers. In order to counter-
act this movement, we gave the DRE and KCUE a list of all
employees who had worked a full year in 1966, their total
hours worked, their W-2 earnings, and their average rate per
hour. The DRE published the list on Wednesday, July 26,
choosing to delete employee names:

"POTTERIES RELEASES EMPLOYEE WAGE LIST
"Red Wing Potteries today made public a complete list of
what its full-year production employees earned in 1966.
"The action became necessary, Potteries President R. A.
Gillmer said this morning, because some striking employees
have misrepresented their actual earnings in conversations
with the Red Wing area public.
"The DRE showed the list at once to Tilfer Chastain, president of the striking Local 6-430, Oil, Chemical and Atomic
Workers, but Chastain declined to make any comment.
"According to the Potteries' list, women who worked the
full year of 1966 averaged $2.10 per hour and men aver-
aged $2.24 per hour. The women ranged from a low of
$1.61 per hour to a high of $2.68. Men ranged from a low
of $1.79 to a high of $3.65.
"The Potteries' list includes 38 women and 43 men - all,
it said, who were working at Red Wing Potteries at the start
of 1966 and still employed at year's end.
"The figures, the Potteries continued, were taken directly
from the W-2 forms which the company uses for income
tax withholding reports to the Federal Internal Revenue
Service. The tabulation shows total hours worked during
the year, total earnings, and average hourly rate."
In retrospect, we should have subtracted vacation and holiday
pay from their earnings to give a more representative picture
of average hourly rates. Removing these two items would have
lowered averages approximately 17 cents. Women would have
averaged $1.93 instead of $2.10, and men $2.07 instead of
$2.24. Publishing the rates served the purpose we had intended

in that many townspeople commented that they had no idea that Potteries employees were "doing so well." On the other hand, the Union was irate that we would resort to such tactics to discredit them and appeal to public sympathy.

On Wednesday the DRE also published a pro-company letter to the editor:

"HOOTING MOB GREETED VISITOR

"Returning to the Twin Cities Sunday (July 23) through Red Wing we decided to visit the Red Wing Potteries sales-room. Approaching the area we were greeted by a mob of jeering, hooting, whistling, shouting, banging on kettles people carrying strike signs. Then, we remembered, the plant had been struck since June 1.

"We wondered if the strikers had ever bothered to consider that the Pottery plant exists and operates solely for the customers, be they retail or wholesale. These customers in effect write the pottery workers' pay checks which in a sense makes the customers the employers.

"If employment is as plentiful in Red Wing as we were told it was by a 64-year-old service station attendant why wouldn't the strikers change jobs and go where they can make more money and obtain more employee benefits? Or, is it their aim to destroy the plant, force its closing and 'help nail the door?' If so, why?"

Also, on Wednesday KCUE broadcasted what we perceived as definitely a pro-company report:

"Both sides will be preparing today for the negotiating session due to start at nine o'clock tomorrow morning at the court house in Red Wing. Neither Red Wing Potteries officials nor members of the union bargaining team seem to have any idea whether anything can come of the session.

"Feelings run high on both sides. The strike, simply as a strike, has badly damaged the image and appeal of Red Wing Potteries, one of Minnesota's prime tourist attractions. What seems to bother Potteries officials even more is the conduct of the pickets, especially on Sundays when outsiders

join Potteries employees on the picket lines. Some of those
who are manning the Potteries salesroom wonder out loud
how it will be to work again with those people who have
said many things to company officials and Potteries visitors
and customers while on the picket line. Union leaders, on
the other hand, speak of provocations by various company
officials. They complain, too, of incidents of mismanage-
ment, in their eyes, and charge various types of deception
and bad faith.

"Company officials had hoped the nature of last Sunday's
picketing would have toned down from the previous Sunday, with the aim of helping cool emotions to lead to a settlement of some sort. Some of the most intense feeling seems
to be directed against the business agent for the Union,
Joe Hammerschmidt. Hammerschmidt has been in the thick
of a number of picket line problems and he has said, 'If
they want a fight, we'll give it to them.' Hammerschmidt
is accused of being not only unfair in presenting the demands but unnecessarily abusive and, as one person put
it, 'absolutely unreasonable.'

"Red Wing police officers are among those hoping for a
cooling off of tempers soon, if not right away. They speak
of last Sunday's picketing as being similar to 'Plymouth
Avenue,' the scene of Negro rioting. Police shifts have been
changed at Red Wing to permit 'in depth' coverage of the
Potteries area on Sunday. A police prowl car has been
on the scene almost all of the time on the Sundays since
the strike began June first. Both the company and the union
have complained about the conduct of the police officers
at various times. Some company officials feel the police
should be doing more to clear the way thru picket lines,
and should not permit obvious harassment of potential
customers. On the other hand, some of the unionists feel
the police should never pull their prowl car away from
the parking lot and salesroom area because things seem
to happen when the police aren't around. Police were not
on the scene last weekend when a fist fight was impending

between a union leader and a company official, nor were the police close by when an effort was made to tip over a small foreign car.

"Red Wing, as a community, has been getting a bad name because of the way the picket lines are functioning. The Potteries draws from a number of states and many of the people encountering the picket line find it is a new experience. However, other motorists have seen strikes before and some of them feel the Potteries pickets are breaking the law with their name calling, use of bad language, and rich hostility to those who want to go in and shop, in spite of the picket line.

"The law is clear in regard to the right of anyone to picket peacefully, while not trespassing on the rights of others. Red Wing Pottery officials have been urged a number of times to seek a court injunction to cut down the number of pickets, and to limit their use of words and gestures. Some feel an injunction to limit or halt the picketing is a must to cool off tempers, and get both sides into a frame of mind so that a settlement can be reached. Some Red Wing business people have suggested to both sides that just the fact there is a strike is enough aggravation for both sides and the picketing serves, in their view, no useful purpose but to antagonize people on both sides.

"Both business agent Hammerschmidt and union head Tilfer Chastain visited Red Wing Chamber president, Ralph Finley, and the Chamber's executive secretary, Mrs. Dorothy Nelson, Tuesday. Hammerschmidt and Chastain sought to point out that only when out-of-town customers seek to ignore the words of the pickets to stay out of the Potteries parking lot do the pickets 'get rough.' "

We checked with Felhaber to make certain he was preparing his case to secure a court order. We felt unable to cope with another weekend's activities. Felhaber informed us that he was preparing the case and would contact the judge on Thursday when he came to Red Wing.

On Thursday, July 27, we gathered at the courthouse at 9:30

A.M. for a negotiating session. In addition to Larson, there were three other conciliators present - one Federal and two State. Hammerschmidt's alleged criticism of Larson's inability to bring about a settlement had apparently caused him to bring in reinforcements. Also, we had heard that the strike had come to the attention of Governor LeVander and he had suggested his State people interest themselves in the situation.

KCUE reported on the meeting in progress and the Union reaction to publishing the employee wages:

"All is not sweetness and light as the labor dispute at Red Wing Potteries is at the bargaining table once again. The high pitch of activity at the picket line has tended to sour prospects that the combatants can get together. The federal mediator who presides over the meeting now underway at the Courthouse in Red Wing faces what many feel is an impossible task. There is a substantial body of opinion in Red Wing which holds that the Potteries will either be forced to close its doors by the Union, or will voluntarily shut down by means of an ownership decision.

"Strikers on the picket lines were given copies of sheets listing wages and hourly wage averages of each employee in the plant on Wednesday. Some of those who saw the figures didn't like the way the information was handed out. One striker said, 'I don't like the way this was done. This is not going to help matters. The figures aren't fair; the sheet lists things which just aren't true.' This man went on to point to the company's listing of his average wage at around two and a half dollars an hour. He said, 'My check stubs show my rate is (and he gave a figure of around a dollar 85-90 cents an hour).' Multiplication, however, of the number of hours the man worked last year into his total wages showed a figure exactly the same as the company claimed.

"An examination of the payroll data furnished by the company shows most workers work about a 40-hour week. Biggest exceptions to this are the three men who work on maintenance tasks. The listing of wages and hours worked and average hourly rates of pay, as prepared by the company, does not show a breakdown in the base pay per hour, plus incentive pay. Unionists feel the payroll should be broken down in a way which does not involve incentive pay. However, the company feels the incentive pay is an integral part of the total wage paid, since workers get incentive pay on top of their regular hourly rate and do not have to work extra hours to achieve it.

"Total incomes for men who work at Red Wing Potteries range all the way from about 35 hundred dollars for the lowest paid to slightly more than 8 thousand dollars annually. These total wages include, as you might expect, varying amounts of time over 40 hours. However, just using averages most get paid around two dollars an hour, with some getting as high as $2.75 and three dollars an hour and as much as $3.65. Women who work at the Potteries earn, as an average, $2.10 an hour. Rates range from $1.61 per hour to $2.68 an hour.

"While many citizens of the Red Wing community feel the strike has gone on far too long now, few can be found who believe the bitterness and mutual antagonism caused by picket line activity, numerous nails, and many personal remarks, will be healed in a bargaining session such as the one going on."

Despite the pessimistic note of the KCUE report, it was an accurate representation of what was to come of the day's session. We did not meet the Union face-to-face that day, but rather met in separate rooms and the four conciliators shuffled from one group to the other. Much of our time was spent reviewing our position for the three new conciliators. The Union flatly rejected the written proposal we had given them earlier in the week. We found particularly depressing the fact that they had rejected our hospitalization insurance offer. This was one area, we felt, where we had gone to the greatest limits of generosity. The fact that the Union was still holding out for a $30.00 daily hospitalization rate seemed to illustrate to us how hopeless it was to ever expect to reach agreement with the Union.

During the noon break Felhaber contacted Milton Holst, company attorney, and Holst informed him that District Judge John Friedrich could not be reached. So, if we were to secure a court order by the coming weekend we would have to appear before a judge in another district.

In the afternoon session the four conciliators made serious pleas to both sides to eliminate those activities responsible for bad feelings. We were to stop all public statements, and the Union was to clean up their picketing tactics. The conciliators felt the anger and hostility between the two sides must be reduced before any progress would be made at the bargaining table. We readily agreed that a "cooling off" was necessary and agreed to do our part. The conciliators reported the Union also had agreed, and would clean up their picketing.

The meeting broke up at 6:00 P.M. with another session scheduled for Wednesday, August 2. In light of the judge's absence and the mutual agreement to cool things off, we decided to wait on the restraining order.

We were to learn that while the meeting was in progress there were incidents of nail setting. President Gillmer's wife and salesroom supervisor, Lorraine Taylor, had, on one occasion, gone out to remove nails from the driveways and suffered an inordinate amount of verbal abuse. One picket had followed closely behind Mrs. Gillmer, swinging his sign at her and calling her "old lady" and "scab." In our estimation this demonstrated a weakness on the part of the Union leadership. We reasoned that they should call a halt to the more obvious picket line abuse during the times negotiating was being carried on. Continuing the provocation during meetings would serve only to anger us further and make a solution more difficult to reach.

That evening Phil Duff ran an editorial in the DRE reflecting the injury to Red Wing's pride caused by the picketing tactics, and calling for compulsory arbitration, although he referred to it as "voluntary arbitration." We felt the editorial was pro-Management and still another strike against the Union:

"POTTERIES STRIKE: A WAY OUT?

"Red Wing has not had to endure this summer the large-scale rioting, arson, and looting which has so shocked and shaken many major cities across the country. But we have had our own hair shirt to wear in the form of the angry, embittered Red Wing Potteries strike, continuing now since the end of May.

"The DRE has avoided expressing a judgment on the wage and fringe benefit issues which have separated the Potteries Management and workers for so long. We can only express our regret, however, that those manning the picket lines have not shown a more courteous attitude, especially toward visitors to Red Wing from afar.

"The Union's defense is that picket line episodes here have been mild compared with what happens elsewhere. We have seen only nasty language, momentary blocking of public drives, nails in auto tires, spitting, verbal abuse. Elsewhere cars were tipped over and heads are bashed. None of that here.

"We suppose verbal harassment on the Potteries picket line is mild compared to what sometimes goes on elsewhere. But this is no justification. Peaceful picketing is the only kind that's acceptable under American law. Picketing is entirely legitimate as a form of free speech, but it should never go beyond words. Farmers Store employees, on strike for some weeks late last year, gave a good demonstration of how workers can maintain a reasonable and responsible picket line in front of a retail store. Pickets made clear they wanted customers to stay away but those who chose to enter were not subjected to abuse.

"Picket line disorder - if relatively mild - has given Red Wing a black eye this summer with visitors. It has injured our standing as a community which enjoys above-average labor-management relations. But these hurts are such as time can heal. They are nothing beside the grave and lasting community damage that Red Wing will suffer if this strike is not soon resolved and the Potteries enabled to continue as a business institution unique in the Upper Midwest.

"Is the Potteries really in danger? We dislike being unnecessarily alarmist, but we think it is. Feelings are already high
on both sides of the strike. It's possible for the situation to
deteriorate further until the company can no longer continue. The Management doesn't want this. The workers
don't want this. But it's possible that, through unwillingness
to compromise, unwillingness to recognize hard economic
realities, unwillingness to go the extra mile in trust in one's
fellow man, the whole house of cards could come tumbling
down.

"Potteries union and management are back in negotiation
today. That's good. Hopefully they are making progress.
Hopefully all concerned - and that includes community
bystanders - will avoid inflammatory statements. But if the
deadlock should persist much longer, we propose this:

"Let's frankly recognize that all Red Wing is involved, not
just Potteries management, workers, and shareholders. Let
each side propose two fellow Red Wingites - two management men from other plants in whom the company has
confidence, two labor men from other plants in whom the
Potteries union has confidence. Let these four have access
to full information, and let them thoroughly study the whole
situation. Let them then propose a basis for settlement, and
let both sides to the dispute agree in advance that they'll
accept whatever proposal the four outsiders unanimously
agree upon.

"Potteries managers, workers, and owners all have vital
interests at stake in this dispute, it seems to us, but there is
also a strong public, a community interest not represented
at the bargaining table. If the deadlock seems unresolvable
through normal negotiations, would the two sides accept
voluntary arbitration as a way out?"

Thursday afternoon and Friday pickets walked in front of
Red Wing's Chamber of Commerce and Finley's Coast to Coast
Store. The DRE carried pictures and reported:

". . . On Thursday afternoon, pickets from striking local

appeared in front of the Coast to Coast Store and in front
of the Red Wing Chamber of Commerce office. Pickets at
the Chamber of Commerce office carried signs saying the
Chamber is unfair to Local 6-430. The pickets were reluctant to say why they were picketing. Two other pickets
marched in front of the Coast to Coast Store with signs
reading, 'Ralph Finley unfair to OCAW.' They too were
reluctant to be identified but one said they were picketing
because of the statements attributed to Finley in a Twin
Cities newspaper."

Finley had our sympathies. We felt the Union's action in
picketing downtown locations was doing nothing to further their
image in town. Their angry efforts at revenge could only serve
to turn the public against them.

The Union had a membership meeting scheduled for Friday
night at 7:30. The purpose, we hoped, was to calm the weekend
picketing. Ralph Finley, in an effort to refute the statements
attributed to him, attempted to speak to the membership that
evening. The next day KCUE reported:

"Red Wing Chamber of Commerce president, Ralph Finley, went over to the Redmen's Hall where the meeting was
held, shortly after 7:45. Finley had hoped to make a brief
statement clarifying his personal feeling about the strike and
the strikers, and also set forth in simple terms the position of
the Chamber on guiding visiting groups and families to the
Potteries salesroom.

"When it was made known that Finley wanted a little time
to address the striking workers a chorus of 'No's' swelled
up from the crowd. After four or five shouts of 'No,' Finley backed out of the room and left, his statement still in
his shirt pocket. Finley's hardware and appliance store is
being picketed by members of the Potteries Union. Finley
feels he was unfairly misquoted in the Minneapolis paper
this week, with his remarks as printed serving to further
antagonize already embittered strikers."

On Saturday, any hopes that we had been entertaining for
more orderly picketing were quickly dashed. The pickets began

on Saturday where they had left off the previous Sunday. As soon as it was clear the direction the picketing was taking, I called the newspaper and radio station to suggest they have a reporter on the scene to witness first hand the near riot situation. Nails were strewn about, customers were subjected to vile oaths and threats, their cars hit and scraped, water thrown, and driveways blocked to all but the most persistent and patient motorists. Of the greatly diminished number of customers many had gained entrance to the salesroom by parking on the street or in the plant lot and walking through the picket lines. The only hope that the Union did not intend their usual level of harassment was found in the fact that Hammerschmidt was not present on Saturday. Perhaps, we reasoned, if he had been there he would have controlled things in light of our agreement with the conciliators.

R. A. Gillmer had spent the day in the Twin Cities, and on his return had suffered two flat tires caused by nail punctures. He was disappointed to learn that the Union had not kept their part of the bargain in cooling picket line activity.

Sunday we were to experience the worst day of picketing in the entire strike. Hammerschmidt was present the entire day. In addition to the many tactics we had come to expect - such as nails, water throwing, blocking of drives, and shouting - the strikers began the practice of pretending injury from contact with incoming cars. They had done this before on occasion, but never to the extent it was practiced on that Sunday. They would pretend to be hurt, and a number of pickets would follow the car into the lot, loudly accusing the driver of recklessness, writing down his license number, and generally intimidating him. Chief Lenway, and up to as many as eight of his officers, was present most of the day, and on occasion, when pickets were overly persistent about their alleged injuries, the police would be forced to fill out an accident report. Lenway and his subordinates acted as observers only, and made no move to prevent the blocking of driveways, the cursing, the throwing of water, etc. He repeatedly refused our requests to clear the drives and put a stop to the other activities. Further, he refused

to issue any tags or make any arrests for the rocking and scraping
of cars - which he must have observed, being present all day.
On one occasion President Gillmer left the store and asked Chief
Lenway, "Why don't you do something to stop this violence?"
Lenway replied, "There's a lot of tough people out there."
Gillmer said, "Then you're afraid!" Lenway offered no response
and Gillmer returned to the store, thoroughly disgusted. As
the day passed the pickets became increasingly bold in their
behavior. It was as if the group in one drive would try to outdo
the group in the next drive. Many cars were not even allowed
to turn their wheels into the driveways as pickets rushed from
surrounding points, spilling into the street and completely surrounding the car. If a motorist did manage to get his wheels
turned into the drive, the pickets would lean on the hood,
scream and scratch the car if he proceeded further.

In the afternoon, at the height of this near riot, a young man
and his wife from St. Paul turned into a driveway, did not come
to a full stop, but rather proceeded to edge their way into the
lot. They parked next to the building very close to the police
car containing Chief Lenway and another officer. Approximately twenty pickets followed the car into the lot. As the young
man and his wife emerged from the car, the pickets pushed and
shoved them, claiming they came through the picket line too
fast. This was the physical violence Lenway had always claimed
he intended to prevent, so he was forced to leave the confines
of his squad car and put a stop to the situation. He managed
to quell the disturbance but made no arrests. The driver of the
car showed the officer the scratches on the side of the car
made as he entered. According to the driver, he said to the officer, "I hope you're not going to give me a ticket," and the officer replied, "I have nothing to give you a ticket for." Shortly
thereafter another officer who had been stationed a distance
away from the incident, approached and ordered a ticket written
for reckless driving. The pickets hooted with glee as they saw
the young man receive the citation.

Mrs. R. A. Gillmer, witnessing the entire incident, was amazed
when she observed the officer issuing the ticket. She immediately

approached Chief Lenway on the matter and, in the presence of
the DRE's Phil Duff, Lenway informed her that the young man
could pay a $35.00 fine or appear in court in ten days. Duff
commented to Mrs. Gillmer, "In my opinion the ticket was
completely unjustified." Mrs. Gillmer, outraged that the police
would issue a ticket under the circumstances while failing to
take action as pickets were rocking and scraping cars, decided
to champion the young man's cause and made arrangements to
see the city attorney on Monday morning.

That same day, one man from Chicago whose automobile
was rocked severely entered the salesroom in near hysteria. In
a loud rage he attempted to call Red Wing's mayor only to find
him in the East on business. He ranted at the mayor's wife,
criticizing her husband for leaving town in such a crisis, and
vowed to get in touch with the Governor.

The Union entered the salesroom later in the afternoon, in-
timidated what few customers there were, called all of us "pigs"
and said our merchandise was "junk," and finally left.

The day was thoroughly frightening. We expected the whole
mob to storm the salesroom at any moment. Also, their all too
evident hatred for R. A. Gillmer and myself was a sobering
phenomenon. We could only guess when and how this hate
would be expressed in action. We were determined to seek a
court order and this time would allow nothing to delay us in
securing one.

That evening as I drove home from work I heard one of
KCUE's public service announcements. I could not help chuck-
ling at the thought of a severely harassed tourist listening to the
same broadcast as he frantically tried to put as much distance
between himself and Red Wing as possible. With the tune "Pretty
Red Wing" playing softly in the background, the broadcaster
seductively said:

"Welcome to Red Wing, an old river town which is one of
the most alert and progressive cities in the Upper Midwest.

"Red Wing is known for the rugged beauty of the bluffs
within the city limits, and in neighboring Burnside.

"It is world famous for Red Wing Pottery, and for Red

Wing boots and shoes. Photos of Red Wing's picturesque Boat House Village on the Mississippi River are found on calendars and in many publications.

"Not so well known is the fact that around 5,000 people go to work in Red Wing every day, helping spur a growing economy. Red Wing is a stable community of home owners and, everywhere, there is found a real warmth of appreciation for the natural beauty and recreational assets of pretty Red Wing.

"If you live in Red Wing, then you live in one of the nicest cities in the Middlewest. If you are traveling through, spend some time at Red Wing, and get to know this fine community better."

Our business had been hurt severely over the weekend. If people did manage to gain access to the store they were either too upset to shop or frightened to let the pickets see them carry purchases from the store.

That evening I had two phone calls without response from the caller. I was truly frightened for my family for, at this point, I did not know to what tactics the strikers might resort. It would not have surprised me to see an attempt made to burn my house or to stone my windows that night. When R. A. Gillmer called at 10:00 P.M. to suggest that I load my shot gun, I informed him that I already had. I phoned the police and informed them that I had been receiving nuisance phone calls, and requested that they patrol my house that night. Then I removed the phone from the cradle and proceeded to sit up most of the night expecting something to happen. Fortunately, nothing did. In retrospect all of this seems melodramatic but, at the time, my fear was very real, and my precautions were not totally illogical based on the hate and the threats of the pickets.

The following day, Monday, July 31, we called Felhaber and told him we were desperate; we could not possibly get through another weekend without a restraining order. He agreed; Judge Friedrich was back on duty and he would arrange a hearing later in the week.

Since Duff had been present at the salesroom most of Sun-

day afternoon we were looking forward to his account of the
situation in Monday's paper. He published a front page editorial outlined in black. While we were generally pleased with
his account, we felt that he had gone out of his way to appease
the Union with his statements of "only momentarily" blocking
drives, and generally underplaying the nails and physical abuse.
On the other hand, he did cite specific exceptions to the statement that there was "no physical force involved." Running through
the editorial was an apparent criticism of Red Wing's mayor and
police chief for failing to take command of the situation from
the beginning.

"END THE STRIKE WITH ARBITRATION

"What judgment should one make about Sunday tactics
and law enforcement along the Red Wing Potteries picket
line?

"This is one editor's attempt to form such a judgment after
spending two hours there Sunday afternoon, dividing my
time between listening to pickets outside the salesroom and
to Potteries management people and customers inside.

"First, what actually happens?

"As a car approaches the salesroom parking lot along West
Main and slows as though it intends to turn in, a crowd of
15 to 25 pickets rush from the sidewalk to meet the car.
They are waving signs and shouting.

"The entrance is effectively blocked by people, and the
motorist must stop if he doesn't want to hit somebody. Then
the pickets crowd around the car and urge the driver not
to enter because there's a strike on. There's a regular din.

"But if the driver persists, he can go on. The pickets get
out of the way, and the car can proceed toward the Potteries salesroom.

"Driver and passengers must run the gauntlet of considerable verbal abuse, but there's no physical force involved. I
don't suppose the car that persists is delayed over 30 seconds
or so in reaching its destination in the parking lot, although
the angry gibes and catcalls may continue as passengers get

out and walk toward the salesroom door.

"One man, Nicholas Kafkis from Chicago, was an exception. His car, including Mrs. Kafkis and their two small boys, was pretty vigorously rocked. But after he got out and objected he was allowed to proceed.

"Another man whose name I didn't get claimed that his car was scratched by one of the picket signs. James Vangen, Minneapolis, said one of the pickets pushed his wife.

"But these were the exceptions. Normally the car went through after making its stop with only the cries and epithets of the pickets - nothing more than words.

"Meanwhile the police.

"Chief Warren Lenway and two officers were on hand all the time. Their general role was to stand back out of the verbal fray as observers. They made no attempt to interfere with the regular massing of pickets which momentarily - but only momentarily - prevented access to the salesroom parking lot.

"Only if something untoward happened, if a specially big crowd of pickets seemed to be gathering around the parked car, would a police officer step forward and quietly clear a path for the car.

"Chief Lenway, obviously perplexed about the proper police role in a situation unprecedented in Red Wing, was frank to say that his main purpose is to maintain order and see that nobody gets hurt.

"Lenway consistently refused the Potteries management requests to prevent the momentary blocking of the driveways and the attempted verbal intimidation of prospective Potteries customers.

"In fact, the police gave a ticket for careless driving to one young fellow who drove through the picket line with his wife and child.

"This fellow - Paul R. Charboneau, Minneapolis - is a Honeywell employee and a Teamsters member, he told me. He's been on strike and manned a picket line, he said, but the Teamster pickets engaged in no tactics like these. He

was outraged, especially at the thought of forfeiting $35.00
in bail money or losing a day's pay to come to Red Wing
and answer the careless driving charge in court.

"The pickets, on the other hand, vigorously defended their
tactics. I would paraphrase their position as follows:

'We don't forcibly prevent anybody from entering the
Potteries salesroom. We just require them to stop so
that they can hear our story about the strike and we
can ask them to go away. But if they insist on going in,
they can.'

"And this is true. So far as I can tell, these picket line
tactics are in a kind of gray, borderline area of legality. A
strike is, of course, entirely legal. And picketing is entirely
legal. But picketing finds its legal justification in our con-
stitutional provisions for free speech. It goes beyond free
speech, in my opinion, when pickets mass in a roadway
and compel a motorist to stop against his wishes.

"Certainly the police would not tolerate a group of people
on any downtown street who systematically got in the way
of approaching automobiles and compelled them to stop,
even momentarily.

"To my mind, strong law enforcement leadership would have
taken command of the situation right at the start of this
strike. It would have laid down firm and fair ground rules
on how many pickets in what places and insisted that these
rules be followed.

"Now doubtless this viewpoint will be labeled 'anti-union'
by those who disagree.

"If so, the DRE's letters column is open to all comers so
long as what's written stays clear of libel. As the DRE has
repeatedly told the Potteries union leadership right from the
start of this strike, they should feel free at any time to bring
us a letter or statement to set forth their point of view or
present the facts as they see them.

"Indeed, the DRE's whole purpose is to report truthfully
what happens in this strike, to give each side full opportunity to appeal to public opinion, but at the same time to

avoid the inflammatory kind of reporting that kindles emotions on both sides and makes a settlement more difficult. "As the strike progresses, there are two points that it would be well for partisans of both sides to keep in mind.

"First, the people on both the union and management side are fundamentally good people. Both think they are right; both believe they are working in a just cause.

"Somebody on the other side may do or say something that seems absolutely outrageous to you, but try to put yourself in his shoes and try to consider how the issues look to him. "And second, it would be possible for individuals to disagree on a strike issue and still remain friends. We don't all see alike politically; we don't all go to church together; but we are all Americans, and part of being an American is maintaining a good feeling toward a fellow citizen with whom you happen to be at odds on a specific question right now.

"So far as the strike itself is concerned, I continue to believe that third party settlement is an eventual solution which should be considered.

"If union and management can get together themselves, fine. But rather than permit an angry deadlock to produce an eventual outcome that injures the workers, injures the company, and injures the whole Red Wing community, why don't both sides agree in advance to accept a settlement worked out by a mutually acceptable set of arbitrators?"

At noon on Monday the Board of Directors met with all directors present. There was further discussion of the possibility of liquidation, but the Board was not ready to take official action in that direction. There was still hope that something could be worked out with the Union. We were heartened somewhat by the perceived swing of public sympathy toward the company.

Management was receiving more letters from customers objecting to the treatment they had received on the picket lines. A good example was the letter from a nineteen year old girl

from Amana, Iowa. The letter apparently was meant for the
president of the local Union:

"I have just returned from a vacation trip with my family
to Minneapolis and stopped at the Red Wing Pottery Factory on the way home. The work of these people is truly
something you can be proud of, but I found their actions
truly inhumane.

"I'm nineteen years old and know the importance unions
play in the economy of the United States. I admit people
need to organize into groups such as these so their wants
may be met satisfactorily. I know, too, that many workers
in this nation live below the standard of living both you
and I are accustomed to. Thus, to get the raise in pay they
no doubt deserve, they strike under pressure built up by
the 'haves' and the 'have nots' and try various means to
get their pay hike.

"I don't know the circumstances under which the Red Wing
Pottery union is striking, but from the actions I observed
today I can certainly conclude that what no doubt was once
an orderly protest has turned into a disgrace to the workers,
the union, and to the right to assemble we inherited from
our forefathers. It hurt us all very much to see these people
act so immaturely as they did. Their actions this Sunday
will have no effect on us next week or next year, but the
workers will never be able to erase the damage they've done
to themselves. What's worse, they'll probably never even
realize the damage they've done. While they were out there
screaming at the tourists they not only came themselves but
brought their little children, some of which couldn't have
been older than seven or eight. These little children I'm
sure didn't know why they were yelling 'scab, scab' at
everyone driving by. I'm sure they'll remember, though all
the fun they had today yelling at the people. This is the
first unfortunate step many children go through when they
learn to hate people for no reason at all. Needless to say,
there's enough hate and destruction in this world without
fighting with people whom you normally would want to

please and impress when meeting them at the local P.T.A.
or general store, or some one who may even become your
neighbors.

"The wood with which one man scraped our car did hurt
us. I'm sure that hurt won't last long, but I'm certain you
know the feeling of owning a new car and searching the
first month or two for the little scratch which you know is
inevitable. Well, we didn't anticipate ours to come in such
a way. Our scrape runs half the length of the right side of
the car.

"Enough of that. I guess I'm lucky if I succeeded in getting you to read even two paragraphs of this letter before
throwing it away. I only hope you impress upon these people
their rights as citizens of the United States and, most important, that they don't abuse these rights."

The Chicago Trade Show had begun the previous day and,
although Red Wing Potteries was represented, our salesmen called
to tell R. A. Gillmer that our strike was general knowledge in
the trade, and customers were reluctant to order when shipping
dates were vague. It looked as though the Chicago show and
the Fall market were all but lost to the company.

Mrs. R. A. Gillmer met with City Attorney Charles Richardson on Monday to discuss the ticket the police had given to the
young St. Paul man on Sunday. After discussing the incident,
Mr. Richardson informed her that he had forgiven only two or
three tickets in his tenure as city attorney. He phoned Editor
Duff regarding the incident and his statement to Mrs. Gillmer
at the time, and Duff told him that while he did not actually
see the incident, he felt the ticket was unjustified "in view of
the existing circumstances." Mrs. Gillmer argued that it was
physically impossible for anyone to come through the driveway
at too fast a speed without hitting several pickets, considering
the fact the driveway was jammed with twenty to thirty people.
Richardson commented that she had a very good point, but
refused to forgive the ticket. Upon leaving, Mrs. Gillmer commented that, as city attorney, Richardson might have come down
to the Potteries to observe at first hand the conduct of the strikers

at least once in eight weeks. Mrs. Gillmer was not ready to drop the matter yet; she intended to discuss the incident with the Mayor and Police Chief.

Thus, the month of July drew to a close. The conflict had passed from the buildup and uncertainties of June, to open and complete hostility in July. There was no longer any question about the other side and their motives; they were completely and totally "no good" and tactics had degenerated to the point of hurting the other side at any cost, regardless of the bearing the tactic might have on settlement. The majority of the Union membership were undoubtedly out of money and desperate. Management was to the breaking point as far as their ability to withstand further picket abuse was concerned. The month of July had brought a decrease in retail sales from $49,000 the previous year to $41,000 this year. All of the loss had been experienced in the latter half of the month when the picketing reached its most deplorable level. It was clear that some decisions had to be made in short order; from a business standpoint we could not hope to recover if the strike lasted much longer. The same was true of the emotional health of top Management. Seven days of work per week and the associated physical and emotional fatigue were beginning to tell. August had to be a month of conclusion, one way or the other.

THE MONTH OF AUGUST — A CONCLUSION

"The vast majority of Union officials endeavor honestly to safeguard the rights and forward the interests of their members and discharge the duties of their office. Yet the reputations of the vast majority and of the labor movement are imperiled by the dishonest, corrupt and unethical practices of the few who betray their trust."
ARTHUR J. GOLDBERG

The doorbell continued to ring in the middle of the night at the R. A. Gillmer home. He had an open garage and, fearing malicious tampering with his automobiles, sealed the hoods from time to time with thin strips of tape. One morning in the first part of August he found the seals broken and asked the police for assistance. The police found that the automobiles had not been visably changed or damaged. The only evidence I found that strikers had been near my home were nails in the driveway from time to time. These minor incidents were enough, however, for us to keep our guns readily accessible.

Phil Duff, DRE editor, called President Gillmer in the first part of August. He informed him that he had two unnamed Union people in his office who claimed that he had refused to meet with Tilfer Chastain. Was it true? Gillmer answered that it was most certainly not true, and that he would meet with Chastain or any other Union representative at any time or any place desired. Gillmer was insulted that Duff would even take the time to ask such a ridiculous and obvious question. Duff must have placed some credence in the Union claim or he would not have called to question him. This bothered Gillmer for a few days to come, and was a frequent topic of conversation.

Our hostility toward the mayor and the police department was very strong. We went so far as to speculate that, had the mayor taken a strong stand in the beginning, feelings would not have run so high and a settlement could have been reached by August.

Felhaber called and informed us that we were to appear in

court on Thursday, August 3, to seek a temporary restraining order. This knowledge gave us some solace, but the question remained as to whether the judge would grant the order.

The first week in August the Union began door-to-door solicitation of local businesses seeking financial support. They reportedly would approach the owner and suggest that the Union, their members and sympathizers, carried a great deal of purchasing power which could be cut off should the business fail to support the cause. We heard that they collected over $500 from the local businesses, and were disappointed to hear that one prominent Red Wing businessman who had been a Potteries Director had given twenty dollars to the Union.

On Wednesday, August 2, at 1:30 P.M. we met with the Union at the courthouse with three conciliators present—Ed Larson from the Federal Agency and the same two State conciliators who had been present at the last meeting. The five company representatives headquartered in one jury room and the Union team was in another. The conciliators moved between the groups.

In the course of the afternoon we offered the Union three alternative proposals:

(1) Our original proposal to reduce all incentive rates to $1.25, raise all base rates 10 cents, and grant the equity raises.

(2) Retain all incentive rates as at present, grant the same equity raises, and raise all non-incentive workers 15 cents the first year and 10 cents the second year.

(3) Eliminate all incentive pay, grant the same equity increases, and raise all base rates 15 cents the first year and 10 cents the second year.

The third alternative was not realistic for either the company or the Union, but was stimulated by the Union pleas to eliminate all incentive rather than cut it in any way. All company proposals included the hospitalization insurance increases we had offered earlier, raises to $1.60 for regular sales girls, and clear withdrawal of the proposal to end the $1,000 life insurance for retired employees. All of the proposals would cost the company between $25,000 and $30,000 per year.

The Union's reaction to the three alternatives could be summarized as "not enough." If the company left incentive pay as it was, the Union wanted 20 cents the first year and 20 cents the second year for all employees, plus the equity raises. If incentive pay was eliminated entirely, they wanted 23 cents across the board initially to cover the $47,000 we had paid in incentive in 1966, and 20 cents the first year and 20 cents the second year, plus the equity raises. They also wanted $30 per day hospitalization benefits, another holiday, improvements in vacation benefits, and a pension plan. We estimated the Union demands at a minimum cost of $100,000—which did not include their pension plan—way out of line as far as Red Wing Potteries was concerned.

At the urging of Duff we gave the DRE our three alternatives for publication. In the same article containing our proposals Hammerschmidt was quoted as saying, "We (the Union) haven't changed our position from the start of the strike." This was one of the few Union statements with which we could wholeheartedly agree; while the company had changed and modified their approach a number of times since June 1, the Union had offered nothing in the way of solutions to the problems we were facing; their position remained unchanged, yet they bitterly attacked anything we set forth.

Before the meeting was over we expressed our anger to the conciliators over the fact that the Union had not kept their part of the bargain made at the previous week's meeting. The intervening weekend had been the worst yet as far as picketing was concerned, and Hammerschmidt had been present all day Sunday. The conciliators had no answer and could only express disappointment that the Union had failed to comply with their request to cool things off.

Before adjourning the meeting, the conciliators set another session for the following Tuesday at 2:00 P.M.

Upon our return to the plant at approximately 6:00 P.M. that day we learned that nails again had been set during the negotiating session. We were thoroughly discouraged at the Union behavior, and felt they were doing nothing to help cool feelings and approach a settlement. The company had offered, for a one-year agreement, the highest cost package ever made in a single year, and still we were nowhere close to the Union demands. Duff summarized it well when he concluded, ". . . It appears that either company or Union or both will have to move a considerable distance from present positions in order to strike a bargain." As far as we were concerned we could not move much, if at all, in the interests of good business judgment and the protection of stockholders. Considering the marginal profit picture of the Potteries in recent years, to raise labor costs much over $30,000 in a single year would assure the death of the company, and probably drain what assets there were in the process. Thus, if there was any changing to be done, it was up to the Union, and, at this point, we had no reason to believe they had any intention of modifying their position. In view of the seemingly unsolvable dilemma, we called a meeting of the company Directors for the following day, Thursday, August 3.

Wednesday evening the DRE published a letter to the editor, written by the president of the local Fur & Leather Workers Union, spelling out labor's position on the strike:

"ALL UNION MEMBERS SHOULD RESPECT POTTERIES PICKETS

"It was with interest I read the article concerning the Red Wing Pottery strike, written by staff writer, Dan Wascoe, Jr., in the July 24 Minneapolis Morning Tribune.

"As in any strike, you will hear such shouts as 'yellow-bellies' and 'scabs.'

"What really hurts the strikers more is the feeling that some of the people still going in the pottery salesroom are members of some unions where they work. If they do belong to a union, they should show respect to their brother members of another union, by not patronizing said place on strike until it is settled.

"We did not read in the article what Mr. Gillmer wanted to do with some of the benefits that the employees now have, which is one of the reasons why they are on strike.

"It is a known fact that the potteries is a tourist attraction, but it is a known fact that people have to live. To work for no increase in fringe benefits or wages just to please the tourists is ridiculous thinking.

"The statement made by Ralph Finley, president of the Red Wing Chamber of Commerce, and also a stockholder in the pottery, was very disturbing. In his statement, we quote: 'They haven't got the best class of people working there.' 'If they're not satisfied, why don't they go somewhere else.'
"So, with that thought in mind, we feel that we should go somewhere else to trade, instead of his Coast to Coast store, which he is co-owner of in Red Wing.

"We feel that the strike at the Potteries will not hurt the town's reputation. It would instead, help it, if the management and workers could come together with a decent settlement in wages and fringe benefits."

On Thursday, August 3, at 11:00 A.M. the company Directors met in the law offices of Director Holst. After much grave discussion of the frustrating lack of progress to date, and the apparent small likelihood of the Union modifying their rigid position in the near future, company Directors concluded that they had no choice but to call a meeting of the stockholders to consider liquidation. If this conclusion was inevitable, any delay would serve only to further deplete the assets of the corporation. After some discussion of who should make the motion, it was moved, seconded, and carried "that the officers of the corporation call a special meeting of the stockholders to be held after due notice for the purpose of considering the adoption of a resolution to dissolve the corporation." It was also moved, seconded, and unanimously adopted "that the officers send with such notice to each stockholder a letter explaining why the Directors felt that such action should be considered by the stockholders." The gravity of the move affected us all; the good possibility that we had just moved and seconded the death of a ninety-year old company and a Minnesota landmark was a sobering fact. A determination of the date of the stockholders meeting and the mailing of the notices was postponed until the next Board meeting to be held on Tuesday, August 8.

At 3:00 P.M. on Thursday, August 3, R. A. Gillmer, Holst, Thomas Vogt of the firm of Felhaber, Larson, Fenlon and Vogt, and I gathered in district court for an ex-parte hearing (only one side, the company, present). We were requesting a court order to prohibit the pickets from the following activities:

(a) From obstructing in any manner the right of any person to gain ingress to and egress from Plaintiff's place of business in the City of Red Wing, Minnesota, specifically including, but not limited to, physically standing or walking in any driveway or entrance or exit to Plaintiff's place of business.

(b) From interfering in any manner with any vehicle entering or leaving Plaintiff's premises, including but not limited to, opening doors of vehicles, striking said vehicles, and placing tacks or any other objects in the streets and driveways used by said vehicles.

(c) From interfering in any manner with the free and uninterrupted use of public roads and streets adjacent to Plaintiff's premises.

(d) From engaging in any mass picketing. Peaceful picketing shall be limited to no more than two (2) persons at any time at each entrance to Plaintiff's premises and there shall be no other picketing, patrolling, or assembly at or near Plaintiff's premises.

(e) From threatening in any manner any customer or employee or Plaintiff.

Our attorneys felt there would be no problem in securing the order. R. A. Gillmer and I were to take the stand to testify. A DRE reporter was present and described the testimony as follows:

"In his testimony R. A. Gillmer said the situation on the picket lines has recently 'gotten worse.' He said as many as 30 pickets have crowded into driveways as cars have attempted to enter the salesroom parking lot.

"He charged that pickets have used abusive language and that cars have been severely rocked as they have crossed the picket line. He said doors of cars also have been opened by pickets who have tried to pull out the occupants.

"There has been shoving and pushing, he said, and customers have been followed from the picket line up into the parking lot.

"He said he has seen pickets scrape signs along the sides of cars, purposely scratching the vehicles. And he said motions have been made as if to strike drivers through windows.

" 'Did you overhear any threats?' Gillmer was asked by his attorney. Gillmer said, 'Yes. People were told if they went into the parking lot they would never get out. They also were told that their cars would be tipped over and that their cars would be pushed over a cliff.'

"Gillmer said he has picked up nails in Potteries driveways and said the nails apparently were set by hand, with the points sticking up. He said tires on his cars have been ruined and said he has paid many bills for customers who have had tires punctured by nails. He said upwards of 100 pickets have appeared at the salesroom on Sundays, both Potteries employees and members of other unions. He specifically cited Hammerschmidt and Chastain as being among the pickets.

"Gillmer testified that Red Wing police contributed 'nothing other than their presence' to avoid incidents.

"He said union members have entered the Potteries salesroom and made statements to the effect that the store 'looked like a pigpen, smelled like a pigpen and that those who worked there were pigs.'

"R. S. Gillmer testified in much the same vein. He said he has observed many nails scattered about and he said he personally observed one picket placing a nail on its head with the point sticking up. He said pickets crowd at times halfway into the street to wave drivers past the salesroom. And if a car heads in he said it may be immediately surrounded. On weekends, he said, pickets may stand immobile in front of a car for three to five minutes."

Following our testimony we returned to the company offices,

and the attorneys met with Judge Friedrich in his chambers. The judge called the Union's attorney, Frances Xavier Helgesen, and Hammerschmidt to court for a conference that evening. Judge Friedrich preferred not to issue a temporary restraining order if he could secure assurance from the Union that they would abide by the picket line restrictions. The only item the judge changed was limiting pickets to four per driveway, rather than two as we had requested. Helgesen and Hammerschmidt agreed that evening that the Union would abide by the provisions, and so Judge Friedrich did not sign a restraining order. A hearing was to be held at 10:00 A.M. Monday morning to determine if a formal restraining order was necessary. News of the judge's decision reached us Friday morning, and despite the fact that our attorneys were in accord with the informal agreement, Management was shaken by the absence of any official court order. Could it be possible that we would have to go through another deplorable weekend?

The DRE made an effort Friday morning to question Hammerschmidt and Chastain on the court action and reported that Hammerschmidt "hung up on a DRE reporter who called with questions on the agreement" and that Chastain "said he knew too little about the situation to comment."

Our alarm was short-lived, however. We learned Friday afternoon that Union Attorney Helgesen had phoned Judge Friedrich that afternoon and asked that the Union be relieved of the commitment on picket line behavior. Helgesen told Friedrich that OCAW Local 6-430 was confident that its own members would obey the rules but that it could not guarantee that other individuals and organizations supporting the strike would respect them. After this notification, Judge Friedrich issued the restraining order. Again, the only change in the order was the number of pickets per driveway. The formal order limited the number to three rather than the four stipulated in the "gentlemen's agreement." The temporary restraining order was to remain in effect until Wednesday, August 9, at which time Friedrich would conduct a hearing in district court with both sides testifying. We would have to repeat our presentation of evidence, and the

Union would have an opportunity to cross-examine and present its own witnesses.

We learned from Friedrich that if anyone disobeyed the order he would be in contempt of court, and could be brought directly into court, given a summary hearing, and sentenced without a jury trial.

County Sheriff Paul Zillgitt began serving the court order on Union officials Friday night and continued Saturday morning. The notice was also served on Red Wing Police Chief Lenway. The DRE reported that Lenway said, "His officers would be at the Potteries salesroom Sunday with copies of the court order and would enforce its terms." It was beginning to look as though we were finally going to receive some help in controlling the terrific abuse and harassment that had been going on for the past eight weeks.

One minor incident occurred on Friday. We were forced to call the police at 3:00 P.M. to report nails in one driveway and that several nails had been discovered in the tires of an out-of-state car.

That afternoon President Gillmer called a meeting with key personnel to inform them of the Board's decision to call a stockholders meeting to consider liquidation. It was a very difficult meeting for Gillmer. He was forced to tell those people who had evidenced the utmost loyalty during the strike, worked long and irregular hours, and weathered the abuse of the pickets that the future of the company looked very grim. While he was not releasing anyone, he explained, "We must face the likely possibility that we will not reach a workable agreement with the Union and will be forced to liquidate the corporation." He added, "Even if the stockholders vote to liquidate there will be work for everyone for a number of months finishing raw materials and work in process, but I would not blame any of you for leaving if a better opportunity presents itself." Of particular concern was Gerry Ross, the new Ceramic Engineer, who had been with the company a short two weeks before the strike began. Ross had moved his family from Ohio, purchased a relatively expensive home, and he and his family were becoming adjusted to the community and growing to like it very much. Telling him that the company was likely to liquidate was one of the most difficult tasks associated with the strike.

On Friday, Mrs. R. A. Gillmer, still obsessed by the injustice of the ticket the police had issued to the young St. Paul man, met with Chief Lenway to discuss the matter. In the course of the conversation Lenway made three statements that convinced Mrs. Gillmer she was fighting a lost cause: (1) "He admitted his guilt to two of my officers; (2) Several of the pickets have contacted me to find out when the trial was to be because they wanted to testify; and (3) We don't know yet how many claims of injury will be made as a result of the incident." These three statements convinced Mrs. Gillmer that the chances of acquittal were slim, so she paid the $35.00 fine and left.

Mrs. Gillmer also had a message in for Mayor Jelatis, and he phoned her upon his return from a business trip in the East. She recounted to him her interviews with the city attorney and police chief. She further recalled all the incidents of alleged law violations she had witnessed throughout the strike, and suggested to the Mayor that if there had been simple law enforcement from the beginning, the hysteria of recent weeks could have been avoided and a negotiated settlement could well have been reached. Jelatis' only comment was that their main interest throughout the strike had been to prevent anyone from getting hurt physically.

On Friday the DRE ran a small front page article casting further question on the role the Red Wing police had chosen to play in the dispute:

"ATTORNEY GENERAL GETS COMPLAINTS ON RW PICKETS

"The Minnesota attorney general's office has received two complaints about Red Wing Potteries picketing, the DRE learned today.

"One from an Edina family objected to rough treatment while driving into the Potteries salesroom parking lot last

Sunday. Red Wing police were asked for help and refused, the complaint asserts.

"The attorney general's office issued an informal request to the State Highway Patrol, it said, to increase its Sunday observation of the Potteries salesroom."

I awoke Saturday morning with a tremendous feeling of relief; a court order had been issued and the strikers would be forced to behave themselves. Reporting to the salesroom early Saturday morning, I was pleased to find the pickets following the rules closely - three to a driveway, and a minimum of noise and driveway blocking.

We left shortly to meet in Holst's office to discuss the legal ramifications of the court order and our role in enforcing it. Attorney Vogt was to spend the remainder of the morning at the salesroom observing the pickets and seeing that they followed the stipulations of the restraining order. To be on the safe side our Industrial Engineer, Ed Alpers, was to be present with his camera all afternoon to secure evidence of any violations.

Shortly before 2:00 P.M. most of the pickets left to attend an "Informational meeting about the Potteries strike" for all members of organized labor Unions in Red Wing. The meeting was called by Red Wing AFL-CIO President Clarence Josephson and held at the VFW hall.

The meeting lasted only a short time, and strikers and sympathizers began assembling near the salesroom lot. Fearing trouble, we notified the police and sheriff's departments. Sheriff Zillgitt was on hand as well as nine or ten policemen, including Chief Lenway, by the time over a hundred sign waving Unionists began to march double file in front of the salesroom. This was a direct violation of the restraining order; yet law enforcement officials watched as it continued. The parade was led by Hammerschmidt and OCAW District 6 President Dale Eggerts. Chief Lenway reportedly tried to serve Eggerts with a copy of the court order, but was brushed rudely aside. We were alarmed; if the strikers could get away with this what guarantee did we have that they would obey any of the stipulations laid down by the court? We called Vogt at his St. Paul home and, other than making certain Alpers was taking pictures, he seemed unconcerned - even pleased about the Union activity. He explained that this would assure making the order permanent at Wednesday's hearing.

After making about five passes in front of the store the large group broke up into smaller groups, and eventually the smaller groups disbanded, leaving the required three pickets per driveway.

Saturday's DRE carried an editorial composed before Judge Friedrich had issued a formal restraining order. Duff criticizes the disorderly picketing and the failure of the mayor and police chief to put a stop to it:

"FOR PEACEFUL PICKETING

"Red Wing Potteries initiative finally put the issue of picket line behavior into Goodhue county district court, and Judge John Friedrich has obtained union agreement to cut the roughhouse tactics which have been marring our community's image. Presumably, the union's choice was to agree or face an immediate court order.

"The agreement is a good one which does Judge Friedrich credit. Under its terms, there will be no more human blockading of access to the Potteries salesroom, no more verbal abuse or 'haranguing' of those who choose to enter the salesroom despite the strike. The Union's right to picket and to tell prospective Potteries customers of the strike is assured. But there will be no more threats, no more mass picketing. The rule of no more than four pickets in a driveway at one time is specific.

"Hopefully the strike will now assume the orderly, peaceable, non-violent aspect which it should have had from the start. If so, it's none too soon as should be plainly evident from the letter on this page today from a Chicago resident who visited the Potteries salesroom last Sunday. No Red Wing visitor should undergo his experience.

"If peace has now been restored to the picket line, we hope the contending parties can now get back to the bargaining table and compose their differences as soon as possible. Meanwhile, a grievous failure on the part of local law enforcement must be recorded. What Judge Friedrich apparently achieved in the courtroom Thursday, Red Wing's mayor and chief of police should have brought about when the strike began."

The letter Duff referred to in his editorial was written by the Chicago man who stopped at the salesroom Sunday, July 30, and attempted to reach the mayor and threatened to call the Governor. The letter was probably the most dramatic public indictment of the picketing and Red Wing police to date. It was addressed to the Vice-President of the United States, the Governor of Illinois, the Governor of Minnesota, the Mayor of Red Wing, and the Editor of the DRE:

"POTTERIES CUSTOMER:
SPEEDING CAR HURLED SPIKES

"This letter is directed to the Governor of the State of Illinois as a citizen's protest, to make his office aware of these conditions and to ask for his active participation in eliminating these acts of violence.

"To the Vice-President because of his intense interest in our guaranteed liberties and because the following criminal injustices occurred in his native state.

"To the other listed officials for their obvious responsibility in these matters.

"While vacationing in Minnesota we drove to Red Wing to see the Pottery works. As we advanced to the store parking lot our entry was blocked by striking pickets. I explained that we were out-of-state tourists and totally non-partisan to any local dispute. I further explained that my children had to use the facilities and again asked for passage. At this point they mobbed my car, bounced it around, opened the doors and manhandled my wife and children. In addition to this we were subjected to the foulest, filthiest language possible.

"The police reacted only after I jumped out of my car to

protect my family and property. They reacted by stopping me and did nothing to stop the mob. For five minutes this melee continued with the chief of police and three other officers standing within a few feet of my car - watching.

"Although I fully realized the danger placed upon my family, I felt that to surrender to this mob violence would be setting the wrong example for my family.

"I insisted on my right of passage, got back into my car and drove through with the mob still screaming and rocking my car. Once inside the store, I found others who had been pushed and kicked and had their cars scratched by the picket signs.

"The severity of the incident was capsulized when my 5-year old son quivering with tears in his eyes asked, 'Daddy, they weren't really going to kill us, were they?'

"After lodging a strong complaint with the mayor's office, I asked for safe escort out of town. This request was refused by the chief of police.

"Three miles beyond the city limits a car with three men sped by and hurled a board, two to three feet long and loaded with spikes, at my car. Fortunately it bounced off my fender and missed my tire. Had this found its mark, we might all be dead today.

"This type of action can only be labeled as gangsterism.

"No amount of grievance between labor and management can justify the attempt to murder innocent children.

"I sympathize with their right to picket, but refuse to give up my rights of free passage. I served my country as a Marine in Korea and was awarded two decorations. I feel I have earned the right to travel this country without carrying a gun.

"It is late, America! Not just for this isolated criminal incident, but totally for the mood of this nation. We must stand up to this mob violence or our country is DEAD.

"Although this type of personal resistance may in actuality accomplish very little, and may again place my family in danger, I will continue to fight it whenever confronted by such hoodlumism. It would be safer and easier to turn the other way, but what lesson does that leave for my children?

"Wake up, Red Wing. Clean up your house."

Saturday night was an anxious one for my family, but for other than the usual reasons. My wife was to be induced early the next morning for the birth of our third child. Due to the confusion of the summer I had had little opportunity to contemplate or look forward to the event. On the one hand, my wife's pregnancy had prevented her from working in the salesroom, as most of the other Management wives had done, but I was thankful that she had not been exposed to the abuse and vulgarity of the pickets. We retired early that night in an effort to see that my wife would be rested for the ordeal of the coming day. At 3:00 A.M. the jangling of the telephone awakened us with a start; I had forgotten to take the usual precaution of removing the phone from its cradle. I stumbled through the darkness to the phone, and as expected, my "hello" went unanswered. The Union had struck again, and at a particularly vulnerable point in time. With the combined shock of being awakened at 3:00 A.M., the anger engendered by the event, and the expectation of the anticipated birth in a matter of hours, we could not find sleep again for the remainder of the night. I was enraged that the strikers' hostility would reach something as inviolable as my pregnant wife and soon-to-be-born baby.

My son was born shortly after 11:00 A.M. Sunday morning, August 6, and without complications. The event was a bright point in an otherwise gloomy summer. While I spent most of the day shuttling to and from the hospital, I learned that things were under control at the Potteries salesroom. Other than a few isolated incidents of more than three pickets to a driveway, the Union was behaving itself and obeying the court order. R. A. Gillmer called the police at 10:05 to report that there were six pickets in one driveway. By 10:25 the police had not yet arrived so Gillmer called again. As he was talking to the desk sergeant for the second time a squad car arrived and dispersed the pickets. Mrs. R. A. Gillmer spent the entire day in

the parking lot with pencil and paper recording names and times
of any minor infractions. Her presence and the power of the
court apparently were sufficient to keep the strikers within bounds.

By Sunday evening we felt safe in concluding that the court
order had emasculated the pickets. On Monday KCUE reported:

"Weekend visitors to the Red Wing Potteries salesroom were
able to drive through picket lines without suffering any
abuse for the first time since the strike began June first.
There were not the usual mobs of pickets, which have num-
bered as many as one hundred, with many of them from
outside unions according to police. Sunday morning a KCUE
reporter counted only nineteen pickets on duty at all but
one entrance to the salesroom parking lot."

While the picketing had returned to an orderly level and
a great deal of the tension associated with the weekend
tumult had been relieved, we still faced the central problem
- ending the strike. A negotiating session was scheduled for
2:00 P.M., Tuesday, August 8. At 11:00 A.M. that morning
the company Directors met to solidify plans for the stockholders
meeting. It was determined that a letter should go out to stockholders as soon as possible informing them of a meeting August
24 at 2:00 P.M. for the purpose of considering liquidation. It
was also determined that the Union should be officially informed
of the company's intentions that afternoon. The company Directors were not bluffing to gain a settlement. They clearly
intended to follow through on their plans. If, however, the Union
did see fit to accept one of the company proposals before the
stockholders meeting the Board would, of course, reconsider
the situation.

At 2:00 P.M. we filed into the courthouse and located, as
usual, in separate jury rooms. The meeting was attended by the
same three conciliators who had been present at the last session,
with Federal Conciliator Larson acting as spokesman. We presented the conciliators with a letter, addressed to Hammerschmidt and Chastain, announcing our plans to liquidate:

"Gentlemen:

"The management of Red Wing Potteries, Inc. has reluctantly concluded that the company can no longer continue in business. This conclusion is regretful and has been reached only after the most careful consideration. Red Wing Potteries has been in business for a period of over 89 years and the decision obviously has a drastic effect upon the company, its employees and the entire Red Wing community. However, in view of the circumstances existing, there is apparently no other alternative available.

"The procedure which will be utilized will be generally as follows:

(1) Liquidation papers will be filed in District Court.

(2) The production facilities will be permanently closed and the manufacturing building and equipment disposed of, as soon as existing inventories have been utilized.

(3) The salesroom will be sold separately as a going business if at all possible. This will be accomplished by bidding procedures under court supervision.

"It is necessary that the stockholders of the company approve a matter such as this and a stockholders meeting will be held shortly. Therefore, if you wish to discuss the decision to terminate or the effects thereof, I suggest that such discussions take place immediately.

R. A. Gillmer

If the letter came as any surprise to the Union we were not aware of it. The conciliators returned with a Union proposal, typed and prepared prior to the meeting. The proposal was totally ridiculous as far as we were concerned. They suggested we eliminate the incentive program, but give all of the incentive money back to the employees in the form of base rate increases. We were certain that the people would not produce at the same level without the incentive system; to think that they would was totally naive. On top of the incentive money, they wanted 10 cents the first year and 10 cents the second for all previous incentive workers, and 20 cents the first year and 15 cents the second for all non-incentive workers. Further, they wanted our equity raises plus an additional 10 cents per hour for the power transporter (who happened to be Vernon Peterson, a member of their negotiating committee). As far as fringes were concerned they wanted an additional paid holiday, more paid vacation, and a $25.00 per day major medical hospitalization plan. The proposal was so outrageous as far as we were concerned that we were amazed the conciliators had the courage to bring it in to us. While they apparently had eliminated their request for a pension plan, their proposal would cost us well over $100,000 in wages alone.

After witnessing our complete shock and categorical rejection of the Union offering, the conciliators trod wearily back to the Union. They returned later and conveyed the Union request to see the company's financial statements. Larson said that it might be a good idea. I told Larson that it was a little late for that now with a liquidation vote only two weeks away. Larson had been aware of our financial picture since the beginning of the strike, and if it would do any good to show the Union our financial picture now, why hadn't he suggested it weeks ago? We had nothing to hide and nothing to lose by showing the Union our finances, so we agreed that Vick and Felhaber would meet with Union officials and their accountant in the offices of our CPA firm, Peat, Marwick, Mitchell & Co., the following afternoon. We had little hope as the meeting broke up that Tuesday afternoon. We were to meet again Friday afternoon.

That afternoon we learned the strikers had diversified still further and had begun picketing the DRE. A lone picket marched in front of the newspaper offices, his sign proclaiming, "Philip S. Duff, Jr. and DRE Unfair to Local 6-430 OCAW AFL-CIO. Please cancel your Subscription." The picket would offer no explanation for the Union's charge of unfairness.

We were anxious about Wednesday's court hearing. The cross-examinations and Union testimony were bound to be unpleasant at best, and we were pleased to hear Wednesday morning that the hearing had been called off. The Union did not wish to contest the action and the order would become a temporary injunction. Our relief was short-lived, however. Holst called back around noon to inform us that the Union had reversed themselves and there would be a hearing that afternoon at 1:30.

In addition to R. A. Gillmer and myself, Attorney Vogt wanted additional testimony from half-a-dozen other salesroom employees. Our group arrived at district court at 1:30 and found approximately twenty-five of the strikers present in the courtroom. I noted the presence of the picket whom I had scuffled with that Saturday in the middle of July, and anxiously guessed that he would testify to my "wanton brutality." We waited nervously in the courtroom pews while the attorneys shuffled in and out of the judge's chambers. These mysterious meetings continued for at least an hour before Friedrich appeared and the court was called to order. We breathed a sigh of relief when the judge announced that the lawyers had come to terms and that no testimony was to be taken in court. The only change in the original order was the addition of a section restraining Management from obstructing, threatening or interfering in any manner with the rights of the Union. We guessed that this was the Union's method of saving face. Union Attorney Frances Xavier Helgesen, asking to address the court, noted that the injunction made the order a two-way street in restraining both sides, and added that the employees had a legitimate right to picket and to the free use of streets and sidewalks. "The public highway doesn't belong to the Red Wing Potteries," Helgesen said. Our attorney Thomas Vogt, countered by noting that the order was very clear in limiting the number of pickets to three at each entrance and not allowing assembly in the streets or elsewhere. He added, "For the record, there has never been evidence of any attack on pickets." That Helgesen was saving face and putting on a show to some extent was evident when he stated that he wanted the record to show that the injunction was accepted after the court (in chambers) had over-ruled his motion to deny any injunction. As far as we were concerned, Helgesen and the Union could save all the face they could as long as the judge granted the injunction, and picketing continued at an orderly level.

The letter we had given the Union the previous day had come to the attention of the press and radio. In reporting the content of the letter KCUE slammed the Union by adding:

"The closing of the business accomplishes a goal set by some of the Union's leaders when the current strike began on June 1. At that time, the Union's President, Tilfer Chastain, and the Union's Business Agent, Joseph Hammerschmidt, told people: 'If the Potteries is to be forced out of business, we will help them nail the doors.' "

KCUE also went on to report some "second thoughts" on the part of strikers:

"Some of the Potteries workers, prevented from building up their anger through picket line actions, are now beginning to feel the current strike began without enough consideration being given to the great financial loss now being suffered by the workers and their families. There has been an undercurrent of agitation and worker resentment in the Potteries for many years and some of the workers have said that, frankly, this led to strong emotional appeals to strike without adequate thought to the consequences.

"If a Potteries worker who normally gets about four thousand dollars a year, takes time now at home to figure it out, it will take him a number of years to make up for the wages lost during the present strike."

Red Wing's DRE carried front page headlines Wednesday evening announcing, "POTTERIES MAY LIQUIDATE." After reporting the facts of the letter, the article went on to describe the Union reaction:

"Joe Hammerschmidt, international representative of the Union, said he understands the sales facilities will be sold and Gillmer is wanting to buy it.

"The Union, Hammerschmidt said, has heard rumors for several months that the production end of the Potteries will close.

"Liquidation, the Union said, will hurt:
— Minority stockholders.
— Red Wing tourist trade and industrial image.

— Plant employees.

"The Union view is that if the company is forced to operate on a low wage scale then there is no alternative."

In addition to the lead article on the impending liquidation, the DRE also ran two letters to the editor that evening. Both letters reflected the Union view of the strike and the picketing:

"WHY DIDN'T CHICAGOAN KEEP GOING PAST POTTERIES?

"I feel I must write something regarding the letter from that 'pool soul' from Chicago.

"He is the first Marine that I've ever heard bellyache. Many of the Pottery workers were also members of the Armed Forces. He should feel free to travel. Why the HELL didn't he keep going when he saw there was a strike? Those folks also feel free to strike and picket.

"I'll bet he belongs to a Union, too. Whether it's a Retailers Association or Chamber of Commerce or Manufacturing Association, it's still a Union.

"As for mob violence - he disproved that himself by saying the police were there and didn't do anything about it. It's a cinch he wouldn't apply for work at the Potteries - not with those miserly wages and miserable working conditions."

"INSULTS ARE HURLED AT RW PICKETS

"As one of the Pottery strikers I would like to tell the people a little of our side concerning the violence we are accused of.

"I have been on duty all through this strike so far, and all this time I have not heard all this rot we are accused of from anyone on the picket line, yes, I have heard the word 'scab,' but that word means one thing, 'crossing the picket line.'

"The people have not heard about the abusive words that are said to us by people who cross the picket line; some words are too foul to mention. There has not been any attempt to scratch or hit cars or molest the occupants, but some have tried many times to run us down.

"Not all people are alike; some do stop to consider what we tell them, not to cross the picket line, but if they insist, we cannot stop them.

"We have been called a 'low class of people.' I really don't think we deserve such; most all of us have worked in this plant over 20 years and have traded in Red Wing all these years, and after all that time to be called a 'low class of people.'

"I do hope people will stop and realize we have a side to consider."

We met with company Treasurer Irving Vick that night after his return from the meeting in St. Paul where Union officials and their accountant had reviewed our past and present financial situation. Vick was optimistic as he recounted the details of the meeting. According to Vick, the Union accountant, after examining the financial statements, had turned to the two Union officials and said, "There is just no fat here." He had added that company profits over the last few years had been at a minimum, expenses were not out of line, officers' salaries and bonuses were reasonable, and advertising expenditures were small. The Union officials then indicated that perhaps they should have stepped into the situation earlier, and that they intended to inform the Committee that their demands were a little out of line under the circumstances. They then asked Vick if the Red Wing Potteries really intended to liquidate. Vick answered that, although he was not a Board member, he understood under the present circumstances the company had no other alternative. The Union officials then suggested that maybe it did not make any difference what they did. On this note the meeting ended and Vick returned to Red Wing. He was confident that now the Union would be brought to reason, their demands would be modified, and the strike could be settled at Friday's meeting.

On Thursday, August 10, the notices went out to the Potteries' stockholders on the special meeting. A proxy form and a letter of explanation accompanied the notice:

"TO THE STOCKHOLDERS OF
RED WING POTTERIES, INC.

"Enclosed you will find a Notice of Special Meeting for the purpose of considering a liquidation of the corporation.

"The employees of this company have been on strike since June 1, 1967. Management has bargained in good faith and has made every effort to reach a settlement of this dispute. All such efforts have failed and the officers and directors have reluctantly reached the conclusion that the possibility of settling this strike on terms which might make it practical for the company to continue are extremely remote. The length of the strike has resulted in loss of income and inability to fill orders. Consequently, the officers and directors have given serious consideration to dissolving the corporation to prevent further losses to the stockholders.

"Will you please be at the meeting if you possibly can be there. If this is not possible will you please sign the enclosed proxy and return in the enclosed envelope by mail."

R. A. Gillmer

"TO THE STOCKHOLDERS OF
RED WING POTTERIES, INC.

"NOTICE IS HEREBY GIVEN That a special meeting of the stockholders of Red Wing Potteries, Inc. will be held at the company offices in the City of Red Wing, Goodhue County, Minnesota on August 24, 1967, at 2:00 o'clock P.M. for the purpose of considering the adoption of a resolution to provide that the affairs of the corporation be wound up under the supervision of the District Court and authorizing certain directors or shareholders to sign and present a petition to the Court praying that the corporation be wound up and dissolved under the supervision of the District Court.

"NOTICE IS ALSO GIVEN That if said resolution is adopted that there may then be presented to the stockholders for their consideration such plan as may be necessary or advisable to implement such dissolution."

R. A. Gillmer   R. S. Gillmer

The local news media were filled with reports on the Red Wing Potteries. KCUE reported the impending liquidation plans in detail and the Union cries of "bluff."

"The President of the Red Wing Potteries, R. A. Gillmer, cleared up a number of cloudy issues today surrounding Wednesday's announcement that management has decided that the Company can no longer continue in business, and it appears an almost certainty that the Potteries will be liquidated. Gillmer said he was the largest stockholder in the Company, which is the key to a stockholders meeting called for August 24th, at which the liquidation decision will be made. He said there are around 160 stockholders, and letters of notification of the meeting are being sent out today. An attorney for the Company, Milton Holst, says ten days notice is required by law. Holst said that two-thirds of the stock must be voted for liquidation before a petition for a court appointed receiver can be filed in Goodhue County District Court. With Gillmer holding the largest amount of stock, and his decision to go out of business already made in a letter to the Oil, Chemical, and Atomic Workers Union and Local 6-430, it appears an almost certainty that Red Wing Potteries will close down.

"Union officials have said all along, even as early as Wednesday, that Company announcements of closing down are all bluffs. Gillmer was asked if this was a bluff, but he had no comment. Gillmer was also asked if it was the impact of foreign imports, or the long-standing labor dispute which forced the Company to announce it would vote on liquidation August 24th. Gillmer said, 'The strike hurt much worse, especially the way this one was handled.' Gillmer also clarified what he meant when he said reports that the Pottery would close were 'not true.' He said, 'The Pottery cannot legally close without two-thirds of the stock being cast for liquidation.' He said, 'You can't say the Potteries will close until this is accomplished.'

"However, the Union is still convinced that this is just another bluff, and local OCAW president, Tilfer Chastain, says picketing will continue at the Pottery salesroom and the union will not disband. Hammerschmidt and the other unionists have sought thruout the strike to set the Gillmer father and son team apart from the other stockholders. Gillmer, as the single largest stockholder in the Potteries, stands to lose the most if the firm is liquidated. Liquidation of such worn-out assets as the big and barn-like Potteries building and equipment which the Union has described as 'antiquated' is expected to bring only a few pennies on the dollar if, indeed, the building and equipment can find a market. The market value of the Potteries salesroom has been further shattered by the strike's impact, as well as by the fact it will not be able to draw tourists as in the past because it will not be associated with any working pottery plant.

"Some of the Red Wing Potteries workers have taken new jobs elsewhere in Red Wing, as well as at Lake City and Hastings. It appears, however, that most of the strikers preferred to go back to the Potteries, and they either spent time on the picket lines or around their homes waiting for the strike to end. Many of the union members will be seeking new jobs now, while some will be forcibly retired on Social Security because they are past 65. Others may have to draw unemployment compensation for a time. The manager of the Red Wing office of the State Employment Service, Norris Mulvania, believes workers will be able to get unemployment compensation just as soon as the strike can be said to be at an end.

"There are some real tragedies in the disaster which befell the Potteries and its workers. One example is the man over 65 who has spent his entire working lifetime, aside from a few years, with the Potteries. Fit and able to keep on working, this man earned $6,500 last year. Now he faces declining years of odd jobs, and never large enough Social Security payments.

"Last year the Potteries payroll was over three hundred fifty thousand dollars, and the payroll up to the time of the strike, June 1, was about the same.

"Many union members are silent and defeated in manner now that the plant is past history. All along from the first day of the strike until yesterday, there were those in the union who felt Gillmer was bluffing. An often-repeated remark was: 'We've heard that bluff before. If they can't pay wages, we'll get a hammer and help them nail the boards over the windows.'

"The prospective closing of the plant, in the eyes of many, gives Red Wing two black eyes. The city's reputation as a friendly community where anyone might come and go as they wished, was all but ruined this summer by wild scenes on the picket line at the Potteries. Now the closing of the Potteries because of strike action would give Red Wing the name of being perhaps the only community in the state where Union action forced a plant to quit. Industrial developers around Minnesota report that employers are still gun-shy over Hastings as a plant site because of the violence of the Smead strike of a few years ago. Incidentally, the same international union was involved in the Smead strike."

The DRE described the notice and accompanying letter to stockholders. Also, Duff wrote an editorial calling for community protest to the possible closing of the Potteries:

"SAVE THE POTTERIES: LET THE PUBLIC SPEAK
" 'Potteries May Liquidate,' declared an eight column banner headline across the top of the DRE's front page in yesterday's issue. This, in our opinion, is the saddest headline this newspaper has been compelled to set in type in many a long year. It bespeaks a really tragic failure in understanding of a company's economic position, in communication between management and labor of the facts of economic life with which the company that belongs to both is faced.

"Surely no right-thinking person has ever wanted Red Wing Potteries to go out of business. Surely not the shareholders, who stand to lose a lot of money; surely not the management, which has done a good job of guiding the company's precarious existence over the last ten years; surely not the long-time workers who have not enjoyed high wages but may find it difficult to get comparable earnings elsewhere at their stage in life; surely not the Red Wing community, for whom the Potteries has long had a unique economic value in making Red Wing known far and wide and in drawing thousands of visitors here every year.

"Is the situation now beyond recall? Is a stockholder vote to liquidate already ordained at the special meeting called for two weeks from today?

"We don't know the answer to these questions, but we do know this: Beginning right now there ought to be a widespread outpouring of opinion from every quarter of our community saying this: We don't want the Potteries to close. We want Red Wing to maintain its ancient tradition of pottery-making. If there is any possible basis on which Potteries owners, management, and workers can get together in a way to preserve the company and preserve the jobs for those who want them, we urge you to do so RIGHT NOW!"

Duff was completely sincere in his efforts to keep the Potteries from closing. He could not, nor could others in the community, imagine Red Wing without a pottery. In fact, it was our feeling that because the Red Wing Potteries had always been such an accepted part of the community, most citizens truly believed a liquidation would never come to pass. The Potteries was like an old ingrained habit; something that one could not imagine being without.

Friday morning, George Fry, senior partner in the St. Paul office of Peat, Marwick, Mitchell, came to Red Wing to meet with company Management. We wanted his analysis of our financial picture as it related to the possible liquidation. We gathered from the meeting that the company would be worth substantially more if the liquidation could be carried out with an intact work force. While Fry did not put it into so many words, it was obviously preferable to sign a contract with the Union, no matter how unfeasible, and then liquidate the company, rather than to attempt to liquidate while the workers were out on strike. The fact that we were not totally committed to liquidation was brought out by the fact that we could not bring ourselves to sign a contract solely for the sake of signing one. If we did sign an unworkable contract, the liquidation course would be unavoidable. While we did not put this line of reasoning into so many words, I am certain that this was the major factor keeping us from signing an impossible contract.

We were very interested in seeing the Union's reaction in the afternoon meeting. As far as we were concerned it was their move. They now knew, or should know, that liquidation was a clear possibility, and they also had had the opportunity to review our rather tenuous financial picture. According to Vick's interpretation of their unofficial reaction to this revelation, they should have been in a "bargaining mood" that afternoon.

At 2:00 that Friday afternoon we gathered in the courthouse and, as had become the custom, the Union located in one jury room and the company in another. At this point in the game we avoided the Union if possible. To meet one of the Union Committee accidentally in the hall or pass one of them on the way to the drinking fountain was extremely uncomfortable. We did glimpse the Union team, however, as they passed our open door and noted that a Mr. Lyman Covert was among them. Covert, OCAW District 6 Director, was Hammerschmidt's boss and one of the Union officials present in Vick's St. Paul meeting where the company's financial state was examined. The presence of this Union "higher up" heightened our interest in the nature of the Union reaction. As far as conciliators were concerned, the customary group was present, including Larson and the two State men.

The conciliators began the session by meeting with the Union group. After a short time they entered our cell and we waited expectantly for their comments. The Union's reaction at this point was crucial, analogous to the play that won or lost the ballgame. We listened in shocked disbelief while Larson reported that while the Union realizes the company has not made exorbitant profits in recent years, they still feel there is enough there to meet their demands. We digested this statement in stunned silence for a few moments, and then Vick exploded. Normally a soft-spoken man of few words, Vick could not believe his ears. He angrily related the complete about-face the Union had taken since their meeting Wednesday afternoon. He recalled the Union statement that "there is just no fat here," and their statement to the effect that maybe their demands were "out of line" under the circumstances. It could not have been a lack of communications because Lyman Covert, who had been present at the St. Paul meeting, was sitting in the next room at that very moment.

The conciliators had no answers. They left and spent the remainder of the afternoon in conference with the Union. The five member company team was left alone to denounce the Union as two-faced, totally unreasonable, and determined to put us out of business. While we had no evidence other than the overt Union position upon which to base this last denunciation, the situation was ideally suited to bring all our latent paranoia to the surface. Was there some deep, dark, unfathomable Union plot operating to put the Red Wing Potteries out of business? While we definitely had feelings of persecution we held no delusions of grandeur; why would an International Union with 170,000 members care enough one way or the other about the insignificant Red Wing Potteries to deliberately try and put us out of business? A more logical answer to the untenable situation, we reasoned, was that the Union had begun by asking for too much, and raised the expectations of their people to such a level that to back down now to any level approaching our offer would mean a great loss of face. Thus, why not let us go ahead and liquidate, if that was what we intended to do, rather than accept a settlement at or near our latest offer, and, in effect, admit that the ten-week strike was for naught? All this was speculation, but we were compelled to try and discover some logic in the Union's position.

The conciliators returned late that afternoon with nothing new to offer other than the assurance that the Union meant to hold with what they had said earlier in the afternoon - they believed the money was there to meet their current demands. At the suggestion of Larson, we agreed to put our proposal in writing for the Union. Hammerschmidt had agreed to put it to a vote of the membership. While their Committee had categorically rejected all three alternative proposals we had verbalized earlier in negotiations, we felt that the Union would find most palatable the one in which incentive was to remain intact and at present rates. All non-incentive people would receive 15 cents per hour the first year, and 10 cents the second year. We were continuing to offer the equity increases. We agreed to write up this proposal and put it in the OCAW box at the local Labor Temple on Monday. Hammerschmidt had agreed to call a membership meeting Monday night to vote on the proposal, although he made it clear the Committee would recommend unqualified rejection.

The conciliators apparently had reached the end of their rope. They had nothing new or creative to offer and, significantly, did not schedule another meeting before we left that day. While they did not announce that they had given up, time was running out before the stockholders meeting and they had not set up any future sessions. We left the courthouse in a confused and totally dejected state of mind. While Vick's report had given us a glimmer of hope prior to the meeting, the events of the afternoon had completely shattered those hopes.

While we initially had entertained hopes that the employees would rise up and overthrow the Union Committee, the events of past months had all but eliminated this as a possibility. We know for a fact that earlier in the strike many of the strikers did not know why they were picketing; did not know the details of the company proposals. As far as we were concerned, most of the people on the picket lines were sheep. We had heard that some employees had tried to voice objections to the Union tactics and position at Union meetings, but were told in no uncertain terms to keep quiet. Rather than insisting on their rights, these people stopped going to Union meetings. To count on approval of our proposal Monday night would be sheer folly, particularly with the Committee's strong negative recommendation.

Yet KCUE reported an undercurrent of Union dissatisfaction: ". . . There is an undercurrent in the Union's membership, apparently quite fragile and slight, which is starting to feel that the Union is going to have to make some adjustments in its position if the workers are to be able to have a place in which to work.

"A few days ago, for example, one Potteries striker remained thoroughly angry with the company and its Management. 'I'd like to see them shut the doors forever,' this man said to his neighbors time and time again. Now with the liquidation of the Potteries near, this same Union worker has said, 'I'd take a five per cent raise and would like to get back to work.'

". . . Many of the strikers have told friends that some of the anger they felt against the company faded with news that the company must prepare to shut down."

As far as we were concerned, this had to be considered idle talk until we saw some sort of action to support it, and we refused to give it any significance.

Friday night's DRE bemoaned the potential ill effects of Potteries liquidation on the city. In front page headlines they proclaimed:

"POTTERIES LOSS WOULD HURT RED WING

"Red Wing stands to lose more than a payroll should stockholders of Red Wing Potteries vote to liquidate August 24. "The 90-year old industry is the backbone of the tourist business here and synonymous with the city's image. Few visitors could think of Red Wing without bringing to mind the potteries. Its loss would give the community a smaller dot on the nation's 'places-to-visit' map.

"From the economic standpoint, the county as well as the city would feel the blow. Lost would be:

— Some $32,000 in local taxes

— A payroll of between $350,000 to $400,000 annually.

— Untold dollars spent here by thousands of tourists whose primary reason for coming is to see the pottery works.

"The pottery is among the top 10 tax payers in the county and the top 5 in the city. Last year it paid $11,923 in personal property and $20,377 in real estate taxes.

"This represents about 6 per cent of the city's mill levy; 1.5 per cent of the county levy and 5 per cent for the Red Wing School district.

"Last year the potteries paid more than $350,000 in salaries to its 100 workers. Some of them are of the age that finding a new job would be difficult.

"Norris Mulvania of the State Employment Service here said the workers could be absorbed by other industry in the city but it would take time - several months. There is no surplus of jobs now but when high school and college youths return to classes more work will be available.

"The loss in tourist trade is immeasurable.

" 'It certainly won't help any,' commented Art Lillyblad at the St. James Hotel. He sees thousands of tourists each year whose main question is, 'How do we get to the pottery?'

"The Potteries is advertised on national television and in a host of tourist brochures. A new tour guide book by the State Department of Business Development cites 'tours through the famous Red Wing Potteries.'

"The potteries is a prominent part of the new Red Wing Chamber of Commerce brochure. It is featured in pamphlets distributed by the Hiawatha Valley Association and the State AAA.

"Mrs. Dorothy Nelson, executive secretary of the Chamber of Commerce, said the potteries is undoubtedly Red Wing's main tourist attraction. 'They come from all over the United States and the first thing they want to see is the potteries,' Mrs. Nelson said.

"Last year Chamber records show 10,337 visitors, 99 per cent of whom wanted to see the pottery works. Some 250 groups have inquired about tours here this year and all expressed primary interest in the potteries.

"Since the strike began June 1, a drop in tourist business has already been felt. By this time last year, 8,863 visitors were listed in the Chamber directory. Currently the figure is 7,454. 'Many people just passing through town have made it a point to stop here because they have heard of the potteries,' Mrs. Nelson reported.

"Some residents feel the twin atomic power plants to be built by NSP on Prairie Island will pick up the tourist interest should the potteries close down. But it's hard to brush off 90 years of tradition and reputation with a new industry.

"By the same token, one can look upon a report made last year by Robert Pohl, Chicago banking executive, on what a community could expect from a new industry employing 100 workers. He said the population would increase by 350. One hundred new cars would be added. Four to six new retail stores would be needed. Bank deposits would climb $500,000.

"In the case of an industry which employes 100 and is forced to shut down, would the figures go in reverse?"

The DRE also ran two letters to the editor that Friday, one pro-Union and one anti-Union. The pro-Union letter was probably the most logical and persuasive pro-Union argument set forth to date:

"PROUD TO HAVE HELPED PICKETS

"Have the people of Red Wing ever walked a picket line? I hadn't, until last Saturday when I went to a union meeting. I'm proud to say I was part of the union working people that helped out the striking workers at the Potteries, even for a short while on this particular day.

"For God's sake look at those workers who feel they have to strike to survive these years ahead of retirement.

"Most of those I saw Saturday were older people who have worked at the Potteries a good share of their lives.

They have earned their pensions and insurance benefits. They aren't enjoying this strike. Have you ever tried standing on a hot, barren sidewalk for eight or more hours a day? I wasn't there nearly that long and believe me I would rather be putting in my eight hours in a factory at my job. As I'm sure most of the Potteries workers would.

"As for the many reports of violence, the picketers I saw never even stood in a driveway. They would step out to stop a car and then back to the side of the road. Cars usually stopped (or went through at a high rate of speed). The cars that stopped, listened to what the strikers had to say, some drove on, some drove in, but I never saw a picket hurt a car, or try to touch or harm the people. The picketers called 'scab,' etc., not using cuss words. There were maybe three or four hotheads in a crowd of about 100 people. They just ran around yelling, using up their energy faster, and perhaps going home sooner, leaving a more quiet, determined group.

"To N. H. Kafkis of Chicago (I can't imagine a man out of Chicago paying any attention to a small town strike), I say don't worry about Red Wing; we are having kind of a bad time right now, but we will never have the gangsters, riots, etc. (I hope) Chicago has.

"Here I might say if any individual or sympathetic unions, on their own, do the things Mr. Kafkis describes thinking they are helping the striking Potteries workers that I talked to a union member, who states, 'You are undoing many days of hard and orderly picketing, by just a few incidents.'

"May I add, wake up, Chicago, clean up your own doorstep.

"I live in Red Wing, I work here, I'm proud of our town. I'm sorry that Management and workers don't see eye to eye right now in these particular matters. Being a member of the working (not lower) class of people I know I'm partial to their side.

"Since reading the paper that the Potteries may close, I like to add, let's put the blame where it belongs on the management and stockholders, who must prefer to invest their money elsewhere, or perhaps keep it in their pockets. It's the management who have let the Potteries stop, not keeping up with the times. Don't blame this on the working people who must make a living."

The anti-Union letter was particularly significant because it was written by a retired Potteries employee and an ex-Union man:

"WHO FEEDS UNEMPLOYED WORKERS?

"Some say it is an idle threat that the Potteries will liquidate. Suppose it isn't. Many potteries have quit in recent years, potteries that were run even more efficiently and were better situated geographically than the Red Wing plant.

"They say, why work for starvation wages? I did for years, and I am not starving or ever was even hungry for food or money either.

"Mr. Varney told me years ago if I didn't like my job I should get another one. I don't think he meant that I should take everybody with me or figured they would go. I didn't go.

"Some could go now and they would no doubt be better off. Then again for some it would be a great hardship.

"I have always believed in good unionism, but not the kind that is dished out by this outfit.

"If they liquidate, are they going to feed you? They won't even know you. I just can't see why the majority of the workers can go along with this kind of a thing. Many of the retired workers have a paid-up life insurance policy which will be voided if they go out of business at the Potteries. That is about all the life insurance some of them have.

"I think that if the workers still have a chance to go back to work they should take it and forget about their agitating big time union agents.

"I think that if some people would start thinking a little more about others, they would in the end be better off."

Editor Duff, judging from the frequency of both pro and con letters being published, was doing his best to remain impartial and give both sides an equal voice.

The weekend was a veritable "utopia" for us as far as picketing was concerned. Any violations of the injunction were so minor as to be considered accidental. Customers came and went unmolested, and business improved. Since the total number of pickets allowed on the scene had been severely restricted by the court order, there was only room for our employees who, by and large, had not been the obnoxious ones during the height of the picketing riots. The real trouble-makers, the out-of-towners, and the members of other local Unions, were eliminated from the scene by the simple fact that their numbers would constitute a violation of the court order. The Union President, himself, was no longer seen on the picket line.

Monday morning I placed our latest proposal in the OCAW box in the Labor Temple. I also saw that a copy of the proposal reached one of our employees whom we knew wanted to return to work. He was to make certain that the proposal was communicated to the membership as written. Also, he offered to spend the day contacting pro-company workers to encourage them to attend the meeting to assure their votes. He was certain of at least a dozen employees who would vote for acceptance.

That morning, R. A. Gillmer and wife, at the insistence of Director Foot and myself, left for a short vacation. They were to return Thursday. With no negotiation sessions scheduled and no real need for his presence, we were determined that he should leave for a few days in an effort to relax. He had lost thirty pounds since the start of the strike, and was understandably tense and low in spirits.

Monday's mail brought a letter from the Chairman of the New Business Committee of Portland, North Dakota, a town of 700, suggesting that "you re-locate in our fair city where you would be very much appreciated in the community, and not be affected by costly labor disputes such as is experienced in the large industrial centers."

Station KCUE reported interest on the part of the Governor and went on to summarize the current state of affairs:

"The Governor is taking a close interest in the Red Wing

Potteries strike, now mid-way in its 11th week. Governor LeVander is asking the State Labor Conciliator's office for reports on progress of strike negotiations.

"Meanwhile, one hundred and seventy-three stockholders have a chance to ponder again this week what their course of action will be when they meet at 2 P.M. on the 24th at the Potteries offices. The major stockholder is Richard Gillmer, the firm's president. He is described as low in spirits now, and is one of those favoring liquidation of the Potteries.

"The Potteries has lost so many orders because of the strike, and has suffered such a financial setback because of the labor strike, that many business leaders in Red Wing wonder whether the Potteries would be able to accept an agreement with the union even if the union would offer concessions at this point.

"One of the ironies of the Potteries situation is that the management was, after ten years, just reaching the point where it might have the capital in order to diversify its business and get into the manufacture of other and perhaps more profitable lines of ceramics. The Potteries' financial position has been precarious for a number of years, but the firm was making better than usual progress up to the time the strike started on June first."

As far as KCUE's report that "Gillmer favored liquidation;" he did not favor it but, under the circumstances, saw it as the only possible alternative. At this point, we were forced to inform our trade customers that "liquidation seemed unavoidable," and suggest that they look elsewhere for a source of supply. We started receiving calls of shocked disbelief from our salesmen, many of whom had represented Red Wing Potteries for ten and twenty years. We had no choice but to suggest that they begin searching for other lines to replace Red Wing.

People were beginning to accept the fact that the Potteries could indeed go out of business. Even the optimistic Duff, on Monday's editorial page, admitted the situation looked very grave:

"GOODBYE, POTTERIES

"We claim no special skill at economic diagnosis, but it seems realistic to observe that Red Wing Potteries is now in its last days as a business entity. Perhaps the company can recover from this apparent death bed - patients do - but the prognosis is not good.

"One of two developments may be the final immediate cause of death. Potteries owners may decide it's no longer worthwhile to risk their capital in the enterprise, and that's surely their right. A special meeting of shareholders has been called for a week from Thursday, and the apparent recommendation from management is to liquidate. Or Potteries workers may well decide that the 100-odd jobs here might as well disappear. If the present U.S. economy can't pay men and women any better to make pottery, these workers may conclude the firm might as well go out of business. And this, too, is certainly the Potteries workers' right. As some of them have pointed out, they have no duty to work at what they consider sub-standard wages in order to continue a tourist attraction here for the benefit of the total Red Wing community.

"Most American pottery makers already have gone out of business, and there's no reason to think it can't happen here. Indeed, if Red Wing Potteries should somehow survive its present seemingly terminal illness, it will only be through a high order of economic statesmanship on BOTH the management and labor sides.

"And this brings us to the point that good labor-management relations today are really an art. Success in this field requires a very high order of human wisdom, a very broad range of human understanding.

"Consider the position of the participants in the kind of economic warfare we call a strike. Their lives, their pocketbooks, what they regard as supremely important principles are all wrapped up in the outcome. And the two sides - the labor man and the management man - approach the field of battle with such a different frame of reference. Each looks through a much different pair of spectacles from those the other wears. Each brings to the conflict different attitudes, different habits of thought.

"People on both sides are usually honorable and sincere, but neither can see these qualities in the other. A word or deed that seems quite reasonable to one is outrageously unjust to the other. A response that one thinks entirely logical and proper strikes the other as something the devil himself would concoct. And so the process sometimes goes, in a descending and self-feeding spiral of animosity and hate. Suspicion begts suspicion, anger begts anger.

"What's exceedingly hard for us mortals to do is to bridge this widening gulf of misunderstanding. A man must suppress his own powerful emotions, mentally put on his adversary's coat and shoes, and understand how the conflict looks from this quite opposite point of view. And then he must make concessions - sacrifices - which seem to him totally unreasonable and unjustified.

"Sometimes human beings do arise to these heights of broadgauge behavior, but it has to happen from both directions at once. And the normal human emotions arising from two and one-half months of angry, embittered picket line conflict make it pretty unlikely."

The editorial brought out very effectively a factor present in all strikes - a lack of empathy. The two sides approach the battle with a completely different frame of reference, and each is unable to place himself in the other's shoes and see the situation as the other side perceives it. The result is a complete lack of understanding of the actions of the other side, the assignment of unwholesome motives to those actions, and an inevitable buildup of animosity.

We had honestly attempted to see the strike from the worker's point of view. We recognized, first of all, that the average employee had no understanding whatsoever of the financial workings of a business, the labor costs, raw materials costs and overhead, and their effects on profits. They looked only at the quantities of merchandise that were shipped to the trade and the weekend hordes of customers that trooped out of the sales-room carrying their packages. This represented income. As far as the workers were concerned, the Potteries was an impene-trable institution with the almost magical powers to produce money and grant higher wages if only they desired. We, the Management, had chosen selfishly to deny them the means for the finer things in life, while we raked in our large salaries for sitting at a desk all day. As the strike wore on and the bill collectors started beating down their doors, these feelings began to intensify and their budding animosity toward us grew logically into hate.

For us to come to hate them was just as logical. While in rare moments of insight we recognized that most of them were the same decent people they had always been, the prevailing attitude was one of bitterness and enmity. It was impossible to step back with objectivity when they called you a "son-of-a-bitch," spat at your wife, called your daughter a "bitch," and were killing the business you had put your heart, soul, and money into for years.

The next day, Tuesday, August 15, we learned that only six Union members voted to accept our proposal. We did not believe it. While we were not expecting majority approval, we were certain there were more than six people who would vote to return to work. The DRE's account of the Union meeting and the statements made by Hammerschmidt evidenced his tremend-ous hostility and unrestrained effort to discredit the company:

"UNION REJECTS POTTERIES OFFER,
ONLY 6 VOTE FOR PLAN
"Members of Oil, Chemical and Atomic Workers Local 6-430 voted Monday night by a reported 'well over 90 per-cent' to reject the last offer of Red Wing Potteries, Inc., union officials said today.
"Joe Hammerschmidt, international representative, said a written proposal which the company called its final offer, was submitted to members and discussed for several hours before a secret ballot vote was taken.

"Of some 70 members present, only six voted to accept the offer, according to Hammerschmidt. He described the meeting as the largest turnout in Union history here.

"The Union official also claimed that during negotiations conducted by state and federal mediators last Friday, it was stated that the company Board of Directors was to meet before noon Monday to come up with the best possible offer.

"Hammerschmidt said the proposal was identical to one received August 2. Equity adjustments were the same at 15 cents this year and 10 cents next year on non-incentive pay. No increase was offered on incentive pay. 'This means that 61 or 62 workers would go without a pay increase over the next two years,' Hammerschmidt said.

"Other proposals concerned vacation and hospitalization plans. Hammerschmidt said at the Aug. 2 negotiations, the company offered to give back some benefits they earlier proposed to eliminate. 'The Union then readjusted its proposal to cost around $70,000 over the two years rather than $80,00 to $90,000,' Hammerschmidt reported. 'They also dropped the demand for a pension plan. The company,' he said, 'is still at the same figure it started with - $16,000 or $17,000.'

" 'Results of the vote show the workers are just as determined as ever,' Hammerschmidt declared, 'even with the possibility of liquidation.'

"He denied that the Union ever said the company was bluffing on liquidation, and said the workers are convinced President R. A. Gillmer 'has had this in mind for a long time. We aren't going to let the threat of liquidation change our request for a decent settlement,' he said.

"Hammerschmidt said the company refused several requests for evidence that it couldn't meet the union requests. When the liquidation notice was sent out the company knew it had no way out because the figures would go to district court, he charged.

"A certified public accountant was then allowed to examine

the company financial records. Hammerschmidt claims the report substantiates the union's position. 'The company has made a profit each year from 1961 through 1966,' Hammerschmidt said. 'In 1966, salaries, bonuses, and dividends paid to the top four officers equals the total union package for two years.'

" 'The net earnings come to the amount of wage increases the union is seeking,' he said. 'We're not saying the company shouldn't make a profit,' he continued. 'We are saying the company can meet the demands and not jeopardize its existence.'

"Hammerschmidt also criticized the news media and the DRE for publishing the wages of workers at the plant. 'It was the most unethical thing I have ever seen a newspaper do. If it hadn't been for a sincere plea by the local president not to publish names, Mr. Duff would have serious legal problems,' he declared.

"Hammerschmidt went on: 'I have made reference to the news media previously, and I would like to state that this paper, the radio station, and the Chamber of Commerce have contributed more to aggravating the situation than any other source.'

" 'Mr. Duff's (DRE editor-publisher) attack on the Mayor, Chief Lenway, and his staff was unwarranted and unfounded. If he was as familiar with the matter as he makes believe, he would understand that the Mayor, Chief Lenway, and his force did not show partiality to either side. They did enforce the laws under the city and state statutes. A court order is a matter of the court and not a matter of the police enforcing it.' "

While I thought I had seen everything by that time, I was truly surprised at Hammerschmidt's statements. What possible purpose could all of these accusations and obvious efforts to discredit us serve at this stage of the game. Our figures on total package costs were in direct disagreement with those Hammerschmidt had given the press. His claim that the Union's proposal would cost "around $70,000" was substantially less than the minimum figure of $100,000 we had arrived at. The "$16,000 or $17,000" figure at which he estimated our proposal also was much less than the $30,000 we had come up with. His denial of the Union claims of company "bluffing" was in direct contradiction to our observations and the earlier reports of press and radio. His allusion to Gillmer's having had liquidation "in mind for a long time" was an underhanded attack completely unsupported by the facts. Had Gillmer in any way desired liquidation he would have signed the first Union contract presented and phased the business out in an orderly fashion. Neither would he have built the Management team by adding his son one year before the strike and Ceramic Engineer Ross just two weeks before the strike. Probably one of the most outrageous statements, in our view, was his claim that the company had refused several requests for evidence that we could not meet the Union demands until we knew we had "no way out" because the figures would be made public in the liquidation process. Prior to the August 8 Union request that they review our figures, to which we complied, they had never broached the subject. His further claim that the review of the figures "substantiates the Union's position" and that "the company can meet the demands and not jeopardize its existence" was a complete about-face from the Union officials' opinions at Vick's St. Paul meeting. Hammerschmidt's statement that the net earnings in 1966 "come to the amount of wage increases the Union is seeking" was false by any stretch of the imagination. In 1966, an unusually good year for Red Wing Potteries, the net earnings amounted to $44,964, an amount substantially less than Hammerschmidt's $70,000 cost figure and even further away from our minimum estimate of $100,000. The whole article was rife with contradictions and obvious hostility.

DRE Editor Duff called the day after the article was published and asked if I wished to counter it with a company statement. He advised against it, and I agreed with him. Most of the charges, as far as the company was concerned, were so outrageous and angry that for us to attempt to counter them would only serve to demean us and give the charges credence in the public eye. Hammerschmidt's outburst could best be met with silence.

Station KCUE reported Hammerschmidt's account of the situation with more emphasis on the alleged attitudes of the Union membership:

"The outlook for a settlement of the strike at Red Wing Potteries is worse than ever. The strike enters its 12th week tomorrow. The business agent for the union local on strike, Joe Hammerschmidt, seems to sum up the situation when he terms it 'an impasse.'

"Hammerschmidt says the meeting of union members held Monday night should dash any hopes anyone may hold that the labor position will change. 'There should be no false hopes,' he says, 'that the union members will throw over their leadership and seek a settlement along lines of the company's offer.' Hammerschmidt said that the union has kept its members informed about the progress of negotiations and he, personally, has clearly warned the strikers that failure to reach agreement on a new contract may force the Potteries to shut down permanently. The union business agent says, 'Many of the workers don't really believe that the Potteries will shut up shop.' But, as far as going back on company terms, he said, 'they've had it.'

"The union has had its own accountant go over the books of the Potteries and, says the business agent, while the company is, to use his words, 'not lucrative,' the check of figures makes the union feel the company could meet what the union wants.

"Company directors met last Friday to go over what Hammerschmidt said was supposed to be the 'best possible proposal.' The union business agent says it was the same offer the company has been making all along. The union has, during the weeks of the strike, dropped one aspect of its request. It is no longer asking for a pension plan. The average age of plant employees is 53 and, says Hammerschmidt, 'we recognize how difficult it would be for the company at this point to start a pension plan.'

"Hammerschmidt feels that some blame can be spread around among all parties and the community for letting the Potteries situation get to the present point. He thinks that there should have been greater awareness of the needs of the workers, as well as of the status of the Potteries, two years ago when workers nearly walked out. Hammerschmidt feels that if the union had stiffened its position then and if the Potteries had clearly understood at the time, then the present impasse might have been avoided.

"Hammerschmidt says it is his own honest opinion that the Potteries will go ahead with liquidation. He says he told this firmly to the best-attended meeting of the striking workers this week, but, as he put it, 'it didn't mean a thing to them.' "

The press and radio were strangely quiet about the strike for the remainder of the week.

Tuesday evening, August 15, Spence Broughton, President of Red Wing's Citizens Security Mutual Insurance Company, called me with a proposal. He was calling to see if we would be interested in community intervention in the form of a Citizens Committee to meet with the two parties and attempt to bring about a settlement. The Committee would be composed of three Red Wing citizens identified with management and three identified with labor. I met the suggestion with less than complete enthusiasm, explaining that both sides were so fixed in their positions and so far apart that any kind of a settlement seemed highly unlikely. Further, the business had been hurt so drastically after two-and-one-half months of labor strife that, even if the Union accepted our last offer, it was doubtful the company could be put back on its feet. Broughton said he realized all this, but that the community representatives would still like an opportunity to see if something could be worked out. The Union would agree to this plan if we would. I agreed to phone R. A. Gillmer that evening to discuss the matter.

I phoned President Gillmer that evening at a northern resort. He informed me that he would be returning on Wednesday, a day earlier than planned, because he could not keep his mind off the strike, so might as well spend his time worrying in his office. When informed of Broughton's suggestion, Gillmer's reaction was similar to mine - "What can they hope to accomplish under the circumstances?" However, in discussing the matter further, we decided that we owed it to the business, the stockholders and the community to explore every possibility, however slight and apparently hopeless, to find a way to salvage the business. While not compulsory arbitration, this was the general approach to settlement Editor Phil Duff had been advocating since the beginning of the strike. Perhaps some avenue remained unexplored, some stone unturned, that could lead to a settlement. We decided that we would request that Broughton; George Bergwall, Personnel Director of Red Wing Shoe Company; and Ora Jones, President of Goodhue County National Bank represent us on the Citizens Committee.

I called Broughton to tell him of our decision. He would be pleased to serve and was certain the other two would, also. He informed me that the three committee members representing labor were likely to be Mayor Jelatis; Clarence Josephson, President of Red Wing's AFL-CIO Council; and Kenneth Tri, newly appointed Assistant State Labor Conciliator who would serve on the Citizens Committee only as a concerned citizen. The Committee was to meet with the Union Friday morning, August 18, and with the company that afternoon to gain the necessary background. From that point on the company and the Union were to meet face to face with the Citizens Committee acting as conciliators. It was the feeling of all parties that the less publicity, the more likelihood of progress, so we agreed to say nothing to the news media. The citizens group had very little time in which to work in light of the stockholders meeting scheduled for August 24.

On Thursday of that week Ceramic Engineer Ross told us he had had a good job offer and was obligated to commit himself the next day. We regarded Ross as one of the prime elements of promise for the future of the company, and the fact that we hated to see him go indicated our unwillingness to admit that liquidation was inevitable. There was still some hope that the Citizens Committee would come up with something, and, on the basis of this, we asked Ross to wait until late Friday afternoon after our meeting with the citizens before committing himself.

Friday afternoon Vick, Mewhorter, R. A. Gillmer and myself met with the Citizens Committee in the conference room at Central Research, Inc. Felhaber's presence was not deemed necessary at this point. Jelatis was Vice-President of Central Research, Inc., a Red Wing firm producing remote control manipulating equipment. He, as Mayor, was to serve as chairman.

President Gillmer summarized our position for the committee. He explained our past and present financial status, and the fact that we felt $30,000 was the maximum we could go in increased labor costs and still expect to remain in business. He recounted the degree to which business had been damaged by the two-and-one-half month strike, the salesmen that had left, the orders that had been cancelled, and the many trade customers that had closed out our lines. He added that he was not certain he could justify going back into production at this point even if the Union accepted our last offer. We needed immediate large-volume orders to begin manufacturing again with any degree of security.

The Citizens Committee had recognized the severity of the situation and had already discussed steps in attempting to insure increased sales. Members of the committee were taking steps to contact Senator Mondale, Congressman Quie, Vice-President Humphrey and Governor LeVander in an effort to see if any State or Federal ceramic purchases could be directed our way. There was talk of a concerted advertising effort on the local level; approaching the State to include the Potteries in any State promotions; and Ken Tri felt sure that certain Union publications could be persuaded to give space to promote the Potteries. According to the Citizens Committee, the Potteries real estate taxes should be reviewed and quite possibly lowered. There was even discussion on municipal financing of a new plant to replace our antiquated structure. All of these ideas were met with enthusiasm on our part. By this time, however, we had learned not to count too heavily on anything. We had had our hopes up and then been let down so many times during the course of the strike that we were extremely wary of again accepting the emotional vulnerability associated with optimism.

While these ideas all sounded interesting, we still had to settle the strike before they could do us any good. When Jelatis told us that Hammerschmidt had left that afternoon for a week-long OCAW convention in New York, the possibilities of settlement seemed even further out of reach. According to the Citizens Committee, Hammerschmidt would return at any time from the convention if an agreement was near, but did not want to be called back and told that the company was now "offering $50,000." This was not enough, and the implication was that any move on our part must be all the way or nothing. This, in itself, was indication enough that we might as well forget any future meetings. Also, it bothered us that Hammerschmidt would have "more important things to do" than work to save the Potteries and the jobs of the one hundred people whom he represented. The liquidation vote was less than one week away and Hammerschmidt was intending to spend that week in New York. However, the Citizens Committee was not to be discouraged so easily. They scheduled a joint Union-Management meeting for the following afternoon, Saturday, August 19.

While the Citizens had agreed, at the request of the Union, that package-costs were not to be discussed in the absence of Hammerschmidt, the Citizens felt a meeting could be of value in alleviating some of the misunderstandings that had arisen over the course of the strike. This was to be our first face-to-face confrontation with the Union since July 21, and we were understandably nervous about sitting across a conference table from people who had become, by this time, our arch enemies.

Late Friday afternoon, following our meeting with the Citizens, we returned to the company offices for a prearranged meeting with Ross. We had no other alternative than to advise him to accept the job offer he had received. While we recognized clearly that in advising him to follow this course we were

losing a valuable company asset, asking him to forego this opportunity would be a serious disservice to him, based on our
current information which could only be regarded as wishful
thinking.

President Gillmer and I were in phone contact with members
of the Citizens group a number of times both Friday evening
and Saturday morning. These people were working full-time to
explore every conceivable possibility in hopes of saving the
Potteries for the community.

In our conversations with the Citizens it was determined to
approach the Union with the idea of profit-sharing. Since any
attempt to put the injured company back on its feet would
involve substantial risk, profit-sharing was seen as the best method
of sharing this risk among stockholders and employees. While
the Union would not be guaranteed their monetary demands,
a plan could be established whereby if the company made money,
the employees would share in the profit. However, if the company failed to prosper, then the employees also would fail to
reap additional monetary rewards. Such a plan would not replace the first-year raises the company had been offering throughout the strike but, in our view, would be a means of bridging
the wide gap between what we had been offering and what the
Union had been demanding. This seemed an extremely sound
and logical solution to the problems we were facing.

We entered the Central Research conference room early Saturday afternoon. The Shop Committee, minus Hammerschmidt,
filed in shortly thereafter. We exchanged strained greetings,
both sides avoiding eye-contact and noticeably embarrassed.
Jelatis opened the meeting with a show of faith, claiming the
two sides could get together if they put aside petty grievances
and worked toward a mutually acceptable conclusion. President Gillmer began by carefully explaining the company's current circumstances to the Shop Committee; the financial condition, the loss of customers and salesmen, and the cancelled
orders. Chastain and the rest of the committee then spent most
of the remainder of the afternoon complaining about the incentive system: "Because standards were so tight, the people

were forced to work for quantity rather than quality; the company was losing a lot of money because of poor quality; the incentive system was no good because a lot of people could not make their one hundred per cent." Most of their statements seemed to me to be criticisms one would find universally in any plant with an incentive system.

Later in the afternoon the two groups split for individual conferences with the Citizens Committee. It was Management's feeling, and supported by some of the Citizens, that the Union's criticism of the incentive program and poor-quality ware was their only defensible position at this point. We concluded that the Union recognized that their demands did not make sense in light of the company's financial status. The money just was not there. Therefore, they were forced to take the position that by correcting the alleged inefficiencies in the incentive system, and by improving quality, the company could realize enough savings to meet their demands. They seemed to be grasping at straws to defend their position.

When the groups were brought back together, we broached our idea of sharing the risks involved in resuming operation through the concept of profit-sharing. The Union group was non-committal, and it was very clear that before any decisions could be made of any nature, Hammerschmidt had to be present. Jelatis suggested that Hammerschmidt be contacted in New York and asked to return for a Monday afternoon meeting. Everyone agreed, and the meeting concluded.

The weekend picketing was very orderly, and this aspect of the strike had all but been eliminated as a source of Management concern. We blamed ourselves for not insisting on a court order earlier in the strike; it would have saved a great deal of tension and hard feelings. On the other hand, our Labor Attorney had hesitated on the court order and we deferred to his vast experience. Also, the possibility existed that had we not waited until the situation reached near-riot proportions the Judge may have balked at issuing the order.

On Monday morning, August 21, two ambassadors from the State Government visited our offices in Red Wing. One of the men was a member of the Governor's staff and the other was, in large part, responsible for State institutional purchases. These men had been sent down in answer to a plea from the Citizens Committee. It was our fervent hope that they could assure us some State business. In addition to R. A. Gillmer and myself, Spence Broughton and Ora Jones were present at the meeting. It began, as do most meetings, with generalities. We discussed the strike and our dim business prospects, and the two men asked general questions and offered personal anecdotes. We patiently waited for them to come to the point at hand and tell us they would purchase so many dollars worth of institutional china, or ceramic bedpans, or whatever. I slowly came to realize, as the time and generalities wore on, that these men had nothing whatsoever to offer. They left with a promise to review their records on ceramic purchases and report back to us if there were any possibilities. The man responsible for purchasing reported that he had nothing to do with purchases for the State educational institutions, by far the largest potential source of dinnerware business in Minnesota. We made no effort to hide our disappointment after the two men had left. One of the men called on Wednesday to report that the State had purchased slightly over $3,000 in institutional china the previous year, an insignificant amount. This was one potential source of business that could be eliminated from our plans. However, the Citizens Committee had contacted the aides of Humphrey, Mondale, and Quie, and were waiting for reports from these sources. The business generated by supplying only one type of official U. S. Army ashtray conceivably could sustain our little business for years.

Monday afternoon we gathered in the now-familiar Central Research conference room. Hammerschmidt was in attendance, having returned from the OCAW conference in New York. Jelatis began the meeting by throwing out the idea of risk-sharing through a profit-sharing plan. He did not get far before Hammerschmidt made it clear he wanted nothing to do with profit-sharing. The Union was definitely unwilling to share in any risks involved in resuming operations. According to Hammerschmidt they wanted all of their demands assured, and deserved this assurance due to the poverty they had been experiencing for years, and were unwilling to take the chance of losing any of it by agreeing to profit-sharing. It was all or nothing. Hammerschmidt said, "It looks as though you people have wasted your time and mine calling me back from New York."

We said we would be willing to sign a one-year agreement, and renegotiate wages again at the end of a year, if this would appeal to the Union. "Not for the amount of money we were talking about," Hammerschmidt indicated. There was more fruitless discussion of the incentive system. The six-member Citizens Committee began exerting some cordial but firm pressure on the Union to readjust their demands. Rightly or wrongly, we felt the Citizens Committee recognized the validity of our position under the company's financial circumstances, and felt the Union had the most readjusting to do. They seemed to spend their time from this point on persuading the Union to come down, rather than us to come up. At the end of the afternoon Hammerschmidt and the Committee agreed that the additional holiday and vacation benefits might be postponed until the second year. They would not move on their wage demands or their proposed increase in hospitalization insurance. The meeting was adjourned and we agreed to meet again the following morning.

Monday evening the Rochester Post-Bulletin editorialized on the likely demise of the Red Wing Potteries and lamented the growing threat of foreign imports:

"RW POTTERIES A VICTIM

"It is unfortunate that the owners and employees of the strike-plagued Red Wing Potteries haven't been able to settle their differences. Death of the 90-year-old firm now appears almost certain, marking the end of Minnesota's once-colorful pottery-making business, plus the loss of about 100 jobs.

"Both parties in the dispute have strong points to make - the owners apparently feeling that it is no longer worthwhile risking their capital in the enterprise, and the employees unwilling to continue working at what they consider sub-standard wages.

"But there may be another factor that makes both the owners and employees unwilling victims of this situation. There have been rather strong indications from both groups that if the pottery-making operation folds, the pottery and ceramics gift shop will continue in business.

"While there apparently is a large stockpile of Red Wing-made pottery to sell, enough for years to come according to some sources, there is the opportunity to supplement and eventually replace this supply by importing pottery and ceramic gift articles from the Orient and other foreign countries. There is said to be a lucrative business in such foreign imports.

"This seems to be a growing trend nowadays - why put up with union and production troubles when there may be as much money to be made another way - in this case foreign imports. While wages of Red Wing Potteries workers are low by U. S. standards, they are high in comparison with the penny-cheap labor costs that characterize Oriental production. It's a sad commentary on a way of life that forces American firms out of their established business and workers out of their chosen jobs."

We reconvened Tuesday morning with the Citizens Committee and the Union. A good portion of the morning session was spent arguing about the incentive system. The Union's position was that we should eliminate all incentive and give them the $47,000 we had paid in incentives the previous year. This $47,000 was to be in addition to the 20 cent across-the-board increase they were asking the first year. We argued that this $47,000 was a bonus we paid for high production, and without the stimulus of extra pay there would be less likelihood of above average production. They claimed, naively we felt, that production would remain just as high without the incentive of more pay.

During one of the periods in which the company representatives were alone with the Citizens Committee, we were informed that the Union was developing a persecution complex.

They felt that everyone was turning against them - the town,
the press, and radio - and felt they were seen as second-class
citizens. While I felt they had brought it on themselves, I did
not say it in so many words. Instead, I suggested that this attitude could contribute to a settlement. The Citizens Committee
was trying to salvage the Potteries for the benefit of the community. Thus, if the Union heeded the pleas of the Citizens and
lowered their demands as a form of sacrifice and public spirited-
ness, they conceivably could come out of the situation looking
like heroes.

We learned that Hammerschmidt was planning to return to
New York the following morning. He had to be present for some
sort of a vote that was taking place at the convention. That meant
something had to be settled at the day's session. We broke for
lunch.

The afternoon session started slowly and we remained hopelessly deadlocked. The Union held fast in their demands for
20 cents the first year and 20 cents the second year. They also
wanted the equity raises the first year and hospitalization coverage increased to $30 per day. They would agree to take the
other fringe benefits the second year. Also, if it was determined
to eliminate incentives they wanted an additional $47,000 the
first year. On the basis of this reasoning we had no alternative
but to continue the current incentive program. The Union's first
year demands amounted to approximately $53,000; $40,000 in
the 20 cent across-the-board increase; close to $5,000 in equity
raises; and about $8,000 in increased hospitalization costs. We
had not moved from our $30,000 package.

In the process of defending the Union position to the Citizens, Hammerschmidt contended that the people were better off
on relief or welfare than they would be returning on company
terms. Hammerschmidt also contended that if the company liquidated, at least then the people would be free to find better
jobs. Neither company representatives nor the majority of Citizens could see any logic in this form of reasoning. While we
were not the best pay in town, neither were we the worst, and
to claim that people would be better off on relief did not make

sense. Further, if the liquidation would "free" people to find better jobs, would they not be better off signing a contract, returning to work, and then looking for better jobs? We were afraid, also, that many of our people would have difficulty finding work, considering their ages and the fact that nearly one half of the work force was female.

By mid-afternoon we had made little progress and in desperation Jelatis asked Hammerschmidt's permission for representatives of the Citizens Committee to appear before the Union membership to explain the situation, answer questions, and get their general feelings on the matter. Hammerschmidt categorically refused Jelatis' request.

The Citizens Committee then split the two groups for a last private consultation before giving up. The Committee had been tremendously persistent in the face of what appeared to be an insolvable dilemma, but understandably was running out of patience and ideas. After brief discussions with both groups, the Citizens told the Union that they saw no further purpose for meeting and that the decision to liquidate on Thursday seemed unavoidable. The Union seemed shaken with this reality; Barbara Hove began to cry, and Chastain indicated an interest in meeting that evening. Therefore, the Citizens scheduled a session for that evening and reported their decision to Management. We were heartened somewhat by the Union's refusal to close off negotiations; perhaps they realized that this was it - the last chance, the end, and would be shocked sufficiently by this realization to moderate their demands. This was the way it looked on the surface, and we anxiously awaited the evening meeting.

We should have known better. It became clear shortly after the meeting commenced that the Union was not prepared to change their position. They remained fixed at the $53,000 first year package. If any of the Shop Committee members had had any intention of weakening at the end of the afternoon session, the feeling apparently had been eliminated in the intervening period. The Union presented a unified front - no change.

The meeting concluded that Tuesday night with a sense of finality. No further meetings had been established; Hammerschmidt was flying to New York the following morning; and the stockholders' liquidation vote was scheduled for Thursday at 2 P.M. We went home that evening with something akin to a sense of relief. At least we knew where we stood and a definite direction had been established. Liquidation was a certainty.

The DRE had gotten wind of the renewed efforts at settlement, and covered the Citizens Committee in brief that evening. The article named the six members of the Committee, reported the series of meetings that had taken place, and stated that the members had "declined all comment on any progress or prospects."

We had underestimated the tenacity of the Citizens Committee; they were not ready to give up. We learned that they had been conferring among themselves Tuesday night and Wednesday morning. Mid-morning Wednesday, two of their members, Ora Jones and Spence Broughton, arrived at the company offices. They wanted to discuss our position.

Given the current rigid positions of the two sides - an agreement was impossible and liquidation the obvious outcome - they wished we would consider raising our first year offer. They reasoned, as we did, that liquidating an operating company was preferable to liquidating a company shut down by a strike. If we raised our offer and succeeded in gaining a settlement, we at least would have an opportunity to see if any of the ideas to increase sales would materialize, such as the local and State advertising and the possibility of new markets through the Federal Government. If after three or four months nothing had materialized and business prospects remained dim, then a decision could be made to liquidate and the company probably would be no worse off in liquidation than it would be in its present state. At least under this plan we would be giving it a fair trial, and allowing the Citizens an opportunity to see what they could do to stimulate business.

Their reasoning made sense. We had very little to lose and, with a good deal of luck, could save the company. Gillmer explained that while he would have to secure eventual Board approval, he would be willing to raise the company offer. Working with suggestions from Broughton and Jones, Gillmer consented to a first year package of $47,000. It included 20 cent per hour raises for all non-incentive workers, 15 cents for incentive workers, an additional $4,700 in equity raises, and the $30 per day hospitalization coverage the Union had been requesting. Second and third year offers were discussed, but nothing specific set forth. We were concerned mainly with the first year and would be willing to sign a one-year contract. As far as the first year was concerned, our $47,000 was only $5,000 or $6,000 short of the Union's demands. There was no question in our minds that this offer would settle the strike, allow us to resume operations, and see if the business could be revitalized.

The two Citizens left to meet with the other members of their Committee to determine how the latest company offer should be handled.

In the meantime, we heard that a member of the Union Shop Committee had been to see Jelatis to tell him that he now felt the Union should accept the company's last offer of approximately $30,000. The Unionist had left, allegedly to begin informing the rank and file of his feelings. While we recognized this as the beginning of a potential uprising among the membership, we did nothing to stop our $47,000 offer.

At the same time the Shop Committee member was purportedly persuading the membership to accept our earlier offer, the Citizens Committee was meeting to decide the best way to proceed with our $47,000 offer. Since it was clear that Hammerschmidt was the decision-maker on the Union side and the Citizens had agreed to discuss money matters with the Union Committee only when Hammerschmidt was present, they had no alternative other than to convey the offer directly to Hammerschmidt. It was decided that Jelatis would inform him of the company's new offer. The Citizens were confident the offer would bring the strike to a close.

Jelatis could not reach Hammerschmidt at his home or the Minneapolis airport, and was forced to wait until he arrived at his New York hotel.

While Jelatis was waiting, the Minneapolis Star came out with

an article on Red Wing's Citizens Committee and their efforts
to settle the strike:

"CITIZENS SEEK TO PREVENT
CLOSING OF POTTERY FIRM

"A 'citizens' mediation committee' was going all out today
in an effort to prevent permanent closing of Red Wing
Potteries, Inc.

"The company, which dates to 1868 and employes about 100
workers in this community of some 11,000, has had no
production (but the salesroom is open) since June 1 when
a strike was called by the Oil, Chemical and Atomic Workers
Union.

"Heading the citizens' committee is Dr. Demetrius Jelatis,
who concedes that he knows more about devices for handling radioactive materials than he does about solving labor
disputes. Dr. Jelatis is vice-president and technical director
of Central Research, Inc., which produces master-slave man-
ipulators used throughout the world in the handling of radioactive materials. He comes by chairmanship of the citizens'
committee, however, through being mayor of Red Wing.
This is his fourth term.

"Other committee members are Clarence Josephson, president of the AFL-CIO Council in Red Wing; George Bergwall, personnel director of Red Wing Shoe Manufacturing
Co., Spencer Broughton, president of Citizens Security Mutual Insurance Co.; Ora Jones, president of Goodhue County
National Bank, and Kenneth Tri. Tri is the only labor dispute 'professional' on the committee, being an assistant state
labor conciliator. It was emphasized, however, that he is
on detached service and is on the committee only as a
resident of Red Wing.

"The committee is working under deadline pressure. A
stockholders' meeting called to determine whether the plant
should be permanently closed has been scheduled for Thursday. The meeting was called by Richard A. Gillmer, president of the company about 10 years, who declines to say

what recommendation he will make.

"No member of the committee will talk about details of the dispute. Dr. Jelatis did explain that the citizens' committee began functioning when it became apparent that negotiators were in an impasse and no longer even speaking directly to each other. At conciliation meetings the company and union representatives remained in separate groups with a conciliator going back and forth between the groups. "The citizens' committee is operating on the theory that if a community can exert itself to get new industry to come to town, it also is worthwhile to retain industries it has."

That afternoon's DRE carried a letter to the editor from a picket who "often wondered at the restraint shown by fellow pickets." In our view, the fact that there had been "no arrests" was no evidence that the pickets' tactics had been within legal bounds. The writer saw the dispute as a class struggle:

"POTTERIES PICKETS HAVE EXHIBITED RESTRAINT

"It is with extreme reluctance that I take pen in hand to write this little missive, as I am not overly ambitious.

"I have noted with interest the exaggerations of violence to be found in the Letters to the Editor column in regard to actions attributed to the pickets at the Potteries salesroom. Yet I note with surprise that if all this were true, that no one has been arrested, no person hospitalized, no reports of injuries, no fights.

"Yet I could tell you of persons entering and leaving the salesroom parking lot, who deliberately antagonized the pickets, with no reprisal but words. Remember the old adage: 'Sticks and stones may break my bones, but words can never hurt me.'

"I have walked the picket line at the pottery, and have seen no violence, and often wondered at the restraint shown by my fellow pickets.

"The person who wrote that his children were molested, apparently did not know there are many family men on the line, who would not have stood to have children verbally abused. It is my belief, and I am entitled to my opinion, that this incident, if it occurred at all, was exaggerated. Children are easily frightened.

"I did see cars followed into the pottery salesroom parking lot. In both incidents these cars came through the driveways at a speed in excess of good driver judgment, narrowly missing pickets. One of the incidents resulted in the driver getting a ticket.

"I read with interest the editor's solicitude for persons making a profit on the tourist trade, as well as the loss in taxes to the city, and the tourist dollar to the county. (DRE Aug. 1.)

"I yet have to see one line written by the editor, expressing like sympathy for residents of the city employed by the pottery whose wages I understand average $3,500 per person per year, before payroll deductions? (DRE Aug. 11.)

"In this day that is not a living wage, though no doubt one could exist on it. I believe an American citizen living in such a land of plenty and prosperity, is entitled to more than existence.

"The so-called better class, to whom we look for leadership, could well ask themselves what kind of world they are building when the sons of working people are expected to fight and die to perpetuate the exalted living standards of the pampered so-called better class, while their fathers are paid a pauper's wage.

"The history of our nation is studded with incidents of heroism, such as Valley Forge, Belleau Wood, Verdun, Bastogne, Korea, Vietnam, and many more, where American workers' sons gave unstintingly of their lives, blood and health, as their fathers did before then, in the hope their sacrifice will make a better tomorrow.

"Why should not the leadership (whose sons generally are provided with sufficient funds to claim exemption from military service on scholastic merit), do their part in making that dream of all servicemen a reality?

"Remember, the last five years of a worker's career are used to compute his social security benefits when he retires. If he is underpaid for those years, he will suffer the rest of his life for this injustice.

"Let us hope something can be done to improve the income of these people of the Potteries, so perhaps they can afford a trip to the states from whence the tourists came.

"I agree the loss of the pottery would be a loss to us all. I sincerely hope a settlement acceptable to both parties can be arrived at.

"I hope you realize I am a union member. I am on the workman's side, but only as long as I believe the workman right. I am on the side of the pottery worker."

Jelatis finally reached Hammerscmidt at his New York hotel at 8:30 Wednesday night. He conveyed the company's $47,000 offer to him, and Hammerschmidt promised to consult with the local Shop Committee and Union officials at the convention, and call Jelatis back. Hammerschmidt called Jelatis at 4:30 Thursday morning and told him that he saw no basis for further bargaining; that Potteries shareholders might as well go ahead and hold their liquidation vote.

We, as well as the other members of the Citizens Committee, learned of Hammerschmidt's refusal Thursday morning. The Citizens were as dumbfounded as we were at Hammerschmidt's lack of interest in the offer. We were a mere $6,000 short of the Union's first year demands, and willing to sign a one-year agreement. The proposed salary increases were far and above any raises the workers had received in past years. We were certain the employees would joyously accept the increases if they had any say in the matter. If not willing to accept the offer on the spot, the very least Hammerschmidt could have done was to tell Jelatis that the offer looked interesting, to request that we postpone the liquidation vote, and return from New York to discuss it. Yet, he had told the Mayor that we might as well go ahead and hold the liquidation vote.

We now had no course other than to go through with the liquidation vote that afternoon at 2 o'clock. Mewhorter, Vick,

R. A. Gillmer and myself had a morose lunch that noon at the St. James Hotel. I do not think any of us had fully accepted the fact that the Potteries would liquidate. While we had openly discussed liquidation plans many times in recent weeks, we had all been nursing a hope deep within ourselves that something would happen to save the company.

Reporters from Twin Cities, Rochester and local news media began arriving after lunch. We had ruled that no one other than stockholders was to be allowed in the meeting; thus, the press and radio people were forced to congregate in the reception area. By 2 P.M. approximately twenty-five stockholders had gathered in the conference room, representing 18,803 company shares. Another 9,517 shares were represented by proxy, bringing the total to 28,320 represented at the meeting out of 31,444 total shares outstanding. President Gillmer opened the meeting. Visably shaken, he explained the circumstances of the strike and the resulting business outlook. He offered to answer any questions the stockholders might have, and a few individuals asked cursory questions which he answered briefly. He then concluded that he had no choice but to recommend liquidation and asked for a motion to that effert. It was moved and seconded that the 90-year-old company be liquidated. In the vote that followed only two stockholders opposed the motion, and were asked by Gillmer to explain their opposition. One man said simply that he felt it "was too early" and failed to elaborate; the other said that he was not sure why he voted "no," just that "it did not seem right" to close the 90-year-old business. Thus, the stockholders had officially voted to dissolve the corporation with 27,830 shares for the motion and only 490 against.

The stockholders filed out of the conference room only forty minutes after they had arrived. It was a somber group of Directors and Officers that remained. The full impact of what had just taken place was sinking in; we had just snuffed out ninety years of history in forty minutes and eliminated something that had been an integral part of Red Wing since nearly the town's beginning. However, Gillmer could not enjoy the luxury of soli-

tude and reflection; he was obligated to face the horde of pressmen that had congregated. This was the last thing he wanted
to do at the moment, but he left the conference room and gave
the reporters a brief statement. R. A. Gillmer, Vick, Director
Holst and myself then gathered in Gillmer's office to give a
more detailed account to the local reporters. While we felt a
great bitterness toward the Union, and Hammerschmidt in particular, at this time we made a concerted effort not to reveal
these feelings to the pressmen. It would accomplish nothing at this
point, and more likely than not stimulate the Union to counter
with hostile accusations. There had been enough bitterness to
last a lifetime and, as far as we were concerned, the thing was
over and best forgotten.

After the press had left, Gillmer called a meeting of all supervisory and office personnel to inform them of the action of
the stockholders. He thanked them for their loyalty of the past
three months, and told them of his intention to seek the court's
permission to finish all in-process ware, so there would be no
layoffs in the immediate future. The group received the news
with a mixture of melancholy and anger, and there were a few
muttered indictments of the Union.

In late afternoon, after most of the confusion had ceased, the
depression we had felt throughout the day took on an aspect
akin to relief. The ambiguity of the strike, the raising of hopes
and the eventual disappointment we had been experiencing over
the last three months was over. We now had a definite course
to pursue and the future was certain. This factor, in itself, provided an emotional balm.

The action of the stockholders had reached the DRE too
late in the day for anything to appear in that evening's paper,
but KCUE reported briefly that "the Red Wing Potteries will
pass into history."

We learned Thursday evening that four of the five members
of the Union's negotiating committee had never heard of the
company's $47,000 offer. Of the five, only Chastain claimed
to have been contacted by Hammerschmidt. According to Chastain, Hammerschmidt had called him at 4 A.M. Thursday to

talk about the offer. What had Hammerschmidt been doing
from 8:30 Wednesday night, when he first talked to Jelatis about
the offer, until 4 A.M. Thursday morning when he allegedly
called Chastain? Further, Chastain claimed Hammerschmidt presented it to him as an "iffy" proposition and he did not learn
until noon Thursday that it actually came from the company -
too late, according to Chastain, to get his negotiating committee
together to meet with the Citizens Committee. The whole thing
did not make sense to us. It seemed, on the basis of the times
and facts, that Hammerschmidt had either used very poor judgment or actually had not wanted a settlement. It also appeared
that he had committed what would seem to be the "cardinal
sin" of an International Representative - not communicating a
last-minute company offer to the people he represented. The
Citizens Committee also was at a loss to understand or explain
Hammerschmidt's action.

We began to speculate as to Hammerschmidt's motives. Could
it be possible that he actually wanted to close us down? If so,
what possible reason could he have? Could he be part of some
mysterious conspiracy? Hammerschmidt had replaced Trout as
our International Rep shortly before the strike. Could the Union
"higher-ups" have thrown Trout out for his poor showing in
past years and told Hammerschmidt to either get something big
out of the Potteries this year or shut them down? Could the
modest raises the Union had received in the past be a source
of embarrassment to them? Could other companies working
with OCAW locals use the Red Wing Potteries as an example,
claiming their wages and pay increases were higher than ours?
Yet, our company was so isolated and insignificant on even a
State-wide basis. Could the time, travel and paperwork involved
in running the affairs of our local be more costly for the Union
than the dues they were receiving from the one hundred employees; was the Red Wing Potteries just "more trouble than
it was worth" for the OCAW? Would the "losing face" argument
apply? Could Hammerschmidt have imbued our people with
such exorbitant desires this year that accepting a $47,000 first
year package would amount to a "loss of face"? Unlikely. Or

could the current state of affairs be solely the unfortunate result of Joe Hammerschmidt's loathing for us? Could he have forsaken the cold, hard objectivity, supposedly a quality of International Reps, for the satisfaction of revenge?

We could not help but ask ourselves these questions because, in our view, Hammerschmidt's actions just did not add up. While we had no answers, there was still a compulsion to try and understand the illogical chain of events. We knew for a fact that some of the Citizens Committee were asking themselves the same questions, and were similarly baffled at Hammerschmidt's actions. We felt that the Citizens had served a worthwhile function. While their efforts had not brought about a settlement, we felt that their presence assured us that responsible people in the community were witness to the fact that we had acted in good faith and done everything we could to save the company. While it was unlikely we could have revitalized the company with a $47,000 increase in labor costs, it had been a good thing that we had made the offer because it proved to us, and hopefully to others, how seemingly unreasonable the Union was.

Friday morning we composed and sent letters to major trade customers and all remaining salesmen telling them of the stockholders' decision to liquidate. The Minneapolis and St. Paul newspapers both carried front page stories of the liquidation. Twin Cities television and radio stations carried the story Thursday night and Friday. The entire front page of Red Wing's DRE was filled with news of the Potteries. Duff had done some spadework and pieced together the events surrounding the company's last-ditch offer. Under one inch headlines proclaiming "DESPERATE FINAL BID FAILS" Duff wrote:

"A desperate, 11th hour bid to save the Potteries apparently sputtered into failure amid a series of Red Wing-New York telephone calls between sunset Wednesday and sunrise Thursday.

"The company agreed Wednesday morning to go considerably farther than ever before in wages and fringe benefits for Potteries workers. But this word never reached the five-man union negotiating committee in time for it to

forestall Thursday's vote of Potteries stockholders to liquidate.

"Here's the sequence of events as the DRE has been able
to piece them together: The six-man citizens committee -
which seems to have earned the praise and respect of both
sides in the long Potteries dispute - held its last joint session
with company and union representatives Tuesday night.
Negotiations stood at an impasse. The company's best offer
stood at $23,000 or $27,000, depending on who figures
it. And the union's latest stance was approximately double
the $27,000. Union and management representatives left the
meeting, but the six-man citizens group put together by
Mayor Jelatis was unwilling to give up. It fully agreed that
Potteries workers should have more money, but the question was where to find it.

"The committee was still exploring such avenues as obtaining more favorable hospital insurance rates for the
Potteries and persuading Minnesota's state institutions to
concentrate a large share of their dinnerware purchases with
Red Wing Potteries.

"(Gov. Harold LeVander's office was asked about the latter possibility, and he showed an immediate interest. Two
state officials were in Red Wing Wednesday to explore the
possibility.)

"Wednesday morning two citizens committee members called
again on Potteries president R. A. Gillmer and won his
consent to a more attractive pay package. Subject only to
board of directors approval, Gillmer offered immediately:

— 20 cents per hour more for non-incentive workers.
— 15 cents per hour for incentive workers.
— $4,700 in additional 'equity' raises for approximate-
ly 24 workers.
— A hospitalization insurance program based on a $30
daily room allowance.

"This total package would have raised the first-year cost
to the Potteries to $47,000. There also were second and
third-year provisions.

"By this time Joe Hammerschmidt, international representative for Local 6-430, was on his way back to New York City for the national convention of the Oil, Chemical, and Atomic Workers. He'd interrupted his convention stay earlier in the week to come home and resume negotiations.

"Mayor Jelatis couldn't reach Hammerschmidt at his New Trier home or the Minneapolis airport but finally got him on the telephone at 8:30 P.M. Wednesday in New York. Hammerschmidt promised to consult and call back. The return call from Hammerschmidt came at 4:30 A.M. Thursday. He told Jelatis that he saw no basis for further bargaining, that Potteries shareholders might as well go ahead and hold their liquidation vote.

"Hammerschmidt told the DRE this morning that he never understood the Mayor's call as relaying a company offer. It was only an 'iffy' proposition - would the union accept a settlement on this basis if the company would? In any event, Hammerschmidt added this morning, 'he had regarded the end of Red Wing Potteries as inevitable.'

"But word of the company's $47,000 pay package never reached the negotiating committee in whom Local 6-430 had placed full bargaining power. Four committee members told the DRE they had never heard of the $47,000 pay plan. The fifth member - union president Tilfer Chastain - said it was presented to him only as an 'iffy' proposition. 'Hammerschmidt called him at 4 A.M. Thursday,' Chastain said, 'but he didn't regard the $47,000 package as a company offer.'

" 'Not until noon Thursday,' Chastain went on, 'did he learn that the $47,000 package actually came from the company. And by then it was too late to get his negotiating committee together to meet with the citizens committee as requested.'

"Thus what the citizens committee went to bed Wednesday night thinking was the basis for 11th hour settlement, or at least continued bargaining, evaporated before dawn.

"The company management, it is understood, was willing

to ask shareholders to defer action Thursday if they had some indication the union would consider the $47,000 pay package. The $47,000 far exceeded the Potteries' average $29,000 profit after taxes over the last 10 years, but the management was willing to give it a try in hopes of saving the company.

"It was encouraged to do so by a series of suggestions - including all-out Red Wing community support - which the citizens committee had advanced as ways of boosting Potteries sales.

"The citizens committee took the company's $47,000 pay package directly to Hammerschmidt, it was understood, because one of the 'ground rules' for the whole citizens committee effort was that money matters would be discussed with the union committee only when Hammerschmidt was present."

We noted with interest the DRE's report that Hammerschmidt claimed that "he never understood the Mayor's call as relaying a company offer. It was only an 'iffy' proposition - would the union accept a settlement on this basis if the company would?" Hammerschmidt's only available course of action became clear to us - he was in the uncomfortable position of having to cast doubt on the authenticity of the offer, or as much as admit that he had been negligent in his responsibilities. We called Jelatis, as other members of the Citizens Committee had been doing, to reaffirm the nature of the conversation he had had with Hammerschmidt. Jelatis assured us that he had communicated the offer to Hammerschmidt clearly and in detail, as a company offer coming from President Gillmer, subject only to Board approval. Hammerschmidt was in a tough spot; he was, in effect, challenging the Mayor's integrity. Also, even if he had somehow, as he claimed, interpreted the offer as "iffy" and not coming from the company, the fact remained that he had still failed to show interest in the offer and had allowed the liquidation to take place. Even if he had regarded the offer as "iffy," it seemed he still owed it to his people to express interest in the hopes of forestalling liquidation. It appeared that he had placed himself in an untenable position; that he had been negligent in his duties and six of the most respected townspeople were witness to this negligence.

Another front page article summarized the entire state of affairs:

"POTTERIES IS DEAD

"Red Wing Potteries died quietly Thursday—90 years after the firm began and 85 days after its production workers took to the picket lines.

"The death scene was the company offices in the rambling old factory on W. Main St. Eighteen shareholders arrived singly and in twos and threes to vote 27,115 to 490 in favor of liquidating the firm that has made Red Wing known around the world.

"The closing and sale of the Potteries appears certain to be the largest single economic disaster here in several decades.

"The overwhelming vote to liquidate means that a petition will be filed in district court - probably sometime next week - asking the judge to appoint a receiver. Once a receiver is appointed, the company will have been taken out of the hands of the officers and directors. The receiver's job will be to sell all assets and get as much money as possible for the shareholders.

"There's no way to know how long liquidation will take - possibly a year or longer. Unless the receiver decides otherwise, the Potteries salesrooms will continue open here and in St. Paul and Rapid City, S. D., so long as merchandise is available.

"Picketing of the salesroom here continues today, just as it did yesterday during the shareholders' meeting.

"As the shareholders arrived, their names were checked off the master list. The list contained 167 names and represented all 31,444 outstanding shares of stock. The voters who filed upstairs for the meeting represented 27,605 shares. Among these shares were the sizable holdings of the Gillmer family. Prior to the meeting, some of the directors gathered in President R. A. Gillmer's office just off the reception room where newsmen were photographing the arrival of the shareholders. The officers were the last to go up to the meeting. Once they arrived, the business was handled rapidly. Only two shareholders spoke against liquidation. Between them they represented the 490 'no' votes. One opposed the liquidation on the grounds that it was 'too soon.' The other said it just didn't seem right to close the Potteries. It was all over in less than 40 minutes.

"President Gillmer made the announcement to newsmen, including the two television crews which had set up their gear on the lawn just outside the office door. He started a short statement with these words: 'It's a very sad day.'

"Representatives of striking Local 6-430 Oil, Chemical and Atomic Workers declined extensive comment on the liquidation vote. International representative Joe Hammerschmidt was contacted at a convention in New York. He said: 'This is no different than what we expected. We expected the vote to go this way.' He added: 'It's a sorry thing - no question about that. But it was inevitable. It was going to happen. I think the end of the Potteries was coming regardless.'

"Local President Tilfer Chastain said picketing of the salesroom would continue as usual and declined further comment.

"Gillmer said the liquidation was made necessary by a combination of 'imports, tariffs and labor problems.'

"The labor problems first came into public focus June 1 when about 100 production and maintenance workers walked off their jobs at the termination of the old contract. As the strike progressed, bitterness increased and picket line tactics were in regular dispute. Up to the final days, only a handful of negotiation sessions were held by union and management. State and federal conciliators were totally unsuccessful in bridging the gap. A massive last-ditch effort was started Aug. 17 by a six-man citizens committee that met virtually around the clock with only last Sunday off.

The sessions brought occasional brighter hopes. But the end result still was failure.

"Gillmer was visibly tired as he sat in his office Thursday with newsmen after the shareholders' vote. Also present were Milton Holst, company attorney, Irving Vick, treasurer, and R. S. Gillmer, operations manager. Gillmer said the liquidation here will leave the nation with only six potteries making 'high style' items for domestic (home) use.

"Current plans call for some small-scale manufacturing to continue here with the supervisory and sales staff that has been manning the pot shops since the strike began. Permission of the court will be necessary once a receiver is named. The production will be geared to filling orders now on hand and it could take a month or longer.

"In answer to a question, Gillmer said: 'We haven't given any thought to having any of the strikers come back.' No formal discharge has been given the approximately 100 strikers. But the company will officially cease to exist when a receiver is appointed.

"Total employment by the firm here and in its out-of-town salesrooms has ranged seasonally from 135 to 150 employees. Annual payroll has been between $350,000 and $400,000.

"Final arrangements are yet to be made with the non-strikers.

"Gillmer discounted the possibility that any other pottery manufacturer might be interested in taking over the plant here. 'Potteries in general have been having a difficult time of things,' Gillmer said. And he believes the Red Wing plant to be additionally hampered because it is not adapted to modern manufacturing processes.

"He declined to speculate on the future of the salesroom with adjacent Country Store and gift shop. 'It could become whatever its buyer wants,' he said. The gift shop and Country Store were opened a year ago last spring. Both places were popular with the hordes of tourists that came to shop and to tour the potteries.

"Gillmer and Holst said they could make no guess on what shareholders would receive per share. In addition to the buildings owned by the potteries, assets include the land on which they're located and 'some cash,' Gillmer said.

"The potteries has been among the top 10 taxpayers in the county and the top five in the city. Last year it paid some $32,000 in personal property and real estate taxes.

"Union spokesmen have since the beginning of the strike pooh-poohed the idea that the company would close. They charged in a paid advertisement in the DRE July 13 that rumors of liquidation were an attempt to 'blackmail the people in the community and the employees.' The statement continued: 'We will assure the company that this method will not work this time. We are determined to continue this strike whatever time it takes to gain a just and necessary settlement. If the company is serious in closing, we are concerned. But we are not afraid. A quick death is better than the slow death we have been suffering for years.'

"The seven driveways to the salesroom were the major source of bitterness in the strike. Weekends until Aug. 5 brought throngs of pickets which the company charged with manhandling customers and using abusive language. In testimony before District Judge John Friedrich the Gillmers said the strikers threw nails under car tires, rocked cars and threatened various forms of violence. On Aug. 4 Judge Friedrich issued a formal restraining order which largely brought an end to the picket line dispute.

"The decision to ask a shareholder vote on liquidation came at a directors' meeting in the first week of August. In announcing the decision Gillmer said: 'We reluctantly have decided we cannot continue in business.'

He said Thursday that his personal plans are not decided. "His son is 'open to offers.' The younger Gillmer said he has been approached on jobs in the Twin Cities and expects he eventually will have to make his home there. 'But I hate to leave Red Wing,' he said.

"The elder Gillmer stubbed out cigarettes in a potteries-made ashtray as he talked. It had obviously been the most difficult afternoon in 85 difficult days."

The fact that the Union planned to continue their picketing mattered very little to us at this point. While it seemingly would serve no useful purpose under the circumstances, it was their choice and we had no method, or real need to stop it. Since their activities had been curtailed by the court, the picketing had become the least of our worries.

Under a large picture of two leering pickets, a man and a woman, the DRE reported:

"STRIKERS UNSURE OF NEXT MOVE
We can still smile

"Pickets at the strike-bound Red Wing Potteries maintained their good humor today despite Thursday's vote by stockholders to liquidate the 90-year-old corporation.

"The strikers were uncertain about their future. Some said they will continue the picketing until the salesroom closes - or at least until liquidation proceedings are filed in Goodhue County District Court. None appeared sure of their next step. Some have already begun looking for new jobs but the picket line is staffed with the same number today as was there a week ago.

" 'Now's the time to start looking, I guess,' one striker said when asked about future employment. 'We didn't win and we didn't lose,' commented another. 'We won as far as working conditions go,' said a woman picket. 'We stood in dirt up to our ankles long enough.'

"Tilfer Chastain, president of the striking Oil, Chemical and Atomic Workers Local 6-430, was not available for comment this morning.

"Union members on the picket line said they expect a general membership meeting will be scheduled for Monday or Tuesday.

"Meanwhile, Norris Mulvania at the State Employment office here said some of the pottery workers were beginning to register for new jobs today. 'This is the first time they started coming in,' Mulvania said. 'But we don't have half of them yet.'

"According to a prior Supreme Court ruling, liquidation of a company ends a strike and workers should be eligible for unemployment pay if they can't find new jobs immediately. Mulvania said, however, the date of liquidation is still a technical point that must be cleared up. If it is from the day of the stockholders vote the workers would be eligible now. The District Court may have to make the determination.

"None of the strikers yet have sought help from the county welfare office. They will be given assistance as needed, officials said."

We were sincere in our praise of the Citizens Committee. These six people had forsaken their own businesses and families and worked tirelessly day and night to save the Potteries for the community. To a man, they had made every effort to remain neutral and keep foremost in their minds the settlement of the strike. While we felt a great deal of bitterness toward Jelatis in his failure to assure us police protection, we applauded him for the role he had played as chairman of the Citizens group. Although, as far as we knew, there had been no replies from the Federal officials contacted by the Citizens, they had made every effort to secure the future of the company and provide a reason for continuing operations.

With our respect for the Citizens, we were somewhat disappointed at the vagueness and indecisiveness of the statement they issued to the press:

"GROUP ISSUES STATEMENT

"The Citizens Committee was established in response to a widespread feeling that an all-out community effort should be made to help in any way possible to resolve the apparent impasse in the labor-management conflict at the Red Wing Potteries.

"The primary reason for public involvement in a private conflict was a deep concern for the welfare of some 140 employees and for a nationally-renowned industry uniquely identified with Red Wing.

"This committee has been in almost continuous session from its inception last Thursday, August 17, until the present time with one day off on Sunday. After the initial private meeting on Thursday afternoon to discuss procedure, the committee met separately with the labor representatives on Friday morning and the company representatives on Friday afternoon.

"Following these, several meetings were held with both groups together starting on last Saturday afternoon. It is the feeling of the committee members that both sides developed some understanding of the other's problems and attempted to bridge the impasse between the union proposals and the company efforts to see an economic future in the business.

"Since numerous confidential matters were disclosed and openly discussed by all parties, the Citizens Committee members feel it would be imprudent to make any public comment at this time regarding the proposals and other details revealed in confidence by both company and labor union representatives."

> /s/ George A. Bergwall, Spencer Broughton,
> Demetrius G. Jelatis, Ora G. Jones, Jr.,
> Clarence W. Josephson, Kenneth Tri.

I called Broughton to discuss the statement and he informed me that because of the fact that certain of the members' positions were dependent on the good will of Labor, the committee had decided not to include anything in their statement that might be interpreted as a criticism of the Union. However, he explained, the Citizens stood ready to publically intervene should the Union representatives make any statements contradicting the facts of the situation.

We learned that afternoon that one of the Citizens had contacted District Judge Friedrich to ask him if the stockholders' decision to liquidate was irreversible. The Citizens Committee reported that the action supposedly was reversible; another meet-

ing of the stockholders could be held and a motion passed to
reverse the decision, if such action were taken before the liquidation petition was filed in District Court and the court appointed a receiver. Thus, we were faced with the prospect of
more negotiating sessions. As far as the Board of Directors and
company Management were concerned, the action the stockholders had taken was final. The Union had had the opportunity
to show interest in our last-ditch offer and failed to do so. Attorney Holst had begun to prepare the necessary papers for the
court, and notices of the liquidation had gone out to customers
and salesmen. The direction was set. Further, there was a question of whether we were equipped emotionally to open the whole
thing up again.

We also learned that Chastain had requested that the Citizens Committee meet with the Union committee. The OCAW
Convention was over in New York and Hammerschmidt was
returning that evening, and would attend the meeting, Chastain
said. Out of curiosity, I asked one of the Citizens to call me if
the meeting broke up before midnight.

No call came, and I did not learn what had taken place until
the following morning. Hammerschmidt had never showed up
at the meeting. Why, no one seemed to know. Thus, the Citizens
met with the Shop Committee alone until nearly 3 A.M. A
member of the Citizens group informed me that they had been
rather rough with the Union, and Chastain had spent much
of his time defending Hammerschmidt's action, or lack of action.
One of Chastain's reported defenses of Hammerschmidt's failure to notify all of the Shop Committee of the company's offer
was that "long distance phone calls from New York were expensive." The general impression of the meeting was that the
Union was still convinced they would be going back to work;
they presented a unified front and were not ready to criticize or
overthrow Hammerschmidt. We reasoned that to overthrow Hammerschmidt at this point would be admitting, in effect, that they
were fools and had been misled for the last three months. This
would be a very difficult admission to make.

In reporting this meeting, the DRE noted that "the parking

lot was crowded at 10 P.M. when the meeting started with cars of strikers. Estimates of the crowd ranged up to fifty persons. The spectators did not enter the meeting." No one seemed to know why these fifty people had showed up at the Central Research parking lot; whether it was to protest the action of their Union, the Citizens Committee, or just because they had nothing better to do.

That weekend, August 26 and 27, the salesroom did more than double the business of the biggest weekend in its history. Customers wanted to fill in their dinnerware sets or buy some Red Wing Pottery before it was no longer available. They literally were buying Red Wing Pottery like it was "going out of style."

From the number of pickets that asked us that weekend "if the company really made that offer" we guessed that the Union leaders were doing everything they could to make the offer appear as unauthorized, "iffy," and not really coming from the company.

Sunday afternoon we were witness to the ultimate in efficient law enforcement. One of Red Wing's policemen came into the store and informed Gillmer that he was going to have to ticket those cars in the parking lot whose bumpers were extending over the sidewalk unless they were moved at once. Gillmer could not believe his ears. Customers' bumpers had been extending over the little-used sidewalk since the salesroom was built in 1954, and we had never heard a word about it. Now, in light of all that had taken place over the summer, this cop had the audacity to come in and tell us he was going to ticket our customers for something that had been going on, unquestioned, for thirteen years. This same officer had been witness to the scraping and rocking of cars, the strewing of nails, the blocking of drives, the pushing of customers, and the vile obscenities and threats that had occurred all summer, and never once had he or any of his comrades lifted a finger to make an arrest or write a ticket for one of the strikers. This, to us, was a blatant effort at harassment, and typified the police attitude throughout the long summer. Gillmer, frantically trying to wrap customer purchases on the busiest day in salesroom history, lost his temper. He told the officer that if he was going to start ticketing he had better get started, because he did not intend to ask every customer in the packed store if their automobile happened to be one of those with the bumper extending over the sidewalk. He added that it must have taken a lot of "guts" to come in to see him on something like this. The officer departed and, to the best of our knowledge, left no tickets in the process.

Jelatis had met with Hammerschmit sometime over the weekend, and called on Monday to tell us the Union wanted a meeting with us that night. Then he asked the inevitable question, "Is the company's $47,000 package still available to the Union?" We answered that, considering what had transpired, the offer was no longer available. We explained that regardless of the legal technicalities that recently had been brought to our attention, company Management and Directors regarded the stockholders' decision as irrevocable from a practical standpoint. We were in a worse position today to offer $47,000 than we were last Wednesday when the offer had been made. Trade customers had been notified of the liquidation and salesmen released in the interim. We had embarked upon a course and there was no turning back. Further, the Union had had an opportunity to forestall the liquidation vote and had chosen not to. Why should we expect them to accept now? Jelatis said he understood completely, but requested that we meet with the Union anyway. We reluctantly agreed.

Jelatis added as an afterthought that Hammerschmidt had claimed that our Labor Attorney, Richard Felhaber, had not been present in any meetings since August 11 because he chose to represent us no longer. The implication was that Felhaber, a highly reputable lawyer, had abandoned us because of "our untenable bargaining position" and a "misrepresentation of our financial position." We found this completely preposterous, and evidence of the lengths to which Hammerschmidt would go in discrediting us. Nevertheless, after closing with Jelatis, R. A. Gillmer called Felhaber to report the story. Felhaber was equally shocked by the allegation and told Gillmer, "Tell them it's a damn lie."

On Monday, August 28, KCUE reported the company's offer and the varied reactions of Union people:

"There is a wide span of views about the nature of the last offer made by the Potteries. What one believes seems to depend on the last person you talk to. Some blame poor communications between the union's business agent, Joe Hammerschmidt of New Trier, and the union bargaining committee. Some in the union think that the Potteries' offer is still nothing the union can deal with, since it was never put down in writing prior to Thursday's stockholders' vote to close the Potteries. 'It has to be made at the bargaining table,' insist members of the union bargaining committee.

"Some unionists feel the Citizens Committee, by being in the picture at this time, is gumming up the works. Other union members, however, feel nothing would have changed in any way if there had not been such a group, half approved by labor.

"At least one member of the union's bargaining committee thinks the 47-thousand dollar offer will not be considered valid until actually presented by Gillmer of the Potteries at a bargaining session.

"Hammerschmidt and other union members feel that publicity about the failure to act on the 'last-ditch offer' is designed to put Union in a bad light. Hammerschmidt conferred Sunday afternoon with Mayor D. G. Jelatis of the committee about the newspaper and radio stories dealing with the 47-thousand dollar company offer.

"A handful of union members have told friends they don't like the way negotiations have been conducted, but they feel powerless to do anything about it. A number of months ago the union membership placed all negotiating power in the hands of its bargaining committee. At least several of those men on strike have told friends they either don't wish to attend union meetings now or, when they go, they say nothing for fear of making enemies among fellow workers."

We were to meet the Union at the Central Research conference room at 9 o'clock that night, and were distraught to learn that the Citizens Committee did not plan to attend. We thought it unwise to meet alone with the Union. We judged that Hammerschmidt's back was up against the wall; that he had to concoct an excuse for not acting on our offer in order to clear himself publicly and with the rank and file. Therefore, we felt he would do anything to anger us into a statement to which he could reply, "See, these people are unreasonable and never had any intentions of a $47,000 offer." We wanted a witness present at the meeting and called Jelatis. He agreed to sit in on the session. Milton Holst, Attorney and Board member, also was to attend. We agreed beforehand that we must refrain, at all costs, from anger and making any statements for which we would later be sorry.

We filed into the Central Research conference room at 9 P.M. for what was to be our last meeting with the Union. We did not know what to expect. Would they realize this was the end, that we were not bluffing, and plead for an opportunity to come back to work on our terms? Or would they cling rigidly to the hard position they had adopted from the beginning? We were interested to find out.

As usual, the room was filled with tension as we took our seats around the conference table. President Gillmer took his usual seat at one end of the long table and Hammerschmidt at the other. Hammerschmidt opened with the inevitable question, "Was the $47,000 offer still on the table?" R. A. Gillmer gave Hammerschmidt the same answer as he had given Jelatis. He explained in detail the company's pessimistic sales outlook and the things that had transpired since the liquidation vote, making the company less able to offer the $47,000. Customers had been notified and found other sources of supply and Red Wing salesmen had taken new lines. Key employees, such as Gerry Ross, had made other commitments. We were too far down the road to expect that any turnabout would be met with even partial success. When Gillmer had finished Hammerschmidt said that that was all he wanted to know, but gave no indication that the

Union would be willing to settle for the $47,000. While the Union had never offered any constructive suggestions to our problem of getting back into business, Hammerschmidt did say that night that he "could bring the national OCAW resources to bear" in our problems of revitalizing the business.

Midway through the meeting the phone rang and Jelatis left the room to answer it. The caller wished to speak to someone from the company. Holst left to take the call. He returned shortly to announce that someone had just thrown a large rock through one of the back windows at the salesroom. All eyes turned to the Union awaiting their reaction. Chastain took the floor to proclaim that he was sure none of his people were responsible. After he had repeated this thought three or four times I asked him how he could be so certain since I could not even be positive that it was not someone from the company who had done it. The matter was dropped, but we derived some private satisfaction from the fact that the incident seemed to confirm our feelings toward the people across the table.

Hammerschmidt resumed the conversation by restating his contention that our employees would be better off on relief, welfare, and social security than they would be returning to work on company terms. We had never been able to see the logic in this argument and we still could not.

We knew that Chastain and many Unionists felt, or claimed to feel, that we had planned to liquidate from the very beginning. I told Chastain that I recognized this was their contention, and asked him if he still felt, at that point, that we had desired liquidation from the beginning. He stated that he no longer believed this to be true, that we had not set out to dissolve the corporation. This admission gave us some small measure of satisfaction.

Jelatis suggested the two groups split and separately discuss a statement to the public on the present impasse. We returned shortly and Hammerschmidt stated that the Union desired to hold off on any public statement. Why they chose to remain silent, we had no idea. We had decided to ask Hammerschmidt's permission to take back certain employees to help finish in-process ware. We explained that it would give these employees an opportunity for some income, however brief. He hedged on the answer, wanting to await "future developments" before giving the go-ahead.

Thus, what was to be our final meeting with the Union ended only one hour after it had begun. We had entered the meeting with no false hopes, and were not surprised at the Union's still uncompromising position. Our main thought as we left the meeting was that we hoped the company could die a peaceful death, and we would be allowed to proceed with liquidation unmolested. We had had our fill of the strike - the picketing, the hostility, and the futility of hoping against hope - and our only desire was to be left alone to proceed with the unpleasant task of liquidating all company assets.

The next morning there were still about fifteen somewhat dispirited pickets on duty at salesroom driveways. Why they chose to continue picketing we did not know, and did not particularly care. The picketing had lost all of its aggressiveness, and was in no way deterring the steady onslaught of customers who desired some Red Wing Pottery before there was no more available.

The six-man Citizens Committee, who had worked so tirelessly for the past two weeks, met for breakfast Tuesday morning and agreed to terminate their activity. The DRE carried Chairman Jelatis' brief statement:

"The Citizens Committee objective was to get the two parties together in the hope of finding a common meeting ground. The two parties met in final session last night. The Citizens Committee members met at breakfast this morning and agreed to terminate their activity. Any further statements at this time will have to come from the Red Wing Potteries Management or the OCAW (Oil, Chemical and Atomic Workers) Union. The Citizens Committee action apparently means that all hopes have vanished for resurrection of the Potteries."

Tuesday's mail brought R. A. Gillmer a sympathy card. The card proclaimed, "With deepest sympathy to you in your sorrow." A newspaper statement had been clipped out and scotch-taped underneath the condolence: "Richard A. Gillmer, President and General Manager, announced the liquidation vote and said, 'This is a very sad day.'" Underneath the clipping were the neatly typed words, "Who do you think you are kidding?" On the back of the card was Gillmer's newspaper picture and words clipped from the DRE to form the statement, "President R. A. Gillmer Killed Potteries." The card concerned us to the extent that a person who would go to the trouble to compose such a macabre message might well be motivated to go to greater lengths for revenge.

We learned during the day that the Union had scheduled a membership meeting at 7:30 that night at the Labor Temple. The situation could likely lead to violence; the membership would have to be told that it was all over, that there was no hope of returning to work, and we guessed that Hammerschmidt would try to absolve himself and the Shop Committee of all blame and make every effort to transfer the blame to the company. Depending upon how it was handled, the rank and file could very well leave the meeting with all the pent-up hate and frustration of the bitter summer demanding an outlet, and we would be the likely targets.

With this in mind we called Jelatis, and found that he had already been in touch with Police Chief Lenway and Hammerschmidt on the matter. Recognizing the potential violence in the situation, he had ordered Lenway to give the salesroom and plant complete surveillance that night, and had asked Hammerschmidt to avoid statements of an inflammatory or provocative nature.

While our fears were proven groundless, I spent a restless night awaiting imagined Union retribution. We were to learn the Union's version of what occurred at the meeting the following day in the DRE:

"STRIKERS BACK LEADERS

"Potteries Union President Tilfer Chastain said members gave a unanimous vote of confidence to union leadership Tuesday night.

"Local 6-430 of the Oil, Chemical and Atomic Workers had its first membership meeting since Potteries shareholders Thursday voted to liquidate the struck firm.

"Chastain said only one vote was taken at the session in the Labor Temple. He said the vote was unanimously in support of all action that has been taken during the strike by the five-member local bargaining committee, the president and the union's international representative.

"International Representative Joseph Hammerschmidt of New Trier attended the session which broke up at about 9:45 p.m. The session was scheduled to start at 7:30.

"Chastain said a detailed union statement will be issued sometime soon. Certain other things have to be done first, he said, and indicated the statement probably would not be forthcoming today.

"Hammerschmidt could not be reached for comment.

"Chastain said the statement would be issued jointly by Hammerschmidt and the local leadership. Chastain said the meeting drew the 'largest attendance yet.' He declined to give a number.

"Union membership includes about 100 strikers.

"Chastain said strike benefit checks were given out at the session, plus 'a little extra.'

"Vernon Peterson, chief union steward and member of the bargaining committee, said Hammerschmidt discussed efforts that will be made to relocate the strikers in other jobs. Peterson said the state employment office in St. Paul will be contacted and he said Hammerschmidt pledged to do 'everything in his power' to find new jobs.

"The strikers were told that some of them might have to organize car pools or even move their families to other towns.

"Other members of the bargaining committee had these comments:

"DON HOPHAN: Chastain can supply full information on the meeting. The relocation of workers was discussed but no action was taken.

"MIKE KERG: There wasn't much to the meeting. It lasted about an hour and consisted mostly of formalities. Very little was done about relocating workers, but we're checking. "The union has no other special meetings scheduled at this time. The next regular meeting of the group is scheduled Sept. 11, but a special meeting could be called at any time. "Attorneys for the Potteries apparently still are preparing the petition to district court asking that a receiver be appointed to take over the company. There were indications that the petition would not be filed today. "Picketing at the salesroom is continuing."

Chastain's claim that the membership had unanimously approved all action taken during the strike by the Union Committee was greeted by management with skepticism and what humor we were able to muster at that point. We viewed it as an effort to paint a rosy picture for the public, absolving the Union leaders of all error, miscalculation and wrongdoing over the course of the summer. That a few Union members would not have questions as to the Committee's strategy was inconceivable. The less enthusiastic comments by committee members Hophan and Kerg seemed to cast further doubt on Chastain's euphoric statements.

Chastain's mysteriously vague promise of a forthcoming detailed statement concerned us. Nothing good could possibly come of it, and more likely than not it would be a full-scale attack on Management. We derived comfort from the Citizens' promise to intervene should Union representatives issue any public statements contrary to fact.

The preponderance of people with whom we talked felt we now "had the Union licked," and that if we desired to resume operations we might do so without a Union. Despite Chastain's claims, certain community leaders felt that the membership was thoroughly dissatisfied with their leadership, that public sympathy had turned strongly toward the company, and that the Union was thoroughly beaten. Although we derived some pleasure from such statements, we explained that the company also was beaten and could resume operations only at substantial and unjustifiable risk to the stockholders and their remaining assets.

On Thursday, August 31, I talked with one of the strikers who had asked to enter the plant to reclaim some of his personal articles. He said mysteriously that we would be receiving a letter from the Union and our reaction to the contents of that letter would determine the Union's next move. We had no idea what to expect and awaited the letter apprehensively. The letter, signed by Hammerschmidt, arrived in early morning and stated simply, "Effective August 31 at 8 A.M. the Union has withdrawn its pickets due to circumstances that appear to have eliminated the labor dispute." The DRE reported the letter and the withdrawal of pickets:

"PICKETS LEAVE PLANT

"The pickets left the Potteries at 6 P.M. Wednesday night and they apparently won't be back.

"Potteries President R. A. Gillmer received this letter from the strikers: 'Effective Aug. 31 at 8 A.M. the union has withdrawn its pickets due to circumstances that appear to have eliminated the labor dispute.'

"The letter was signed by Joseph L. Hammerschmidt, international representative for the Oil, Chemical and Atomic Workers.

"The 'circumstances' mentioned in the letter apparently was the vote last Thursday by Potteries shareholders to liquidate the firm that has been struck since June by Local 6-430.

"The liquidation will be started when a petition is filed in district court asking that a receiver be appointed. The petition had not yet been filed this morning.

"Local President Tilfer Chastain said today that a statement will be issued by the union 'in the near future.'

"First word of a statement came Tuesday in advance of a special membership meeting. But Chastain said today that 'futher developments' will be awaited before a statement is issued.

"Chastain said the five-man bargaining committee of the

local will work with Hammerschmidt in preparing the statement.

"Chastain said he plans to meet today with Norris Mulvania of the State Employment office here. Chastain said methods of re-locating Potteries workers will be discussed, along with the possibilities for unemployment compensation. "Chastain said Hammerschmidt will be in Red Wing 'from day to day,' and that no specific meeting times have been set."

Thus, on the last day of August, exactly three months after the strike had begun, the Union had withdrawn their pickets and the strike was officially ended. We were at a loss to guess what kind of reaction the Union was expecting from us. Were we expected to be overwhelmingly grateful to Hammerschmidt and the Union for withdrawing pickets? It was only logical for them to stop picketing after what had taken place in the last few days. The pickets were no longer hurting the salesroom business in any way and, in light of the liquidation, further picketing would be a total waste of time for all concerned. We made no reaction to the letter whatsoever, and whether this disappointed the Union we never learned.

Chastain's further reference to a forthcoming Union statement continued to bother us. His statement that "further developments" would be awaited before a statement would be issued completely puzzled us. What "further developments" could he possibly be referring to? We imagined all sorts of Union plots, from monumental law suits to attacks on our personal integrity.

The sight of the salesroom without pickets was unique. The pickets had become such an accepted part of the landscape after three months that the empty driveways and sidewalks gave one the feeling an integral part of the whole had been removed. Their absence recalled the catastrophe of the summer and the many indignities customers had suffered. We were still receiving angry letters.

From Batavia, Ohio, a woman wrote of the disgraceful conduct of the pickets, but diminished her argument by revealing underlying racial prejudices:

"The Red Wing Potteries is very well known therefore while vacationing in Minnesota the latter part of July, we made it a point to drive to Red Wing with the intention of visiting the Pottery and selecting a few gifts. A group of hoodlums blocked the entrance to the parking lot, they threatened us with black paint to be splashed all over our car, another came racing down the road slamming his brakes within inches of our car. Rather than risk bodily injury by these ruffians we drove away.

"It is certainly appalling, in a free country to be antagonized by people conducting themselves so disgracefully. The colored are shocking the country with their riots but we apparently have many whites who are just as disgusting. Such actions do very little to attract tourists to Minnesota, not to mention the economy of Red Wing.

"If these people are so unappreciative and dissatisfied with what this country has to offer, there is public transportation leaving daily for their homeland. I am unable to convince myself that American born white individuals would act in such a manner."

In addition to the letters complaining of picket line abuse, we had received many letters from salesroom customers and trade accounts expressing sympathy for the shutdown.

From a Northfield, Minnesota, woman:

"It is with real sorrow that I learned of the closing of the pottery at Red Wing. We always looked forward to a trip to Red Wing to the pottery on various trips during the year.

"The people of Minnesota were proud of Red Wing Pottery. I have heard people with wonderful backgrounds in classical art speak highly of some of the designs and products at Red Wing.

"It really seems as if this should be a 'cause' for the people of Minnesota. I wish very much that the economic problems could be overcome to save Red Wing Pottery."

From a retailer in New Orleans who saw great political implications in the situation:

"I received your letter telling us that you were closing down

the company and I just had to extend my sympathy in this
American tragedy. It is being repeated over and over in
every area and I could weep for this great and wonderful
country. Every one is the loser because, as you say, foreign
competition helped by our own government policies is gradually taking over field after field and it looks like the idiots
in Washington are tumbling over themselves trying to give
away or make easier the give away of the American strength.
I watched the cotton business go down the drain some years
ago—cotton was priced out of the world market, then the
government subsidized it to make it competitive, then they
shipped it cheaper to foreign countries than it could be
bought here, and it was spun on modern mills that had been
built with the tax money of the American business man who
was being put out of business.

"As long as they use the Fabian tactic of nipping off one
small part of the economy at a time, there will be no organized and general outcry until eventually we will have a
completely Socialized government and the United Socialized Soviet Republic has said that Socialism is just the first
step to Communism.

"You had a good American product and I used to sell it
on that basis. It is like watching a giant being shredded by
ants—our great country getting deeper in debt, becoming
more and more mired in foreign affairs, meddling in things
that are not our business, giving away our sustenance and
getting hated for doing it."

From a Chicago woman:

"Thank you for sending the newspaper to me, I've been
most concerned and of course had no way of knowing the
progress of this devastating thing.

"I feel so sorry for everyone involved, it certainly is an
end to a proud and upstanding organization and an era of
a town.

"It is disgusting to think that any group (Union) can be
so ruthless and un-American in its operation. Causing hardship and panic to so many, to say nothing of the heartbreak

and physical and mental despair to those who have worked so hard and so faithfully.

"I know you'll all be very busy for a long while with the unpleasant work which lies ahead.

"My devotion and loyalty is with you as well as my wish for a brighter tomorrow for each of you."

From a retailer in Newton Highland, Massachusetts:

"Your letter of August 28 brought sadness and gloom to our store. Although we have never been one of your biggest customers, we did at one time, operate our own small pottery and each news of a closing of one is met here with the greatest sympathy—as though a special way of life is fast disappearing—never to be seen again. We extend our thanks for your past service and good product."

From the president of a competitive pottery:

"We were all shocked to learn of the closing of Red Wing Potteries. What a shame that our country has reached the stage where it is almost impossible to talk to employees concerning the basic facts of life.

"The misunderstandings that now exist over the profits, costs, etc., are a deep concern to me. I would appreciate very much your suggestions as to how we can better present this information to employees to avoid a stalemate such as you have experienced.

"There are not many of our companies left in the United States, and it hurts to see one as old as Red Wing close its doors. You have my complete sympathy."

Thus, the month of August brought a conclusion to the bitter three-month struggle. The strike was officially ended and the 90-year-old business had drawn its last breath. Salesroom business for the month was slightly over $56,000, off from $63,500 the previous year. Business had fallen off drastically the first half of the month, but picked up significantly in the second half when word of the court order reached customers and they learned that it was once again safe to visit the Potteries salesroom.

The month of August had been one of anguish. We had been frantic with the state of affairs in the first days of the month. The picketing had reached unimagined levels of abuse and we were distraught over what we perceived as the Union's unwillingness to bargain. Business prospects were getting worse with each passing day. The situation was such that a conclusion was mandatory, both from an emotional and a business stand-point. We could not continue under those circumstances. Any conclusion was better than no conclusion at all. In retrospect we felt we had offered the Union a reasonable alternative; they had chosen to reject it. Thus, a conclusion was reached, perhaps the least beneficial for all concerned; yet with it came the comfort of future certainty. Employees could look for new jobs, Management could proceed with the liquidation, and we could all stop hoping in a situation that lacked hope.

EULOGY

"In the final analysis, no union can gain any-thing—I am speaking now of American unions, not a Communist-controlled union—no union can gain anything by putting the fellow out of business who fills the pay envelope. The interests of the worker and the employer must be iden-tical in an industry because they have both got to get their livelihood from whatever is pro-duced by the industry."

GEORGE MEANY

The Red Wing Potteries was officialy and irreversibly dead. The Management and the Citizens Committee acting for the community had explored every apparent avenue to save the dying company; yet she had passed on in spite of all efforts.

The community, however, found the Potteries' death a diffi-cult fact to accept. In the first week of September we had two community groups approach us in an effort to raise the com-pany from the grave. Other than the emotional feeling that "Red Wing just cannot lose its Pottery" these representatives had nothing original to offer. President Gillmer patiently an-swered their questions and gently rejected their time-worn ideas for salvation. While they undoubtedly had honorable intentions, it was improbable that these people could suggest something, as outsiders, that we had not considered dozens of times in the course of the strike. We were cast in a role not unlike the foot-ball coach who falls victim to the "Monday morning quarter-backs." More likely than not our strategy was second-guessed at every coffee session in town.

On Wednesday, September 6, District Judge John B. Friedrich signed the liquidation petition and appointed R. A. Gillmer as the receiver in charge of liquidating the firm. With this action, any hopes were quashed that there could be another vote of Potteries stockholders reversing the decision to liquidate. Thus, we were left with our bitterness and memories. We reviewed many times the events of the summer and speculated on the Union's motives.

In retrospect we saw June as a month of uncertainty. Both employees and Management were novices in the ways of a strike; we were experimenting and feeling our way. There was no panic and the strike had begun on almost an amicable basis. We expected a settlement by the middle of July and felt we could weather the shutdown without serious detriment. There was no question in our mind that we would keep the retail store open; the busy summer season was upon us and the income generated by the store was critical to our survival.

As it turned out the salesroom became a logical outlet for the hostilities of the strikers. We were unique as manufacturers in having a company-owned retail outlet on the premises. Without the store, we would have shut down operations and, as in most strikes, pickets would have patrolled the factory without any real target for their animosity. The strike would have been an economic test of endurance. However, the activity at the salesroom and the evidence of continued income served as a source of irritation for the Union and, as such, provided the pickets a very concrete object upon which to concentrate. As the month of June progressed and the mere presence of pickets failed to discourage customers, the strikers became desperate and resorted to more severe tactics on the picket line. Under the tutelage of Joe Hammerschmidt, the strikers became more "proficient" at their picketing. Outsiders began to appear on the picket lines and, protected by their anonymity, led the crowds to greater forms of harassment. With the absence of a clear-cut police position the pickets moved logically toward greater disorder, testing their limits to see just how much they could get away with.

By the end of June we knew we were in a war - the positions had been defined. We were sick of the strike by that early date; the weekend picketing and the seven-day work week was beginning to make itself felt psychologically and physically.

Despite the lack of progress in negotiations we entered July with the conviction that the strike would be settled by the middle of the month. The picketing increased in intensity, and when the strikers celebrated the Fourth of July by strewing nails in the drives, a new dimension was added to the picketing. Company Directors began to push for a settlement in the first weeks of July but our feelings, supported by Attorney Felhaber, that the time was not yet "ripe" for a settlement resulted in July 15 passing with no meetings. By this time the rank and file had reached such a peak of anti-company feeling that some mellowing of feelings was necessary if we were ever to reach an agreement. Their hate, anger and frustration were matched by our own. We felt it was Hammerschmidt's job to bring the people back down to a reasonable level; yet to our knowledge he never made any efforts toward this end. The nail strewing during negotiating meetings, and Hammerschmidt's failure to heed the conciliator's plea to cool down, were proof to us that we were dealing with an uncompromising man.

When the middle of July passed with no settlement, we were faced with the uncomfortable realization that there was no logical end in sight to the strike. Company salesmen and trade customers began to sever their Red Wing ties. By the end of the month pickets were engaging in practices which in our view were clearly illegal, yet the police remained passive. The last two weeks in July salesroom business fell off substantially. We felt completely alone in our struggle during most of July. The last week in the month, however, we began to feel the tide of public opinion swing to our defense. People were beginning to recognize what was occurring on our picket lines and were beginning to voice disapproval of the Union tactics. The small solace we felt at the emergence of this public opinion did nothing to alleviate the basic panic we felt at the apparent hopelessness of the situation. As we entered August we were desperate for a conclusion.

While we had talked continuously of a court order to limit picketing, we had allowed ourselves to be detained in this effort on the advice of Attorney Felhaber. However, in the face of our total desperation, Felhaber pursued a court order in the opening week of August. The order took effect the first weekend of the month and did a great deal to relieve the anxiety and tension we had experienced as part of the weekend picketing. It left us free to concentrate solely on the major problem confronting us - settlement of the strike.

Despite the increasing frequency of negotiating meetings in the first weeks of August no progress was made, and company Directors saw no alternative but to call stockholders together to consider liquidation. Revealing our financial statements to the Union on August 9 could logically have been a turning point, but the Union's refusal to modify their demands at the next meeting eliminated this hope. The conciliators apparently had also lost hope because they scheduled no further meetings after August 11. We were emotionally exhausted from the re-occurring experience of sensing a ray of hope and then having this hope evaporate. By the middle of August it looked as though all hope was gone and we would unquestionably liquidate the company.

However, the patient was not to succumb so easily. A group of Red Wing citizens asked if they might act as conciliators in an effort to save the company. So the flame of hope flickered weakly again. The Citizens Committee worked night and day for the next ten days exploring every alternative to achieve a settlement. The Union's first year demands were modified slightly to $53,000, but we held to our offer of $30,000, feeling it was all we could offer and expect to remain in business.

Hammerschmidt returned to an OCAW Convention in New York the day before the stockholders were to hold their liquidation vote. As a last-ditch effort, the Citizens Committee persuaded President Gillmer to offer a first year package of $47,000. Jelatis was to convey the offer to Hammerschmidt in New York, and the Citizens and Management felt totally confident the Union would accept the offer and the strike would be over.

After a series of phone calls and a mysterious lack of communication between Hammerschmidt and the local Shop Committee, Hammerschmidt took it upon himself to reject the offer and told Jelatis that Potteries' shareholders might as well go ahead and hold their liquidation vote. Management, as well as the Citizens, listened with disbelief as Jelatis reported the results of his conversation with Hammerschmidt. Thus, stockholders voted on August 24 to dissolve the ninety-year-old corporation, and the labor dispute, for all intents and purposes, was brought to an unsatisfying conclusion.

In an effort to be objectively critical of our own actions over the summer, we concluded that we would have done little differently had we to do it all over again. We would not have included in our original proposal the elimination of the retired employees' life insurance policies and dependents from hospitalization coverage. While these were low priority items, the Union used them to prove our "cold-hearted, take-away" attitude. We probably should have made formal revelation of our financial situation at an earlier date. Such a move may have given the Union time to modify their position comfortably and without risking a "loss of face." We should have pursued a court order at an earlier point in time. Rather than creating animosity, it may have served the opposite purpose and saved the hard feelings and growing antagonism that occurred over the picketing tactics. Finally, we should have avoided all conversation with the pickets. Angrily approaching the pickets served no constructive purpose and, if anything, worked against us in the resulting loss of stature. It also provided them the assurance that they were "getting to us."

Regarding the role of the conciliators, the best criterion upon which to judge their effectiveness would appear to be settlement of the labor dispute, and this they failed to accomplish. They held very few meetings during the three-month period. The strike began on June 1 and the only meeting the first month was on June 15. We were to wait nervously for over a month until they scheduled the second meeting on July 21. This second meeting was the last time we were to meet the Union on a face-to-face basis; the remaining four meetings Union and Management were located in separate rooms. If one holds the opinion that the only way to "clear the air" and reach a point of understanding between the disputants is to meet face-to-face, then the conciliators were in error in keeping us apart. After the

July 21 session we met four more times - on July 27, August 2, August 8, and August 11.

In our view, the conciliators were unaggressive in their approach to Management and did very little "arm twisting." Whether they used a like approach with the Union we have no way of knowing. Their role could best be characterized as one of "message carrier."

We felt, further, that Conciliator Larson made a mistake in not suggesting at an earlier date that we reveal our financial situation to the Union. He was aware of our tenuous financial position in the early days of the strike and did not recommend revealing this to the Union until August 8, and then only at the suggestion of the Union.

Another major factor in the strike was the role of the Red Wing Police Department. We said many times during the summer that had the police done their job, the great bitterness between company and Union never would have occurred and the strike would have been settled. This is at best unsupported speculation. Nevertheless, the action, or lack of action, on the part of the police was a source of bitterness very difficult to forget. In their defense, they had had very little, if any, experience in policing labor disputes or mass civil disobedience of any kind. Thus, they were at a loss as to how to deal effectively with the situation, and probably somewhat frightened of the disorderly mob. They needed direction, but failed to receive it from either Chief Lenway or Mayor Jelatis.

Had Jelatis or Lenway taken a strong stand in the very beginning - you can do this and you cannot do that - the strike may not have been settled, but the pickets would have been kept within reasonable limits and Red Wing would have been saved the embarrassment of being criticized by thousands of visitors. Instead, the police remained passive and the pickets gradually expanded their activity searching for limits that they never found.

With the advent of shouted threats and obscenities, unabashed driveway blocking, and the setting of nails, we met with Mayor Jelatis to plead for police protection. Despite his argument that more policemen would only breed more violence and that their job was only to prevent physical abuse, he did assure us that we would receive police protection. We were relieved until it became clear on the following weekend that the police had not changed their approach in any way. The pickets became more blatantly abusive over the weeks while the police stood by.

However, the police were not entirely passive. To the delight of the pickets, they ticketed a customer on July 30 for entering a driveway too fast. On August 27 an officer threatened to ticket customer automobiles for extending over the sidewalk. The police took this action without once ticketing or arresting anyone for setting nails, scratching and rocking cars, throwing water on cars, blocking access to the parking lot, and shouting threats and vulgar abuse. In our opinion, there was no justice in the situation and we lost all respect for the local police department.

Despite Jelatis' apparent lack of decisiveness as far as the police were concerned, we sincerely felt that he had done a good job as chairman of the Citizens Committee. In fact, all of these men - Jelatis, Jones, Broughton, Bergwall, Tri, and Josephson - brought us closer to a settlement than had the professional conciliators. We were deeply indebted to these men who had given so generously of their own time solely for the benefit of their community. Yet, their efforts went unrewarded.

In many ways the real losers in the situation were not Joe Hammerschmidt or company Management, but the fifty to sixty-year-old workers who had been at the Potteries fifteen or twenty years, knew no other trade, and now faced the unpleasant task of finding new employment at an age where prospects were vastly diminished. This man or woman was purely a victim of circumstances. He paid his Union dues, but attended few meetings, and when they told him they were going out on strike he had no choice but to go. Who was he to openly question the decision of the others? Anyway, maybe it would be a short strike and he could come out of it with a few more dollars in his paycheck. This man was swept along in the tide, never really knowing what the basic issues were, but taking his cues from the most available leader. To outwardly question this leadership or to challenge the decisions of his fellows was unthinkable, so he went along with the majority who were carbon copies of himself. They accepted the dogma of the most available leader and this constituted a democracy. This was the most pathetic figure when the smoke of battle cleared.

In looking back over the events of the summer we recalled Hammerschmidt's July 3 statement that "the OCAW has never put a company out of business over economic issues," Chastain's cocky July 24 statement that "if he must close the place, we'll pick a committee and help him nail the doors," and the many Union references to our "bluffing" about closing down. The mysterious Union statement that Chastain had promised at the end of August never came into being. Perhaps the Union thought that, under the circumstances, the less said the better.

Our bitterness remains and we continue to ask ourselves, "why?" - a question for which we have no answer and probably never will have. The final actions of Joe Hammerschmidt suggested to us that either he handled the matter with total incompetence or that for some reason he desired to put us out of business. His unqualified rejection of our final $47,000 offer, when the Union was asking only $53,000, and his failure to communicate this offer to four of his five Shop Committee members suggested to us that he had no interest in stopping the liquidation vote. Giving him the benefit of the doubt and assuming he interpreted the offer as "iffy" in talking with Jelatis, the very least he could have done would have been to tell Jelatis that the offer was "close," asked him to try and hold up the liquidation vote, and return from New York. This seemed to be the very least he owed the hundred people who had entrusted their jobs and their futures to him.

Yet, what possible reason could Hammerschmidt or other OCAW officials have for shutting down the Red Wing Potteries? We began the frustrating process of trying to piece together possible motives. We arrived at three hypotheses that seemed to hold together and make the most sense to us:

Hypothesis #1. "Loss-of-Face." The Union had started out in the beginning with high demands, believing at the time that

the company could afford them. Our early allusions to going
out of business were thought indeed to be bluffs. By August 9
when they saw our actual financial status they realized that they
had been demanding too much. But they had committed themselves to these high demands for so long that backing off to any
level approaching our offer would be, in effect, an admission
that we were right and they had been unreasonable. It looked
as though we were serious about liquidation at that point, so
why not let us proceed with liquidation rather than experience
any loss of face? Thus, at the next negotiating session on August
11 they reversed themselves and said our figures did indicate
that we could meet their demands.

Hypothesis #2. "Source of Embarrassment." The Pottery
wage scale, while in the average range on the local scene, was
very low in the OCAW's scheme of things and quite possibly
a source of embarrassment to them. On a nationwide basis the
170,000 OCAW members worked in highly-paid industries such
as oil refineries, atomic installations, chemically-oriented plants,
etc., where wages were far and above the $2.00 average paid
by the Potteries. Our wages did indeed seem paltry in their
frame of reference. Rather than have this blot on their record,
this dragging down of their average, why not eliminate us entirely? Could Hammerschmidt have been assigned the Red Wing
Potteries and told "either bring them up to an acceptable level
or shut them down?"

Hypothesis #3. "More Trouble Than We Are Worth." A
one-hundred man plant in Red Wing, Minnesota, is out of the
way and insignificant as far as the OCAW is concerned. The
necessary paperwork and the representative's time and expenses
could have been more costly for the OCAW than the dues
of the one hundred people they represented. Could Hammerschmidt have been told to "shoot for the moon and get it or,
as an alternative, eliminate the whole bothersome situation?"

The three hypotheses it will be noted are not mutually ex-
clusive. The driving motive behind the OCAW's actions could
have been any one, combination of two, or elements of all three.
On the other hand, the motive behind their actions could have

been something entirely different, something that has not yet occurred to us. Yet, driven by the human compulsion to explain the misfortunes that befall us, we have arrived at these answers which provide us some satisfaction in their apparent logic.

Many of the twenty-five employees who returned to assist in finishing the in-process merchandise told us that they were displeased with their Union leadership, ashamed of their picket line tactics, and very sorry about the outcome of the strike. — Responding to the most available leadership? We listened and said nothing.

Receiving the apologies of the employees and finding a logical answer for the injustices that befell us did nothing to negate the fact that the Red Wing Potteries had been killed - not allowed to die a natural death - but wilfully destroyed. The death of the Potteries marked the end of an historic era in the pages of the city, and 1967 will be cited as the regrettable conclusion to ninety years of pottery manufacturing in Red Wing, Minnesota. The impact on the community is yet to be felt, however — somthing far more intangible and far-reaching than the loss of one hundred thirty jobs or the Potteries' payroll; Red Wing has lost a nationally recognized symbol, a reason for a "place on the map," and a very critical piece of its heritage.

———————————————————

INDEX

189, 190, 191, 192, 193, 194,
195, 197, 198, 199, 200, 201,
202, 203, 204, 206, 207, 208,
209, 210, 211, 212, 213, 214,
215, 216, 217, 218, 219, 220,
221, 222, 223, 224, 225, 226,
227, 228, 230, 231, 232, 233,
234, 236, 237, 238, 239, 240,
241, 242, 243, 244, 245, 246,
247, 248, 249, 250, 251, 252,
253, 254, 255, 256, 257, 258,
259, 260, 264, 266, 267, 268,
269, 270, 271, 272, 273, 274
Olson, Sheriff Lenus, 24

Paulson, Officer, 65
Peat, Marwick, Mitchell &
Company, 191, 200
Pepe (dinnerware), 11, 29, 116
Peterson, Vernon, 30, 31, 191,
257
Philleo, W. M., 5
Pierce County Highway
Department, 142
Pierce County NFO, 104, 142
Pine Bend, Minnesota, 63
Pittsburgh, 24
Pohl, J., 5
Pohl, Robert, 206
Police Department, 4, 55, 56,
57, 59, 60, 61, 62, 64, 65, 66,
67, 77, 78, 81, 82, 84, 89, 90,
91, 97, 105, 106, 109, 110,
111, 112, 113, 114, 115, 117,
118, 119, 120, 121, 122, 123,
125, 126, 132, 133, 134, 135,
136, 137, 138, 141, 142, 146,
147, 151, 155, 156, 163, 164,
165, 166, 167, 168, 169, 172,
173, 174, 180, 182, 183, 184,
185, 186, 187, 188, 189, 194,
215, 232, 233, 247, 250, 251,
256, 266, 267, 270, 271
Portland, North Dakota, 209

Prairie Island, 206

Quie, Congressman Albert, 220,
224

Rapid City, South Dakota, 10,
242
Red Wing, 3, 4, 5, 6, 15, 18,
19, 24, 48, 52, 55, 59, 63, 69,
70, 72, 79, 82, 84, 85, 86, 93,
99, 100, 102, 103, 105, 106,
107, 108, 112, 113, 114, 120,
123, 124, 125, 126, 127, 128,
133, 134, 141, 142, 143, 144,
145, 146, 147, 150, 151, 152,
153, 154, 155, 156, 157, 158,
159, 160, 161, 162, 165, 166,
168, 169, 170, 174, 178, 179,
184, 185, 186, 188, 190, 193,
195, 196, 198, 199, 200, 204,
205, 206, 207, 208, 210, 211,
218, 219, 220, 222, 223, 227,
231, 232, 233, 235, 238, 239,
241, 242, 244, 245, 247, 248,
258, 260, 261, 262, 265, 267,
268, 270, 271, 273, 274
Red Wing AFL-CIO Council,
62, 63, 184, 219, 231
Red Wing Bus Line, 63
Red Wing Chamber of
Commerce, 3, 63, 106, 143,
144, 145, 148, 150, 152, 156,
161, 162, 178, 205, 206, 215
Red Wing City Council, 145
Red Wing Court House, 149,
154, 156, 157, 175, 179, 189,
192, 201, 203
Red Wing Industrial Development Corporation, 58, 145
Red Wing Labor Temple, 203,
209, 256, 257
Red Wing Shoe Company, 219,
231

331.89
G48

113661